Public Employee Relations in West Germany

WILLIAM H. McPHERSON

INSTITUTE OF LABOR AND INDUSTRIAL RELATIONS
UNIVERSITY OF ILLINOIS

ANN ARBOR
INSTITUTE OF LABOR AND INDUSTRIAL RELATIONS
THE UNIVERSITY OF MICHIGAN—WAYNE STATE UNIVERSITY
1971

This monograph is one of a series prepared under the direction of Professors Russell A. Smith and Charles M. Rehmus of The University of Michigan, and is a part of their comparative international study of labor relations in public employment. Financial support of this research project has been derived from a. number of sources. Basic grants came from the comparative law research funds of The University of Michigan Law School; the Institute of Labor and Industrial Relations, The University of Michigan—Wayne State University; the comparative economics research funds of The University of Michigan Economics Department; and the research programs of the New York State Public Employment Relations Board and the United States Department of Labor.

Preface

THE most rapid change in employee relations that this country has seen in the last three decades is that which is presently taking place in our public sector. This current restructuring of our public employee relations system confronts all participants with a number of major problems, such as those concerning union recognition, extent of the bargaining unit, scope of the subject matter of negotiations, regulation of strikes, structure of the grievance procedure, the impact of inability to pay, and the appropriate degree of mandating.

To provide some guidance for government and union officials, who are the main participants in the restructuring of our system, there has recently been extensive research on our own experience in the public sector, but as yet there has been only limited study by Americans of foreign systems to pinpoint those aspects of the experience of other countries that may offer ideas concerning the optimal solutions to our problems.

The German employee relations system is one of those that should be of most interest to us in this respect. By studying a country whose political and economic institutions are not too unlike our own we increase the possibility that successful aspects of its system might be transferable with proper adaptation to our own institutional setting.

Some general aspects of the German background closely related to employee relations in the public sector are presented in the first chapter, while recent political and economic developments are covered in Chapter II as the setting for an analysis of the 1969-70 negotiations. This exposition of the institutional enviornment will serve the double purpose of facilitating an understanding of the German system of public employee relations and of alerting the reader to those international differences that may limit the transferability of certain practices.

The main body of this study describes the principal features of the structure and operation of the German system. With reference to structure, questions such as the respective roles of negotiation and legislation, the nature of the bargaining units, the organization of the parties, the scope and timing of negotiation, the avoidance of strikes and quasi-strikes, and the structure of employee representation within the agency will be considered. One of the major questions to be studied is whether the system is well adapted to the peculiarities of the public sector or is just a duplicate of the private sector system. The dynamic character of the system will be shown not only by sketching its postwar development but also by emphasizing significant recent changes and noting others that seem likely to occur in the near future.

Just as a study of the structure of an automobile will not tell us all we might want to know about how it performs, so a knowledge of the structure of an employee relations system will not alone permit an accurate evaluation of how well it operates. For this reason a special effort has been made to investigate the actual functioning of the German system. Among the matters to be assessed in this regard are the spirit of the bargaining relationship and the extent of the union impact on the terms of agreements and legislation. In order to present a more vivid picture and to enable the reader to evaluate the generalizations and conclusions regarding negotiation, lobbying, strikes, and grievance handling, the study includes an analysis of the major day-to-day developments in two recent negotiations, of union strategy and tactics concerning the enactment of a key civil servant bill, of the issues and outcome of nearly all the postwar strikes, and of the activities of the staff councils in two federal agencies.

In the final chapter an attempt is made to evaluate the success of the German system with respect to sixteen criteria, which constitute a proposed model of an ideal system, and to point out some of the specific aspects of German experience that may have special applicability to the future development of our own system. It is hoped that the reader will find in this volume many other respects in which that experience can be helpful.

This study is based largely on six months of field work in West Germany during the last half of 1969 (with the help of a Fulbright research grant) and updating to cover major developments that occurred up to September 1970. It was found that German literature provides considerable material on the structure of the system, but only two significant studies of certain aspects of its operation. It was therefore necessary to rely to an unusual degree on extensive interviewing. One or more interviews were held with over thirty government and union officials at the federal, state, and local levels and with several employee representatives within federal agencies. For the details of developments during the past year or two the study relies heavily on accounts in the newspapers and news magazines. The comprehensive "business reports" issued by the unions prior to their national conventions every two or three years were also invaluable in tracing earlier developments. Large volumes on the history of two major unions in the public sector provided additional historical information.

Fortunately, all those whose guidance and information were sought, offered their complete cooperation. Their patience with my difficulties in mastering their language and in grasping the special German concept of the status of the civil servant is deeply appreciated. All were so helpful that it is impossible to single out any few for special mention, and a complete listing is scarcely appropriate. I can only say that I am extremely grateful for their help, without which this study would have been impossible, and for their geniality, which made the interviews as enjoyable as they were fruitful. Special thanks are due to a number of them who took the time to read the first draft of this manuscript and pointed out many of its inaccuracies. Dale Good, Labor Attaché at our embassy, and Hans Schrinner, his assistant, provided essential initial background information and ultimate factual corrections. Special mention of indebtedness is due to Rainer H. Kluge, a doctoral candidate at the Law Faculty of the University of Bonn, who was willing to spare some time to serve as a research assistant during the latter part of my German sojourn, and whose help was invaluable in keeping me informed regarding significant developments following my departure from Germany last December.

William H. McPherson

Institute of Labor and Industrial Relations
University of Illinois
Urbana, Illinois
October 6, 1970

Contents

ABBREVIATIONS

BAK	Bundesassistentenkonfereng Federal Assistants Conference
BAT	Bundes-Angestelltentarifvertrag (Bund, Länder, Gemeinden) National Master Agreement for Salaried Employees
BGBl	*Bundesgesetzblatt* *Federal Law Gazette*
BMT-G	Bundesmanteltarifvertrag für Arbeiter der Gemeinden Master Agreement for Wage-earners of Local Governments
BDA	Bundesvereinigung der Deutschen Arbeit geberverbände Confederation of German Employers Associations
CDU	Christlich-Demokratische Union Christian Democratic Party
CGB	Christlicher Gewerkschaftsbund Deutschlands Federation of German Christian Trade Unions
CSU	Christlich-Soziale Union Christian Social Party
DAG	Deutsche Angestellten-Gewerkschaft German Union of Salaried Employees
DBB	Deutscher Beamtenbund German Civil Servants Association
DGB	Deutscher Gewerkschaftsbund German Trade Union Federation
DPG	Deutsche Postgewerkschaft German Postal Union (in the DGB)
FDP	Freie Demokratische Partei Free Democratic Party
GdED	Gewerkschaft der Eisenbahner Deutschlands Union of German Railway Employees (in the DGB)
GdP	Gewerkschaft der Polizei The Police Union (independent)

xi

ABBREVIATIONS

GEW	Gewerkschaft Erziehung und Wissenschaft
	Union for Education and Science (in the DGB)
GGVöD	Gemeinschaft von Gewerkschaften und Verbänden des öffentlichen Dienstas
	Alliance of Unions and Associations in the Public Service
GtV	Gemeinschaft tariffähiger Verbände
	Alliance of Negotiating Unions (in the DBB)
ILO	International Labor Office
KAV	Kommunale Arbeitsrechtliche Vereinigung in Württemberg-Baden
	Local Labor-Law Association in Württemberg-Baden (regional employers association of local governments)
Marburger-	Verband der angestellten Ärzte Deutschlands
bund	Association of German Salaried Doctors
MTB	Manteltarifvertrag für Arbeiter des Bundes
	Master Agreement for Federal Wage-earners
MTL	Manteltarifvertrag für Arbeiter der Länder
	Master Agreement for State Wage-earners
ÖTV	Gewerkschaft Öffentliche Dienste, Transport und Verkehr
	Union for Public Services, Transport, and Communication (in the DGB)
SPD	Sozialdemokratische Partei Deutschlands
	German Social Democratic Party
TdL	Tarifgemeinschaft deutscher Länder
	Bargaining Association of German States
VDF	Verband Deutscher Flugleiter
	Association of German Air Traffic Controllers
VKA	Vereinigung der kommunalen Arbeitgeberverbände
	Federation of Local Government Employers Associations

Public Employee Relations in West Germany

The Institutional Environment

THE STRUCTURE OF GOVERNMENT

SOME understanding of the form and operation of a country's government is essential to an analysis of its public labor relations. The government of the Federal Republic of Germany (hereafter called Germany) somewhat resembles that of Great Britain. Its parliament consists of two houses. The Bundesrat is composed entirely of state officials appointed by the state governments to represent their interests. The Bundestag consists of 496 elected members and 22 appointed by the government of West Berlin for four-year terms. The latter have very limited voting rights. The country is divided into 248 voting districts. The voters designate their preference for both an individual candidate and a party. The candidate winning the largest number of votes in his district is elected. The other half of the elected members are chosen from party lists of nominees in proportion to the number of votes cast for each party. This permits some representation of small parties even if none of their candidates receive a plurality, provided the party wins at least 5 percent of all votes. The Chancellor is elected by the Bundestag. He may be replaced by a vote of no confidence, but only on condition that his successor is named at the same time, thus greatly increasing the stability of government as compared with that of Italy, for example.

The nature of the executive-legislative relationship has some bearing on public labor relations because negotiation is highly centralized and because both of these branches of government participate in the drafting of all legislation concerning the civil servants. The members of the federal cabinet—the ministers who head the fifteen departments or ministries—all have direct personal access to the floor of the Bundestag. A group of seats to the right of the rostrum is reserved for them. A similar section on the left is reserved for Bundesrat members who may wish to hear the debates. The ministers, with rare exception, are chosen from the elected members of the Bundestag and may consequently come down from their section to the floor to speak or vote on all issues. Any who are not members have the right to speak on matters related to their particular ministry. All are expected to reply to any questions put to them by the membership. The minister may be represented by his state secretary, who is the next highest official in the ministry. The latter is one of the highest of the civil servants, but, unlike nearly all of the others, he may be retired when there is a change of government, because of the political importance of his position.

Another link between the executive and the legislative branches of government has been introduced within the last few years. This is a position called the parliamentary state secretary. A member of the Bundestag is named to this position in each ministry to serve as the minister's personal assistant. The appointee is not a civil servant, has no tenure in the ministry, and has no general authority over the staff of the ministry. His appointment does mean that the Bundestag has an additional member who is intimately informed regarding the functions and problems of that ministry and who has a position of loyalty to the minister.

The fairly close contact between the cabinet members and the legislators means that the former should be well informed regarding legislative views and sensitive to them. It also means that the ministers and their representatives have ample opportunity to explain and defend their actions before the parliament. Thus there is little likelihood that the results of employee negotiations that have cabinet approval will encounter serious opposition in the Bundestag. And civil servant legislation drafted by the administration should usually find widespread support in parliament, even though some revision of the proposed bills is to be expected.

The federal-state relationship is sufficiently different from that in the United States that most American authors do not translate the term *Land,* but instead use the German designation. The difference may be significant for the political scientist, but for our purposes it seems too slight to preclude translation.

We shall therefore speak of German states rather than *Länder*. When the Federal Republic was established in 1949 it consisted of eleven states, including the two city-states of Hamburg and Bremen. The three states in the southwest subsequently merged to form Baden-Württemberg. The Saarland was added after a plebiscite in 1957. West Berlin is technically not a state, since it is still under control of the occupying powers. However, its form of government is similar to that of Hamburg and Bremen. Like the states, it is covered by federal laws on public employment and also has supplemental legislation of its own on this subject. For the sake of simplification, we shall in this study take liberties with international law and follow the German practice of referring to it as a state. Thus we shall consider that after the merger and the two additions there are again eleven states. The governments of the three city-states have both state and municipal functions. Bremen is in a slightly different situation than the other two in that it includes the two cities of Bremen and Bremerhaven. The legislation in the eight other states[1] controls not only the state government but also to a large extent the county and municipal governments. The larger cities typically do not belong to any county, but the towns are a part of their surrounding counties.

LABOR RELATIONS IN THE PRIVATE SECTOR

The union structure in Germany is relatively unified, centralized, and nonpolitical. In these respects it is in sharp contrast to the situation that prevailed during the period of the Weimar Republic (1918-33). At that time the unions were divided along political, religious, and policy lines into the "free" or socialist unions, the Christian unions, and the "liberal" Hirsch-Duncker unions. Each of these groups had its own federation, and each enlisted members from all types of employment. In the early 1930s, as the union movement found itself increasingly threatened by the Communists on the one side and the Nazis on the other, union leaders became convinced of the need for unification to gain strength for self-defense.

1. Baden-Württemberg, Bavaria, Hesse, Lower Saxony, North Rhine-Westphalia, Rhineland-Palatinate, Saarland, and Schleswig-Holstein.

Plans for mergers were discussed, but the union structure was taken over by the Nazis before any consolidation was accomplished.[2]

At the end of World War II union leaders who had survived Nazi persecution were nearly unanimous in their desire for the building of a unified labor movement. The American, British, and French Occupation Forces insisted that the union structure be rebuilt from the bottom up rather than from the top down. At first they were willing to recognize only local unions; subsequently they permitted the development of unions at the state or zone levels, and eventually at the trizone level. The insistence on starting unionization at the local level retarded organizational development but reduced the possibility that the new union structure might be dominated by Communist and other political groups. This policy supported the desire for a unified structure, since it prevented the growth of competing unions within any one plant. The natural result of subsequent consolidation was an industrial union structure.

Hans Böckler, who emerged as the strongest union leader, favored the formation of a single union, with several industrial sections. British union officials were instrumental in dissuading him from this goal. The eventual result was a central federation of quasi-autonomous industrial unions. The confederation, which emerged first in the British Zone, was composed of twelve member unions; but when it was established as the German Trade Union Federation (Deutscher Gewerkschaftsbund or DGB) for the trizone area in 1949, there were sixteen constituent unions, since the railroad workers, the postal workers, and the teachers had withdrawn from the government workers union and the leather workers had split from the textile and clothing union. The 1949 structure has continued to the present day.[3]

2. For a brief history of labor relations in prewar Germany see P. Taft, "Germany" (Ch. 4), in W. Galenson (ed.), *Comparative Labor Movements*. New York: Prentice-Hall, 1952.

3. For a survey of early postwar labor relations see C. Kerr, "Collective Bargaining in Postwar Germany" (Ch. V), in A. Sturmthal (ed.), *Contemporary Collective Bargaining in Seven Countries*. Ithaca: Institute of International Industrial and Labor Relations, 1957.

DGB membership at the end of 1969 was 6,482,390, which represented a decline of about 3 percent during 1965-68 and a recapture of half that loss in the latest year. Of these members, about 76 percent were wage-earners, 14 percent salaried employees, and 10 percent civil servants. The constituent unions and their percentage of the total membership were as follows:

Metalworkers	31.9
Public services and transport	15.0
Chemical, paper, ceramic	8.5
Construction, stone, earth	7.7
Mining, power	6.2
Railroads	6.2
Postal service	5.5
Textiles, clothing	4.8
Food, hotels, restaurants	3.8
Trade, banking, insurance	2.3
Printing, paper	2.2
Wood, plastics	2.0
Education, science	1.7
Leather	0.9
Agriculture, forestry	0.8
Arts	0.5

In spite of the wide desire for a unified labor movement, the DGB is not the only federation, even though its membership represents nearly 80 percent of Germany's union members. One rival organization is the German Union of Salaried Employees (Deutsche Angestellten-Gewerkschaft or DAG). It had a separate existence from the start in the American and French zones, but was originally part of the single federation in the British Zone. Böckler, in his insistence on industrial organization, wished to confine it to the area of trade, banking, and insurance. Its leadership, however, was equally insistent on a broader field. A compromise was nearly reached on the basis that it would have jurisdiction for salaried employees in all industries, with the exception of government service (including the railroads and the postal service) and the coal, steel, and chemical industries—in the expectation that these would soon be nationalized. In the end Böckler decided to hold to the principle of industrial organization. The leaders of the salaried employees were expelled and established the independent DAG, while the DGB formed its own union for trade, banking, and insurance. The DAG had about 470,000 members at the end of 1969.[4]

Another major rival is the German Civil Servants Association (Deutscher Beamtenbund or DBB). This was the reconstitution of a similar organization that existed during the Weimar Republic. In September 1969 it had 718,914 members. Some of its constituent unions have recently been seeking increasingly to enlist wage-earners and salaried employees in government service. These two groups now constitute about 10 percent of its membership. It has no members in the private sector.

Finally, there is the Federation of German Christian Trade Unions (Christlicher Gewerkschaftsbund Deutschlands or CGB). It was established in 1959 but has never received much support and is of minor significance except in the Saar. Its total membership is approximately 190,000.

In addition to these four federations, there are a number of small independent unions, whose membership we will guess to be about 380,000. Thus the union organizations as a whole probably have in the neighborhood of 8,250,000 members. Since at least 15 percent of these are retirees or widows, we estimate that the unions as a whole have enrolled 7,000,000 members of the labor force. These are about 26 percent of the 26,766,000 persons in the total labor force or 33 percent of the 21,330,000 in the employed labor force (excluding the self-employed and family workers). This degree of organization has been achieved without benefit of any union shop provisions in labor agreements or other special inducements, since recent efforts of some unions to obtain special benefits (such as longer vacations) for their members alone have been disallowed by the Federal Labor Court.

The unions negotiate in rare instances with a single employer, but nearly all labor agreements cover a particular industry on a regional or national basis. Supplementary agreements for a company or plant are common. For negotiating purposes most employers belong to one or another of the regional

4. For further details on the history of the DAG see G. Hartfiel, "Germany," in A. Sturmthal (ed.), *White Collar Trade Unions*. Urbana: University of Illinois Press, 1966.

industrial employers associations, which in turn are members of national industrial federations. These latter then are joined in the national all-industry organization, the Confederation of German Employers Associations (Bundesvereinigung der Deutschen Arbeitgeberverbände or BDA).

Since the postwar union structure is quite different from that of the interwar period and entirely different fom that of the Nazi era, the present bargaining system is little more than two decades old. During that time, however, it has shown high stability; and the long, if interrupted, history of collective bargaining in Germany has produced a relatively mature system. At least it is very mature for its young age. The total system of German labor relations is undergoing some change, but there is no indication that the structure of negotiations will soon be significantly affected. The Chemical Workers in Hesse attempted in April 1970 to negotiate separately with the nine largest companies in that industry in the hope of winning higher wage rates from them than could be obtained from the whole industry, but the employers association vehemently rejected the proposal.

Labor legislation is of major importance in setting some of the terms of employment in German industry. The unions seek many of their goals in the legislative chambers rather than at the bargaining table. Although there is a considerable body of state labor legislation, only federal laws will be mentioned at this point. In addition to the usual protective labor legislation, such as the Youth Employment Protection Act[5] and the Maternity Protection Act,[6] there are, for example, the Work Hours Order[7] (setting maximum workday and workweek) and the Vacation Act[8] (setting minimum terms for

5. Aug. 9, 1960. *Bundesgesetzblatt,* 1960, I, 665; International Labor Office *Legislative Series,* 1960, Ger. F. R. 2.

6. Jan. 24, 1952 (rev. Nov. 9, 1965). *BGBl.,* 1965, I, 67; I.L.O., *Legislative Series,* 1965, Ger. F. R. 2.

7. April 27, 1965. *BGBl.,* 1965, I, 349.

8. Jan. 6, 1963. *BGBl.,* 1963, I, 2; I.L.O., *Legislative Series,* 1963, Ger. F. R. 1.

9

annual vacations). There is also the Dismissal Protection Act,[9] regulating the length of notice that either party must give in terminating the individual employment contract and specifying conditions under which discharge without notice is permissible. It also regulates questions of layoff. Some of these laws have little effect, because they are surpassed by the agreements. The Collective Agreement Act is of major significance for the structure of collective bargaining. It sets the conditions under which organizations may be parties to an agreement, the legal effect of the various parts of an agreement, the obligation of the parties to maintain industrial peace regarding the terms of the agreement, and the conditions under which the agreement may be extended by the federal or state government to cover employers and employees in the industry who are not members of the contracting organizations (see pp. 28-30).

Labor relations at the plant level are governed by the Works Councils Act of October, 1952 (see pp. 124-35). These councils, elected by all the employees regardless of union membership, take the place of an American union local in handling grievances at the plant level. They also have the right of consultation on some matters and codetermination (joint decision) on certain others. The act further entitles the employees of a corporation to elect one third of the members of the board of directors.

The Codetermination Act of May 21, 1951, applying only to the mining and iron and steel industries, provides that boards of directors shall consist of an equal number of labor and stockholder representatives plus one additional member and that the personnel manager shall be appointed only with the approval of a majority of the labor representatives (see pp. 133-34).

Since negotiation is highly centralized and the parties have seldom reached an impasse during the postwar period, there

9. Aug. 10, 1951. *BGBl.*, 1951, I, 499; I.L.O., *Legislative Series*, 1951, Ger. F. R. 4. See also F. Herbst, *Notice of Dismissal and Protection against Dismissal.* Bonn: Federal Ministry of Labor and the Social Structure (Social Policy Monograph No. 13), undated.

has rarely been any need for mediation. Indeed, there is no federal and but little state legislation on this subject. Throughout nearly all of Germany the Control Council Law No. 35 on conciliation procedures for labor disputes,[10] issued by the Occupation Forces on August 20, 1946, is still in force though little used. It provides for a mediation service in the Ministry of Labor of each state. At the request of both parties the service appoints a mediation board consisting of an equal number of employer and employee representatives and a neutral chairman. The representative members are named from panels proposed by the unions and employers associations. The chairman is named from a panel proposed by the service and approved by the organizations. If agreement on the dispute is not reached through mediation, the board concludes its efforts by presenting its recommendations for settlement, which are not binding unless the parties have so agreed. The state of Rhineland-Palatinate and the former state of South Baden (now part of Baden-Württemberg) abrogated Law No. 35 in 1949 and replaced it with legislation which differs chiefly in permitting the state, in cases that seriously jeopardize the public interest, to initiate mediation without a request and to declare the recommendations binding.

The major union and employer confederations reached agreement on September 7, 1954, concerning a model mediation provision, which they recommended to their members for inclusion in their industry agreements for use in case of deadlock in negotiations regarding future revisions of those agreements.[11] The model is fairly similar to the provisions of Law No. 35 except that the parties obligate themselves to establish a board in case of deadlock and that they, rather than the government, name the board members. The model provisions have been adopted with various minor modifications by many parties, but there has seldom been occasion in the last decade to use either them or Law No. 35. More frequent has been the use of a staff member of a state Ministry of

10. *Labour Gazette for the British Zone*, 1947, p. 8.
11. See *Recht der Arbeit*, 1954, p. 383, for the terms of the agreement.

Labor as a single mediator in the absence of a mediation service at the federal level.[12]

Private arbitration is rarely used in Germany. Under the terms of the Labor Court Act of September 3, 1953,[13] unsettled grievances are normally taken to a Labor Court with limited appeal to a State Labor Court and the Federal Labor Court. Each court operates through several chambers or senates, which consist of a jurist as chairman and two or four representative members appointed from lists of nominees presented by unions and employers associations. The local courts make a preliminary and frequently successful attempt at mediation.[14]

LABOR RELATIONS IN GOVERNMENT-OWNED INDUSTRIES

The local public utilities (gas, water, electricity, and local transit) are operated sometimes by a municipality or county as an integral part of the governmental administration and sometimes as a separate legal entity partly or wholly owned and supervised by one or several local governments. Usually the staff contains a large proportion of wage-earners and few, if any, civil servants. If the utility is organized as a separate company, it operates like any private company, and the members of its work force are not considered as government employees.

Intercity bus service is operated as a part of the postal system in the Postal and Communications Ministry (including telephone and telegraph service, but hereafter referred to as the Postal Ministry).[15] Postal employees are largely civil servants and all are public employees.

12. For more details on German mediation see H. Reichel and H. Zschocher, *Conciliation and Arbitration and the Law as Applied to Labor Disputes.* Bonn: Federal Ministry of Labor and the Social Structure (Social Policy Monograph No. 20), 1963.

13. *BGBl.*, 1953, I, 1267; I.L.O., *Legislative Series,* 1953, Ger. F. R. 2.

14. For more detail on the labor courts see H. Sahmer, *The Labor Courts.* Bonn: Federal Ministry of Labor and the Social Structure (Social Policy Monograph No. 24), undated, and W. H. McPherson, "Basic Issues in German Labor Court Structure," *Labor Law Journal,* 1954, p. 439.

15. The federal government has announced its intention to merge the Postal and Transport ministries. As a first step in this direction it has named the same individual as Minister in both of these ministries.

The federal railway system, which includes all but about 2,500 miles of the nation's railroad trackage, does not have a ministry of its own, but is operated as a separate legal entity under the general control and supervision of the Transport Ministry. Of its some 400,000 employees, approximately 57 percent are civil servants, 2 percent salaried employees, and 41 percent wage-earners. All of them are government employees.

The federal government—and in some cases a state government—is sole or part owner of numerous corporations in a wide variety of industries, including coal, steel, power, shipbuilding, shipping, aluminum, machinery, and autos. At the end of 1967 it had capital holdings in excess of one billion dollars and a direct or indirect capital interest of 25 percent or more in 580 enterprises.[16] Many of its direct investments are in housing development firms and research institutes. Its industrial investments have been made chiefly through a very few giant holding companies. This type of government ownership frequently resulted from financial difficulty that was resolved by government investment. Labor relations in such firms are exactly the same as in all of private industry. They are governed by civil and labor law, and have no relation whatever to public employment.

THE UNIONS AND POLITICAL ACTION

Unlike the conditions in several other West European nations and in sharp contrast to the situation in Germany during the Weimar Republic, the postwar German unions are politically neutral. The goal of the old-time labor leaders as they started to rebuild the labor movement after the Nazi debacle in 1945 was a unified union structure. This could be achieved only on the basis of political neutrality. Therefore the leaders, most of whom had belonged during the 1920s to the "free"

It is anticipated that by 1971 the postal service will be reorganized as a government corporation with its board of directors and management committee, as has long been the case for the railway service.

16. "Beteiligung des Bundes in Haushaltsjahr 1967." Appendix to Financial Report 1969 in Federal Finance Ministry *Annual Report*.

unions, which were closely related to the Social-Democratic Party, tried to learn new ways. It was hard for many of them at first to separate political activity from union activity, and members of other political parties often felt themselves disadvantaged in seeking leadership roles in the new labor movement. Union members have since gradually managed to be politically active as individuals without involving their unions. There appears to be much more tolerance now than twenty years ago in the DGB unions for leaders who are active in other parties. Union leaders have learned from experience that it may be very helpful to the labor movement to have politically active members in each of the major parties. For example, most of the twenty DGB members allied with the CDU (the relatively conservative Christian Democratic Party) in the Bundestag probably belong to the Labor Committee of the CDU caucus, which in effect constitutes the liberal wing of the party and has a very appreciable—though far from dominant—influence on party policies.

Unlike the practice in the United States, many German union officials run for public office. Of the 518 members in the 1970 Bundestag (including Berlin delegates), 291 hold union membership. In spite of the policy of political neutrality, unions do inevitably have their party leanings. Some 90 percent of the 237 SPD (Social Democratic Party) Bundestag members are trade unionists, and nearly all of them belong to DGB unions. The four DGB unions that focus on public employees have 131 member-parliamentarians. On the other hand, DGB unionists constitute only 10 percent of the 201 CDU legislators. Clearly, the vast majority of the national and local leaders of the DGB unions, whose membership consists primarily of wage-earners, feel a strong tie to the SPD. It is said that about a tenth of the union legislators hold a significant union office. The union membership of many of the others is only nominal. There are 163 civil servants in the present Bundestag. The party and union affiliations of the Bundestag members are approximately as follows:[17]

17. Source: DPG Parlamentarische Verbindungsstelle, Bonn, Rundschreiben Nr. 42/1969 (December 29) and DBB correspondence.

Union	SPD	FDP	CDU/CSU	Total
DGB	208	2	21	231
DBB	3	1	23	27
CGB	—	—	21	21
DAG	4	1	6	11
GdP	1	—	—	1
All unions	216	4	71	291
Nonunion	21	27	179	227
Total	237	31	250	518

Although union officials complain that union members often fail to vote in accord with union policy, the voting record indicates that nearly all deputies tend to follow party discipline on major bills.

In spite of this high degree of unionist political participation, the union federation and the party are not just different aspects of the same entity, as was practically the case in the 1920s. During the Weimar Republic it could have been said that the free union federation was the union wing of the party or, with perhaps equal validity, that the party was the political wing of the union. Today, DGB leaders, in spite of their feeling of affinity with the party, recognize that it cannot rely solely on the labor movement for support, but must have a broader appeal if it is to aspire to majority status. If union leaders should in some instance face a choice between loyalty to the union and loyalty to the party, the former would usually prevail. In the twenties union leaders were more likely to think in terms of using the union to help the party rather than using the party to help the union. Today, the reverse is probably true.

Support for this view can be found in the tactics of the ÖTV (Union for Public Services, Transport and Communications) concerning the municipal wildcat strikes just before the national elections in September 1969 (see p. 67). Interpretations of that event will vary, but in the view of this author the union leadership, in order to obtain some gain for its membership and to strengthen its own position within the organization, took steps which could not benefit and might well have harmed the chances of the SPD in the election.

Another situation that may serve as a test of the relative

15

strength of union and party loyalty was developing in 1970. The unions had for several years been urging that full codetermination, as practiced in the mining and steel industries, be extended by law to large companies in other industries. The SPD supported this demand, but all that it could obtain as junior partner in the grand coalition was the appointment of an ad hoc committee of experts—mostly professors—to analyze the experience of the two industries under full codetermination and make recommendations regarding the possible extension of the system. The committee was appointed early in 1968, but had not made its report by the time of the 1969 election. Since it was chaired by a professor who had been very active in the CDU, it was widely anticipated that the report would not support the union demands.

Immediately after the election it appeared possible that the SPD might become the senior partner in the government by forming a coalition with the FDP (the small Free Democratic Party). Exploratory discussions revealed sufficient agreement on all major issues of domestic and foreign policy except on extension of full codetermination. The FDP insisted that the SPD renounce any hope of such a change for the life of the coalition. The SPD decided to accept these terms. It was agreed that the Works Councils Act would be revised in some respects favorable to the unions, but that the changes would not include the extension of full codetermination. The SPD assigned its new Minister of Labor—formerly president of the Miners Union—to meet with the heads of the other DGB unions and explain the situation. Presumably the union leaders agreed to acquiesce, though their subsequent public statements have not supported this assumption.

In any case, they were faced with a situation to test their relative loyalty to their party and their union. If they did acquiesce in shelving for a time their codetermination demands, one might perhaps conclude that party loyalty proved to be the stronger. On the other hand, they may have reached their conclusion in the belief that the unions would gain more in the long run if the SPD were the senior, rather than junior, partner in the new government. Consequently, this issue does not yet present a clear test of conflicting loyalties.

The issue, however, is far from dead. It will be very much alive when the Works Council Act comes up for revision. Will the SPD then be able to hold its members in line on the codetermination question? If it cannot, will the coalition then be broken and the SPD relegated to its former role as government junior partner or even to its earlier role as the opposition party? The present coalition has only a twelve-vote majority (not counting the Berlin deputies). In the meantime, the codetermination issue has become more explosive. Four months after the election the committee of experts submitted its report.[18] To the consternation of CDU leaders and perhaps the dismay of top SPD officials, the voluminous report proved to be largely favorable to the codetermination claim. The committee found very little in the experience of the mining and steel industries to support the chief arguments that have been raised against it. The members had largely reconciled their originally conflicting views, and presented a set of unanimous recommendations. To be sure, they did not suggest the extension of full codetermination, but they did propose a considerable strengthening of the codetermination rights currently operative in other industries and an increase in the proportion of labor representatives on the boards of directors. They also sanctioned the application of this change to a much larger number of firms than was covered by the union proposal.

This report may result in a continuing test of party vs. union loyalty. It may well make it harder for the SPD to keep its pledge, and thus may increase the possibility of an FDP withdrawal from the coalition, unless the Free Democrats should decide that they will go along with the committee's recommendations.

The union point of view on political action was well expressed by ÖTV President Kluncker in his major address at the last quadrennial congress of his union in 1968:[19]

> The conditions of work and life of the wage-earners, the salaried employees, and the civil servants are so decisively

18. *Mitbestimmung in Unternehmen*, Bundestag, Drucksache VI/334.
19. ÖTV, *Tagesprotokoll*, 6th Ordentlicher Gewerkschaftstag, 1968, pp. 69–70.

influenced by the political action or inaction of the parties, the parliament, and the government that the use of political pressure has become an obvious necessity for the ÖTV. In so doing we shall respect the jurisdiction of the political authorities, and will not fall into the error of considering ourselves a substitute party. . . . The executive committee has endeavored to develop improved contacts with all the democratic parties and their parliamentary organizations. Practical cooperation with the political parties and with parliament and government authorities naturally depends on their political principles and their behavior toward the union in matters of practical politics.

Our analysis of the close relationship between the DGB and the SPD does not imply that all unions lean toward the Social Democrats. The DAG, consisting of salaried employees, has a lesser preponderance of SPD members in its ranks. The DBB, with its strong position among the civil servants, has a relatively conservative membership that results in a much closer relationship with the CDU than with the SPD. Indeed, the DBB, as a strong rival to the DGB in the civil servant area and following somewhat different policies and decidedly different tactics, finds itself on less than cordial terms with most SPD leaders. The growing power of the SPD is not a good omen for the DBB.

Although the unions *as such* concentrate their efforts on winning economic goals for themselves rather than promoting the interests of some political party, this does not mean that they do not engage in some form of political activity. Their political activity, however, is designed to win concessions from the parties rather than to advance the interests of a party. It takes the form of lobbying rather than electioneering. All German unions strongly emphasize their lobbying activity, because many union goals are sought through legislation rather than collective agreement.

Strikes for political purposes were not unknown during the Weimar Republic. They were called by the Communist Party rather than the unions. Since there are now no Communist unions in Germany, as in France and Italy, there has not been any instance of a politically motivated strike during the postwar period. The earlier Communist Party has been outlawed. A small one recently formed (the DKP) has not yet been challenged, pending observance of its willingness to abide by the standards of the federal constitution. There are undoubtedly Communist cells in a number of the larger plants, especially in the Ruhr area. Some works councils have a Communist chairman, and at least one has a Communist—or in any case an anti-DGB—majority. In general, Communism has few advocates in Germany, except in small student groups at some universities. These students find themselves sharply divided as supporters or followers of Lenin, Mao, and even Luxemburg and Liebknecht.

The possibility of a political strike, in the sense of a work stoppage intended to force specific legislative action by parliament, cannot be entirely ruled out. Indeed, a few instances of strikes intended to influence legislation have recently occurred (see Chapter V). Some union leaders have talked about the possibility of a strike in support of their codetermination demand. As yet this is just a way of saying that they are very serious about this issue. If such a stoppage should ever be called, it would probably be a brief "demonstration" strike. The prospect seems remote, for such action would surely be bitterly criticized as an illegitimate form of political pressure; and it would probably be ruled illegal, if the matter were to reach the courts. On the other hand, the unions have not forgotten that the special negotiations that led to the formulation of the Codetermination Act of 1951 were probably influenced by their strike threat on that occasion.

HISTORY AND TRADITIONS OF THE CIVIL SERVICE

Germany has 3 percent of the area and 33 percent of the population of the continental United States. Its labor force is also 33 percent of the U.S. Yet if its railroad workers are excluded, its full-time federal employees are only about 29 percent of the U.S. and public employees at all levels only about 24 percent. The figures used in this calculation are not exactly comparable, but it is at least a rough approximation to say that, although the U.S. has only three times as many inhabitants, it has four times as many public employees. Including the railway service, U.S. public employment of 3 million is 11.5 percent of the labor force; excluding it, 10.3 percent. Full-time public employment by level of government and type of employee is shown in Table I.

German public employees, whether working for the federal, state, or local governments, are divided into three groups: wage-earners (*Arbeiter*), salaried employees (*Angestellten*), and civil servants (*Beamte*). The civil servants differ from the others not only in their rights, their duties, and their terms of employment, but also in the procedures by which these

TABLE I
FULL-TIME GOVERNMENT EMPLOYEES
1968-69

	Civil Servants	Salaried Employees	Wage-Earners	Total
Federal agencies[1]	78,013	96,461	105,388	279,862
Postal service and Ministry[1]	254,129	49,557	93,469	397,155
Railway service[1]	222,688	8,088	163,608	394,384
Unincorporated Indl. Enterprises[1]	46	699	3,527	4,272
Indirect employees[2]	11,361	74,389	4,537	90,287
Total federal employees	566,237	229,194	370,529	1,165,960
Direct state employees[3]	638,371	338,292	144,039	1,120,702
Indirect state employees[4]	8,200	60,451	7,440	76,091
Total state employees	646,571	398,743	151,479	1,196,793
Local government employees[3]	136,250	333,155	250,292	719,697
Total government employees	1,349,058	961,092	772,300	3,082,450

1. As of October 2, 1969 (preliminary).
2. As of October 2, 1968. Includes the Bundesbank (Federal Reserve Bank), Bundesanstalt für Arbeit (Federal Institute for Employment Service and Unemployment Compensation), and social insurance funds under federal supervision.
3. As of October 2, 1968.
4. As of October 2, 1968. Covers social insurance funds under state supervision.

Source: Correspondence from Statistisches Bundesamt (Federal Statistical Office), April 10, 1970. Similar earlier data may be found in *Statistisches Jahrbuch*, 1968, and *Wirtschaft und Statistik*, September 1969, p. 510. Excluded are judges, members of the armed services, and more than 150,000 who work at least half-time but less than full-time.

are determined. They not only were the original public employees, but are still by far the largest of the three groups, comprising nearly 45 percent of the total. It is impossible to understand the nature of their special status and the reasons for it without a review of the unique history and traditions of the German civil service. This review should also serve to emphasize that the terms "civil servant" and "civil service" as applied to Germany have a very special connotation quite different from what they have in other countries. Unfortunately a more exact translation of the terms *Beamte* and *Beamtentum* is not possible.

Very early in German history—certainly by the time of Charlemagne as the Holy Roman Emperor—the civil administration was an important part of the social structure. Church lands were a considerable part of the empire, and every monastery and bishopric was required, because of the precepts of St. Paul, to have a secular official to represent it in legal and military controversies that were considered unsuitable for the clergy. The *Vogt*, or advocate, was an administrator of secular affairs, a judge representing the church, and a leader of armed defense. The position carried with it power and prestige and, because of its desirability, often became hereditary.

Centralized administration broke down after Charlemagne. The many independent duchies struggled with each other, with the church estates, and with the invaders from the north. During these feudal times the administration of the estates of the nobles was often placed in the hands of persons known as *Ministeriales*. They owed absolute loyalty to their lord, who had the power of life and death over them. Although their position was one of complete subservience to the lord, it involved considerable authority and was often very profitable. The *Ministeriales* typically had little training that would enable them to supervise the efficient use of the lands or keep accurate accounts, and they frequently abused their considerable powers. They were generally envied for their status and acquisitions, not necessarily respected. This ancient nature of the "governing" function is mentioned not because of its similarity to the modern concept of civil servant but because of its contrast.

With the decay of feudalism and the rise of the monarchy, there came in Central Europe a sharp change in the nature of the administrative class and its position. Friedrich Wilhelm I (the "Soldier King") is regarded as the father of the modern German civil service. As the son of the first king of Prussia, he felt the need of having an independent army of his own rather than one supplied by the lesser nobility on the basis of unreliable alliances. The support of such an army required a substantial increase in the royal revenues. This could be achieved, he felt, only by the establishment of a well-trained and highly efficient civil service. As his higher civil servants, he sought young men with university training who could increase the productivity of his estates and had an understanding of accounting principles. He demanded absolute loyalty, efficiency, and frugality.

His son, Frederick the Great, continued his father's policies. Regarding himself as a servant of the state, he too practiced frugality, set high standards for himself, and demanded them of his civil servants. The high standards set for entrance and promotion in the civil service brought a significant increase in efficiency and productivity. Frederick remained a despot, but he enlisted the bureaucracy in his concept of absolute devotion to the state, which in turn had the responsibility of assuring the livelihood of its civil servants.

This gradual transition in the concept of the civil servants' loyalty from "loyalty to the monarch" to "loyalty to the state" was completed as the monarchy gave way to the modern state. It was accompanied by a change in the generally accepted concept of the state. The notion that people exist to serve the state was gradually reversed to the view that the state exists to serve the people. Von Humboldt's claim that "the state is merely a means to which man, the true end, must never be sacrificed" achieved eventual acceptance.

At the end of World War II the Occupation Forces, believing that the civil servants had been too acquiescent in accepting Nazi rule, urged the abolition of the traditional German civil service. This policy was widely resisted by the Germans, and, after much debate, the new Constitution of the Federal Republic provided (Art. 33, Sec. 5) that "the law regarding public service shall be determined with due regard to the traditional principles of the professional civil service."

The present concept or "theory" regarding the status of the civil servant derives from this history. The civil servant is not an employee; he is an embodiment of the state and its sovereignty. His is a service relationship, not a contractual one. He has no individual contract of employment. He is governed by public law, not private or civil law. He is almost always the subordinate of a superior, and the superior of a subordinate. His relationship of service, trust, and loyalty affects his whole person, not just his occupational activities. Even his conduct in private life must not bring discredit upon the state or the civil service. He may lose his position or his pension rights as a result of serious misconduct quite unrelated to his professional life. In other respects he has exceptional security, one purpose of which is to assure his independence and integrity by protecting him from improper influence. Although he may be released from the service on his request at any time, it is assumed that he has entered upon a lifetime career. He is not hired, but is named or appointed to the civil service, which action is symbolized by the administration of an oath and the presentation of a certificate. Once he has met the entrance requirements of education and training, has served a probationary period, has passed the required tests, and has reached the age of 27, he receives a "lifetime" appointment. Thereafter he cannot be severed because of unsatisfactory work, though in rare instances he may incur a lesser penalty.

He does not receive wages or salary, and is not paid on the basis of his performance. But the state has the obligation to see that his income is adequate to assure the subsistence of himself and his family at a level that is appropriate to his education, training, and position. Thus he has an attractive noncontributory pension plan that provides not only for him after termination of his active service, but also for his survivors. The nature of his remuneration is perhaps best symbolized by the fact that he receives his monthly payment in advance!

Considering his relationship of service and loyalty to the state, it is quite "inconceivable" that he might strike against the state. The incongruity of such action was felt to be so clear that it was considered unnecessary and inappropriate to spell out a strike prohibition in the public law. This is still the prevailing view although a few labor law specialists have recently challenged it (see pp. 164-65).

The realism of this total concept of the civil servant at the present day may well be questioned. It seems probable that many civil servants consider their pay as a salary, that they are as concerned as other government employees with their level of remuneration and with promotion, and that they do not consider themselves as servants rather than as employees. On the other hand, it appears probable that most of them do think of the civil service as a lifetime career and that there is relatively little transfer between the civil service and private employment. Because of the difficulty of translating the special terms that Germans use in referring to civil servants, we will make no attempt to conform to the "theory" of their position, but will consider them as employees who receive pay rather than a salary. Their special status, however, must be borne in mind in order to understand the reasons for many aspects of their employment relationship.

With the change in the role and functions of the state toward the last turn of the century came a change in the structure of public employment. Whereas most earlier government functions involved some application of the concept of sovereignty, newer functions took the form of services. Municipalities and other government units undertook the provision of public utility services. Various types of public welfare projects involved much routine record keeping. In particular, World War I, with its rationing and other controls, required the employment of many young women who had little thought of a lifetime career in government. Also, changing technology led to the need for technicians in many branches of government.

Thus the early years of this century saw a great increase in government employment of wage-earners and salaried employees, who were not civil servants. Up to the present they remain employees, not servants. They are paid on the basis of performance. They tend to receive a higher salary, but their pension plans are contributory, whereas such contribution would be inconsistent with the concept of the civil servant. Unlike their counterparts in the private sector, they may, by additional contributions, raise their pensions to the level received by the civil servants—75 percent of final pay, excluding certain bonuses. Their terms of employment are set by collective agreement rather than by legislation. Their right to strike is the same as in private industry. Their unsettled grievances and other legal disputes go to the labor courts, while those of civil servants go to the administrative courts. Their employment relationship is governed not by public law but by civil law, just as in the case of their counterparts in private industry. In fact, the only major difference in the legal situation of these public and private employees concerns their representation within the workplace. While the latter are subject to the Works Councils Act, the former are covered by the federal or state Staff Representation Act (see Chapter IV).

In practice, the distinction between work performed by each of the three types of public employees (wage-earners, salaried employees, and civil servants) has grown increasingly vague. A number of positions are now occupied by persons in two of these groups. For example, a postman may start as a wage-earner and after a few years may, under certain conditions, become a civil servant. The young lady behind the counter at the post office may be a salaried employee or a civil servant. The job budget of any public agency specifies for each position the appropriate type of employee, but the actual incumbent may be of a different type. Although the boundaries between the three groups are vague, most positions fall clearly within one category or another.

The differences in the terms of employment for the three types are gradually diminishing. The wage-earners and salaried employees in public employment are winning more and more of the security and other provisions enjoyed by the civil servants. A study conducted by the Bundesrechnungshof (the German counterpart of our General Accounting Office) concluded that on the basis of the conditions existing in October 1966 it was cheaper for the federal government to use civil servants rather than corresponding salaried employees. Total payments to salaried employees prior to retirement would run about 15 percent to 20 percent higher, and even the lifetime payments were slightly higher than for corresponding civil servants in the lower career levels. The reliability of this study has, however, been questioned.

Changes in the status of the civil service have been accompanied by changes in its prestige. There is reason to believe that the position of.civil servant is in itself no longer so highly honored or so greatly coveted as formerly. The nature of the civil service will probably continue to be as dynamic as it has been in the past decade. It appears that nearly all Germans who, as government or union officials, are concerned with the civil service believe that the present situation contains many incongruities and are seriously considering further modifications. Proposals of this type range from a revision of the four career levels for the purpose of broadening opportunities for advancement to the abolition of the civil service and the merging of the three types of public employees into a single new type (see Chapter VI for probable changes).

·II·

Public Sector Negotiation

LEGAL BACKGROUND OF NEGOTIATION

FREEDOM of association for employees and employers, public as well as private, is guaranteed in the Federal Constitution.[1] Article 9, Section 3 reads in part as follows: "The right to form associations to safeguard and improve working and economic conditions is guaranteed for everyone and for all occupations. Agreements that seek to restrict or impede this right are void; measures directed toward such purpose are illegal."

Federal agencies are under legal obligation to negotiate the terms of employment of public employees. This is in contrast to the situation of the private employers, who are not forced to bargain collectively, even though they may be obliged by their federal or state government to conform to the terms of employment that have become prevalent in their industry as the result of negotiation by other parties. Strangely enough, the obligation to bargain with the representatives of federal wage-earners and salaried employees is set forth in the Federal Civil Servants Act of July 14, 1953, which contains the foundations for legislation regulating the terms of service of the civil servants, concerning whom there is no obligation or even permission to bargain. Section 191 of the act states: "The legal relationships of the salaried employees and wage-earners in the service of the Federal Republic or of a public law corporation, institution or foundation directly responsible to the Federal Republic shall be regulated through collective agreement."

This same act elaborates on the constitutional provision of freedom of association with reference to civil servants. Section 91 reads as follows: "(1) On the basis of freedom of association civil servants have the right to join together in unions or professional societies. They may authorize the appropriate

1. I.L.O., *Legislative Series,* 1949, Ger. F. R. 1.

unions or professional societies to represent them, in so far as legislation does not provide otherwise. (2) No civil servant may be disciplined or disadvantaged because of activity for his union or professional society." In their case, however, there is no obligation to bargain, since their terms of employment are set by law and not by contract.

The form and content of collective agreements is regulated to some extent by legislation, especially the Collective Agreements Act of April 9, 1949, issued in its latest revised form on August 25, 1969,[2] which is equally applicable to the private and public sectors. It requires that all agreements be in writing. This means that they must be signed by the representatives of the parties and that any revisions or supplements must be in similar form. It is also required that copies of all agreements be deposited with the federal Ministry of Labor. The ministry has no function of approval or disapproval, but merely serves as a depository and analyst.

The specific provision of the act on content of agreements (Sec. 1) reads: "The collective agreement regulates the rights and duties of the parties and contains the legal standards that can govern the content, the establishment, and the termination of employment relationships as well as questions concerning the enterprise and employee representation."

Legal commentaries and court decisions have given these provisions rather more specific substance than might be inferred from a quick reading. There is no definite requirement regarding what must or must not be included in an agreement. It is understood, however, that the agreement consists of two basic parts, which are termed "contractual" and "normative."

The contractual provisions deal with the rights and obligations involved in the relationship between the parties to the agreement and have no direct effect on the terms of employment. These include the implicit or explicit obligation to maintain industrial peace (p. 196) and the obligation to strive for the obser-

2. *BGBl.*, 1969, I, 1323. See also H. Reichel and O. Wlotzke, *Collective Bargaining and the Law Governing Collective Agreements.* Bonn: Federal Ministry of Labor and the Social Structure (Social Policy Monograph No. 19), 1963.

vance of the agreement by the members of the contracting associations.

The normative provisions set the standards for the individual employment contracts between the employers and their workers. As indicated in the legislative provision quoted above, these provisions may deal with several types of questions. The most important group is the one related to the content of the employment relationship. It covers the details that constitute the basic terms of employment (such as wages, hours, and fringes), and constitutes the major part of the agreement. Terms dealing with the establishment of the employment relationship are rarely found, though a few agreements may supplement laws dealing with employment preference for the handicapped or the prohibition of employment of women or children under certain conditions. On the other hand, agreements do typically cover the conditions under which dismissal and resignation are permissible, even though this matter is also covered by law. These provisions specify the length of notice required to terminate employment in the absence of grounds for immediate dismissal.

The act makes vague reference to "questions concerning the enterprise." This is considered to refer to provisions regarding employee conduct and discipline or matters benefiting the employees as a group, such as accident prevention, health measures, and welfare projects (e.g. canteens, vacation homes, and supplementary pension funds).

The final area mentioned in Section 1 of the act is matters of employee representation. This area is covered in considerable detail by the Works Council Act for private industry and the Staff Representation Act for the public service, but there is still room for the negotiation of supplementary details.

A final area of negotiated provisions, though not mentioned in Section 1, is effectively implied in Section 4, Paragraph 2, which states: "If joint organizations of the parties are set forth and regulated in the agreement (wage equalization funds, vacation funds, etc.), these regulations directly and compulsorily control the statutes of these organizations and the relationship of the organization to the employers and employees who are subject to the agreement." This applies to any joint funds that may be created, such as those for welfare or training purposes. It is not of much importance in actual practice, but it completes the legal listing of items that may be covered in an agreement.

No instances were found in which a union had attempted to obtain in an agreement covering German public employees a provision not closely related to the terms of employment. Possibly such a provision might be permissible, if it were phrased in terms that·brought it within the contractual part of the agreement, concerning the relationship between the parties themselves. Its permissibility within the normative provisions is much more doubtful. Such provisions must relate directly to the employment relationship, and should not cover any point that might not appropriately be included in the individual contract of employment. "The employment norms must govern the content of this employment relationship. It can be said that they must concern provisions that could be agreed to in an individual contract of employment. . . . The regulated points must *directly* concern the content of the employment relationship, and may not stand in only a loose relationship to it. . . . [O]nly that which has a close connection with the employment relationship may be regulated by collective agreement."[3] This is apparently a question that has not been clearly tested in the courts, nor much discussed by commentators. Issues other than terms of employment are sometimes discussed by unions with certain government officials, such as state Ministers of Education, but there has apparently been no thought of trying to deal with them in collective agreements.

PUBLIC EMPLOYEE UNIONS

The sixteen unions in the German Trade Union Federation (DGB) include four whose members are largely or entirely in government service. By far the largest of these is the Union for Public Services, Transport, and Communication (Gewerkschaft Öffentliche Dienste, Transport und Verkehr or

3. A. Hueck, H. C. Nipperdey, E. Stahlhacke, *Tarifvertragsgesetz* (4th ed.), Munich: Verlag C. H. Beck, 1964, p. 61.

ÖTV). It enrolls all three types of public employees (wage-earners, salaried employees, and civil servants) at all three levels of government (federal, state, and local), excluding only those employed as railway or postal workers or teachers. Like all other German postwar unions, it has no direct ties with any prewar union. The obliteration of unions during the Nazi period was so complete that no present union can claim direct descent from earlier ones. They can at most claim to have been patterned more or less after some forerunner.

Organization of government employees began in the municipal public utility plants, especially in the gas works in Berlin and Hamburg in 1896-97, and spread to local transit and hospitals.[4] The next decade of organization and affiliation saw the establishment of two major organizations: the Association of Municipal and State Wage-Earners and the German Transport Workers Association. Both grew substantially during the first quarter of the century, though the former found itself frequently thwarted in its jurisdictional claims by the priority given to craft organization by the General Commission of German Trade Unions, which served as the federation of the socialist unions from 1891 until replaced by the General Federation of German Trade Unions (ADGB) in 1919. In 1920 the Transport Workers Association developed into the German Transport Association and in 1929 finally merged with the Municipal and State Wage-Earners. Efforts toward merger with the Railway Workers were unsuccessful. The new postwar union for the public services, the ÖTV, long waged a vigorous struggle to encompass the entire public sector. It was unable to prevent separate organization of the railway and postal workers and the teachers, but has preserved for itself a vast domain that covers nearly all the other forms of public employment.[5] It is the second largest of the DGB unions. Its

4. F. J. Furtwängler, *ÖTV: Die Geschichte einer Gewerkschaft.* Stuttgart: Union Druckerei, 1955, p. 152. This is a voluminous history of German public employee unionism.
5. For an account of these struggles see E. Fritz, "So entstand die ÖTV," in ÖTV, *Zwanzig Jahre ötv.* Stuttgart: Verlagsanstalt Courier, 1966. This volume contains 23 essays on various aspects of the problems and achievements of this union during its first two decades.

total membership at the end of 1969 was 977,031. Of these, 147,270 were retired, unemployed, or otherwise inactive, leaving 829,761 employed members. Of these, 65,994 were in the Transport Department, which includes almost entirely workers in private employment, such as trucking, warehousing, airlines, harbors, and inland waterways. Deducting them leaves 763,767 active public employees divided into eight departments as follows:

Department	Wage-Earners	Salaried Employees	Civil Servants	Total
Local Transit	70,585	9,557	182	80,324
Power and Water	89,388	34,879	436	124,701
Health	31,403	35,786	2,154	69,343
Police	3,070	3,621	28,716	35,407
Social Insurance Funds	3,127	29,347	10,411	42,885
Other Local	131,804	94,856	34,175	260,835
Other State	30,322	36,438	13,451	80,211
Other Federal	44,415	20,385	5,261	70,061
Total	404,114	264,867	94,786	763,767

One unique aspect of the membership of this union is that it obtained the permission of the government in August 1966 to enroll members of the armed services. It appears, however, to have made slight headway in this unusual area of its jurisdiction. The membership figures show that it has relatively little strength among the civil servants, but that on the other hand it includes more than half of all public wage-earners. If we combine the local transit and power and water with the "other local" department, it is obvious that this union has tremendous strength at the municipal and county level. It is in effect the sole bargaining agent for all public wage-earners at all levels of government except those in the federal railway and postal services. Some public wage-earners belong to the Christian unions, but they are almost insignificant in number as compared to those in the ÖTV.

The Christian unions would, of course, like to negotiate jointly with the ÖTV, but the latter refuses to accept such a situation. Since unions negotiate on behalf of their members, the Christian unions are free to conduct separate negotiations, and they do so. The government agencies, however, naturally refuse to sign anything other than an identical agreement with a minor union. At the national level the Christian unions must therefore await the conclusion of negotiations by the ÖTV before signing their own agreements. These duplicate agreements are separately registered with the federal Ministry of Labor, but are given the same identification number with the addition of an "A" or a "B." Since the agencies do not inquire into the union membership or nonmembership of their wage-earners and salaried employees, they conclude with each one an individual contract of employment, specifying the agreement that governs the relationship. In this way nonmembers are also brought under the terms of the appropriate agreement.

Three other DGB unions enroll almost entirely persons related to the public sector. Two of these, the DPG (Postal Union) and the GdED (Railway Workers) are very strongly entrenched in their respective areas of jurisdiction. They are of course active only at the federal level. Their dominance in their two areas, where civil servants play such a large role, apparently justifies the DGB claim that its unions as a whole contain more active civil servants than the unions in the DBB (Civil Servants Association). These two unions are the sole bargaining agents for both the wage-earners and salaried employees in their respective agencies. Their agreements must in practice be very similar to those concluded by the ÖTV, except insofar as additions and omissions are related to the peculiarities of the tasks and services involved. Agreements with these two unions are not concluded until the corresponding ÖTV settlement has been reached, through the negotiations may be held simultaneously. This does not place the two specialized unions at the mercy of the ÖTV, however. Since all three belong to the DGB, there is a high degree of coordination in their bargaining, both before and during the negotiations.

The fourth DGB union focusing in the public sector is the GEW (Teachers Union). Unlike the DPG and the GdED, it is relatively small and faces strong opposition.[6] Since nearly all teachers are state civil servants, it has little occasion to negotiate and directs its efforts chiefly toward consultation and lobbying.

In addition to these four DGB unions, whose membership is exclusively or predominantly in the government area, there are some that have a few public employees. The Union for Agriculture and Forestry has over 3,000 civil servants and presumably a number of wage-earners who are employed in the state forests. The Union for Mining and Power has approximately 175 civil servants, presumably mine inspectors. And the Union for the Arts has some public-employee members, since the opera houses and many of the theaters are operated by a municipality or a state. The DGB public service unions are closely coordinated with each other through their membership in the confederation. The coordination occurs largely through the activities of the Salaried Employees Department and the Civil Servants Department of the DGB. As a result of the work of these departments and their committees of representatives of the constituent unions, a high degree of concurrence on all major policy questions is achieved.

While the DGB unions have the field to themselves when negotiating for public wage-earners and the DPG and GdED have a similar monopoly regarding the salaried employees in their two agencies, the ÖTV, when bargaining for its salaried employees in all other public agencies (federal, state, and local), must share honors with a major independent union federation. As mentioned, the DAG (Union of Salaried Employees) was involved in constant dispute during the early postwar years regarding affiliation with the union federation in the British Zone, but in 1949 was definitely denied admission, due to its refusal to confine its jurisdiction to the trade-banking-insurance "industry." It was presumably influenced in this stand by the fact that during the Weimar Republic separate organizations and even separate federations for wage-earners and for

6. For a recent account of teachers unions in postwar Germany see W. D. Fuhrig, "West Germany," in A. A. Blum (ed.), *Teacher Unions and Associations: A Comparative Study.* Urbana: University of Illinois Press, 1969.

salaried employees were the general rule. Although 72 percent of its membership is in the private sector, the DAG has so many members in nearly all areas of public employment outside the postal and railway services that it joins with the ÖTV in negotiating for such salaried employees. Thus these two unions are at the same time competitors and partners.

Another major independent union federation is the DBB (Civil Servants Association). This union comes closer than any other to tracing its history back to prewar days because of the existence of a very similar organization with the same name throughout the Weimar period. Efforts at consolidation of the numerous civil servant organizations took place during World War I. In February 1916 four of these unions in the postal and railway services joined in forming the Interessengemeinschaft Deutscher Beamtenverbände. By June 1918 it had acquired 72 groups with some 600,000 members. Under the pressure of revolution, most other civil servant unions joined it on December 4, 1918, in forming the Deutscher Beamtenbund with some million members. It followed the same principles of independence and political and religious neutrality as its present counterpart. It refused to align itself with the socialist unions, which soon formed their own civil servant federation. The Christian and liberal unions also formed their civil servant branches, but with only moderate success. By 1928 the Beamtenbund had nearly two thirds of the more than 1,600,000 organized civil servants in the German Reich, in spite of the serious internal strife occasioned by its refusal to support the unsuccessful strike of its railway affiliate in 1922.[7]

There has been considerable controversy concerning the details on DBB activity in the first months after Hitler came to power on January 30, 1933. On March 14 the organization issued a statement of support of the new government. Ten

7. For more details on civil servant union history see Ch. 2 of D. O. Schoonmaker, *The Politics of the Deutscher Beamtenbund: A Case Study of a Pressure Group, 1949–1963*. Ann Arbor: University Microfilms, 1966. This excellent Princeton doctoral dissertation in political science contains a wealth of material on the structure, policies, and tactics of the DBB.

days later its president resigned and was replaced by an appointee of that government. Although the other unions were dissolved on May 2, the DBB continued on under government control until it was reorganized under a new name at the end of the year.[8]

After the war the Occupation Forces, believing that the civil servants of the early 1930s had been too ready to follow Hitler and mistrusting those who had held significant office since then, at first refused to allow the organization of separate civil servant unions. At this time many civil servants joined the mixed organizations of public employees of the federation in the British Zone. They came especially from the postal and railway services, which had supplied most of the membership for the socialist civil servant unions in the 1920s. This explains in part the dominance of the DPG and GdED among even the civil servants in those two agencies today. The ban on separate unions was lifted early in 1948, with the limitation that the new groups be restricted to small areas. This requirement tended to mold the new unions along geographical lines rather than the career-level and occupational lines that had predominated in earlier times. A federation known as the Gewerkschaft Deutscher Beamtenbund developed. With the creation of the Federal Republic in 1949 the earlier limitations ceased and the federation was reorganized on March 24, 1950, as the present DBB. The inevitable disputes as to whether the constituent unions should be organized along the lines of agency or type of work or career level or state demarcations was never completely resolved, and its 43 groups include various types. Aside from the state organizations there are several based on the type of agency. There is one for the postal service and two for the railways, one of which is for the engineers. Other illustrations are the unions for police, teachers, tax officials, customs officers, and social insurance employees.

Since the DBB is primarily a representative of civil servants,

8. For documentation on this controversy see DBB, *Deutscher Beamtenbund: Ursprung, Weg, Ziel*. Bad Godesberg: Deutscher Beamten-Verlag, 1968, pp. II/171–73. A fascinating presentation of civil servant union history with close reference to major political developments.

it and its constituents are not (as yet) negotiating unions. It reports, however, that about 10 percent of its members are public wage-earners or salaried employees. At its last triennial congress in November 1969 it emphasized its interest in representing these two groups by changing the subtitle of its name from "Union Federation of Professional Civil Servants" to "Federation of the Unions of the Public Service." Its structure includes an Alliance of Negotiating Unions[9] (Gemeinschaft tarriffähiger Verbände or GtV), to which twelve of its constituents belong. It reports[10] that the GtV during the three years 1966-69 signed 148 agreements. This represents chiefly a signing of agreements already negotiated by other unions. Thus far the GtV has been unable to win the right to participate in the actual bargaining (except on behalf of the employees of some social insurance funds), and has been limited to the role of presenting its demands in advance to the appropriate government agencies, for it faces the adamant opposition of the DGB and DAG to its inclusion in the negotiating process. The law is not entirely clear on its right to full participation, but some authorities on labor law are of the opinion that its exclusion may be unconstitutional. This is perhaps the least stable aspect of the bargaining structure.

The GtV has recently made another push for participation. In December 1969 it joined with five independent unions (two for public salaried employees in general, two for social workers, and one for highway maintenance) to form the Alliance of Unions and Associations in the Public Service (Gemeinschaft von Gewerkschaften und Verbänden des öffentlichen Dienstes or GGVöD). This does not involve withdrawal of the GtV from the DBB. The new alliance claims to represent 216,000 wage-earners and salaried employees who at present are not represented in the negotiation process.

A final federation, the CGB (Christian unions), plays only a minor role outside the Saar. Although it has not submitted any membership data, its total membership is thought to

9. Literally: Alliance of Unions Authorized to Conclude Collective Agreements.
10. DBB, *Geschäftsbericht der Bundesleitung,* 1969, p. 77.

be about 190,000, but the proportion of these in public service is not available.

In addition to these four federations, there are a considerable number of independent unions. Although many of them are comprised of public servants and thus are not bargaining agents, many do include some wage-earners or salaried employees. It will therefore be best to mention them at this point.

As stated above, the GEW includes a relatively small proportion of all organized teachers and faces strong competition from a number of other unions. There has always been a strong tendency to form separate unions for male and female teachers and for Catholics and Protestants. A still more important divisive force has been the inability to agree on a common program because of the rivalries between the teachers in the various kinds of schools to protect or improve their relative status. Thus many unions are for teachers of a single type, such as those in the primary, secondary, vocational, or high schools. Most of the teachers in the higher academic type of schools have been unwilling to join with those in the vocational or grade schools and do not support their demands for higher training requirements and a reduction in pay differentials.

One independent union, the Bavarian Association of Male and Female Teachers, joined with the GEW for nearly twenty years in a Working Alliance of German Teachers Associations. In the spring of 1969, with a membership of about 30,000, it discontinued this relationship and in June joined with four DBB teachers unions in forming the German Teachers Association (Deutsche Lehrerverband) with a claimed membership of about 100,000. The four DBB unions remain in that federation, but the Association is independent. This anomalous situation is perhaps temporary and transitional. Presumably it is hoped by many that the Bavarian union, although unwilling to move from its long relationship with the GEW into the DBB in one jump, will eventually enter the latter after a trial period with this halfway measure. Other independent teachers unions are too numerous to mention.

In higher education the senior members of the teaching

and research staffs of the thirty-eight state Universities (the *Dozenten* and full professors) typically do not belong to a union, but to a professional organization known as the University Association (Hochschulverband). Its functions are somewhat similar to those of the American Association of University Professors, but with a greater emphasis on lobbying, and not unlike those of a number of unions affiliated with the DBB. Junior faculty members belong to the Federal Assistants Conference (Bundesassistentenkonferenz or BAK). In this particular case membership is, under university statutes, automatic and compulsory. The BAK is not technically a union, but recently it has been acting very much like one in its lobbying and organizing of protest demonstrations in an effort to influence the content of new state laws on university governance.

Although the ÖTV and DBB both have police affiliates, by far the largest organization in this area is the independent Police Union (Gewerkschaft der Polizei or GdP), with about 75 percent of the organized police officers. During the postwar occupation period the formation of police unions was prohibited in the British and French zones. Police associations were formed, but functioned only for social and welfare purposes. In the American Zone there was no such prohibition. The police unions formed there early became a part of the ÖTV. When the restrictions in the other zones were lifted with the establishment of the Federal Republic, the police associations joined in November 1950 to form the GdP. This union has sought to affiliate as a separate unit with the DGB, but these efforts have been blocked by the ÖTV, which believes that, since it already has many police members, the GdP should enter as a part of the ÖTV rather than as a separate national union. Except in several of the larger cities, the police are state civil servants. The GdP, in addition to its civil servants, has many wage-earners and salaried employees who work for the police authorities, but it does not presently have the right to participate in the negotiations affecting them.

Another independent union, which has attracted considerable public attention as a result of several slowdowns, is the Association of German Air Traffic Controllers (Verband Deutscher Flugleiter or VDF). At the end of the war, air traffic control was a new civilian occupation. The controllers were salaried employees of the Occupation Forces until they were eventually taken over by the Federal Institute for Flight Safety. At that time they belonged chiefly to the ÖTV. They have long sought special terms of employment and retirement because of the alleged tension of their work. Meeting with little success in these efforts, they eventually formed their separate union. Following a strike in 1962, most of them accepted transfer to civil servant status. Those who continued as salaried employees and other groups in the Flight Safety Institute are represented in negotiations not by the VDF but by the ÖTV and the DAG. The latter claims to enroll two thirds of the 1,200 civil servants and 600 salaried employees in this service.

One more independent union, which has been noted for protests over long hours of overtime without extra remuneration, is the Association of German Salaried Doctors (Verband der angestellten Ärzte Deutschlands or "Marburger Bund"), which also includes a number of civil servant physicians. The two groups are employed chiefly on the medical faculties and in the clinics of the state universities and in state and municipal hospitals. The Bund, like the other independent unions, is not a direct participant in negotiations. For this purpose it has a working alliance with the DAG.

After this survey of the union structure in the public sector, an estimate may be made of the degree of organization of public employees in certain agencies and as a whole. An exact statement of the extent of unionization is impossible for a number of reasons. A major problem is that all unions include in their total membership a considerable number of retired employees and widows or others who are not in the labor force, and many of them are reluctant to disclose the proportion of their inactive members. Fortunately, the number of the unemployed has been so low in recent years that their inclusion or exclusion can have little effect on the estimate. Unfortunately, the government does not collect any useful union membership data. In most cases it is impossible to obtain enough breakdown of union figures to permit relating the members of specific agencies or types of work. Finally, the data available on employment and membership are not all for the same date or even the same year. This is of little concern since changes from year to year have recently been minor. Therefore, the most recent data readily available in the desired detail have been used in most cases.

The railway system is certainly the best organized among the larger government agencies. The GdED reports[11] that at the end of 1967 its membership included 123,412 *active* civil servants or 53 percent of the number then employed; 6,376 active salaried employees or 81 percent of the total; and 157,419 active wage-earners or 91 percent of the total. It thus claimed as members at that time 70 percent of all federal railroad employees. (It has a few members who work on nonfederal railroads. It is not clear whether or not these are included in the above figures, but in any case the percentage of organization would not be greatly affected.) The two DBB unions in this field (the Gewerkschaft Deutscher Bundesbahnbeamten and the Gewerkschaft Deutscher Lokomotivbeamten) had in September of the same year 99,948 employed civil servants (out of a total membership of 145,049) representing 43 percent of the civil servants then employed on the federal railways or 24 percent of all employees of that system. An additional 2 percent of the total are attributed to the Christian unions. It thus appears that at least 96 percent of federal railway employees belonged to some union in 1967. The percentage was actually higher to the extent that the two DBB unions included active wage-earners and salaried employees. For this agency it has been necessary to use membership and employment figures for the same year, since railway employment has been declining.

The postal service is also well organized. The DPG reports[12] that it enrolled at the end of 1967, 182,885 *active* civil servants (and postmasters) or about 64 percent of the 283,736

11. GdED, *Geschäftsbericht, 1965–1968*, p. 368.
12. DPG, *Geschäftsbericht, 1965–1968*, pp. 612–13, 616.

total; 22,584 salaried employees or about 42 percent of the 53,220 total (indicating the difficulty of enlisting female clerical employees); and 84,692 wage-earners (including apprentices) or over 66 percent of their total of 127,487. Their indication that their membership includes about 75 percent of the total employees appears to include members in retirement. If these are deducted, they probably have not more than 63 percent of the total. This union, unlike most others in the DGB, has steadily increased its membership in recent years.

The DBB postal union (the Deutscher Postverband) had in September 1967 a membership of 50,652, of whom 37,209 were employed civil servants. These were 13 percent of the civil servants and 8 percent of all postal employees. On the assumption that the Christian unions have 1 percent of the total, the postal service is at least 72 percent organized. Again, the actual percentage is slightly higher because the unknown number of wage-earners and salaried employees in the DBB union have not been included.

In contrast to the United States, the police officers are more highly organized than the postal employees. This estimate is based not on exact figures but on approximations as of the first half of 1970. There were then about 145,000 authorized positions, of which about 10,000 were vacant because of the labor shortage. Out of a total membership of 120,000, the independent GdP had 90,000 active officers or 67 percent of the total. The ÖTV had another 28,700 or 21 percent. The number of active officers in the Polizeigewerkschaft in the DBB is not presently available, but it would need to be only 2,800 to bring the extent of unionization of police officers up to 90 percent.

The only other group for which a separate estimate is available is university instruction. The University Association states that its 1969 membership of about 6,800 constituted 67 percent of the senior faculties of the state universities. It is not known whether they include persons beyond 68 years of age in their membership and employment data. Retirement has a unique connotation for German full professors, unlike any other group of civil servants. Their obligation to serve is ended, but their right to teach and conduct research continues for life, as does their full basic salary.[13]

For an estimate of the overall degree of government employee organization the latest figures available at this time will be used. They date from late 1968 to early 1970. Here again the major problem is estimating what proportion of a union's members are in the active labor force. A second problem is the need to estimate the membership of some of the independent unions that have not been contacted. The conclusion of this estimate is that the unions have perhaps enrolled some 2,312,-000 public employees, distributed by union and employee type as follows:

Union	Date	Civil Servants	Salaried Employees	Wage-Earners	Total
ÖTV	12/69	94,786	264,867	404,114	763,767
DPG	12/69	186,000	25,000	86,000	297,000
GdED	12/69	121,000	6,000	154,000	281,000
GEW	12/69	87,000	9,000	—	96,000
DBB	9/68	486,000	54,000	—	540,000
DAG	6/70	7,500	90,000	—	97,500
GdP	6/70	90,000	16,500	—	106,500
Others		83,000	34,000	13,000	105,000
Total		1,155,286	499,367	657,114	2,311,767

Some explanation and justification of the estimate are called for. The ÖTV is the only union for which precise current figures are at hand. They have already been listed (p. 32). For the DPG and GdED it is assumed that their proportion of active members remains the same as in 1967. Since it is known that the number of inactive members in the ÖTV

13. The professors have indeed a favored position, but it is not quite as attractive as it sounds. They formerly received in addition to their basic salary a share of the student fees. This fee-sharing was discontinued by the various states about 1965, partly because it unduly favored the teachers of courses that students were required to take and because it gave all professors an incentive to resist expansion of the curriculum to keep classes large. The fees were replaced by an individually negotiated bonus, which in a few cases may be even larger than the basic salary. The bonus ceases upon retirement. Even so, the continuing annual salary may run as righ as 36,000 DM. (Prior to the autumn of 1969, the Deutsche Mark was valued at 4 to the dollar. Since then the ratio has been about 3.65.)

and DPG is about 15 percent, the same proportion has been applied to the total membership of another DGB union, the GEW. In the case of the DBB, since it is known that about 25 percent of the members of its three unions in the postal and railway services are not employed, the same proportion has been applied to its total membership of 718,943. The DAG reports for June 1970 a total membership of about 470,000, of whom some 120,000 salaried employees and 10,000 civil servants were related to government service. Since it does not indicate how many of these are inactive, the ratio is assumed to be high, and 25 percent has been deducted. The GdP has made its own breakdown, which indicates that 11 percent of its 120,000 members are inactive. Some of its members listed here as salaried employees are in fact wage-earners.

The data for "other unions" involve much more guesswork. As to civil servants, it is assumed that 25,000 of the 30,000 members of the Bavarian teachers union are active, and an arbitrary 25,000 are added for the many other independent teachers unions. The 6,800 members of the University Association are included along with some 3,200 civil servants belonging to DGB unions other than the four already listed. The air traffic controllers are said to have some 1,000 members. It was noted in Chapter I that the Christian unions have about 2 percent of all union members. It is assumed that they have the same percentage of organized government employees, so they are credited with 22,000 civil servants. As to salaried employees, perhaps 25,000 of a reported 47,000 salaried doctors belong to the Marburger Bund, and 9,000 are included for the Christian unions. Finally, 13,000 wage-earners attributed to the Christian unions have been added. If some of these guesses prove to have been on the high side, that may perhaps have been balanced by the omission of various small organized groups, such as the forestry wage-earners in the Union for Agriculture and Forestry.

Comparing the results of this estimate with the official data on total government employment presented on page 20, it appears that about 86 percent of the employed civil servants,

52 percent of the public salaried employees,[14] 85 percent of the public wage-earners, or 75 percent of all public employees are union members. Earlier it was estimated that 33 percent of the total employed labor force is organized. From this it follows that if the public-sector labor force is 75 percent unionized, the private sector is only 26 percent organized. This seems a very surprising difference in the degree of organization. It is probably futile to speculate on its cause. It seems unlikely that union organizing drives are any less aggressive in the private sector. Can it be that the opposition to unionism of private employers in the smaller plants could make this much difference?

GOVERNMENTAL BARGAINING STRUCTURE

The federal government has three agencies that are involved with negotiation of the terms of employment of its wage-earners and salaried employees. The management of the federal railway system negotiates, under the general supervision of the Transport Ministry, for its employees. The Postal Ministry bargains for the staff of that ministry and the postal service. This may be changed very soon. The new government that came into power under the chancellorship of Willy Brandt following the national election in September 1969 announced its intention of eventually establishing the postal service as a separate federal corporation, somewhat similar to the Railway System, and placing it also under the control of a merged Transport and Postal Ministry. A government bill to accomplish this reorganization was submitted to the parliament in August 1970 after consultation with the DPG. Presumably there will continue to be separate negotiations for postal employees.

The Ministry of the Interior represents the federal government in negotiations concerning all of its other wage-earners and salaried employees. This responsibility rested originally with the Ministry of Finance, but was transferred to Interior in 1960,

14. This conclusion, and perhaps the entire estimate, must be viewed with some skepticism in view of the oral statement of a DAG official that about 25 percent of the salaried employees in the public sector have been organized (and the same proportion in the private sector).

because there was a widespread belief that the Finance Ministry was too exclusively concerned with the goal` of minimizing expenditure. Finance continues, however, to have a representative present as observer in all federal negotiations. Similarly at the state level the negotiating function is assigned to one of the state ministries—in some states it is the Interior Ministry, in others the Finance Ministry. The states, however, seldom negotiate individually. Following a brief postwar experience with separate bargaining, major negotiations have been conducted jointly by all.

At the end of the war collective bargaining was not immediately introduced because of the wage freeze imposed by the Occupation Forces. This was lifted in the American and British zones in March 1948 and in the French Zone in the autumn. Unions immediately pressed for negotiations with the individual states. The first such agreement was concluded in July and obtained Occupation approval in September. The states were interested in maintaining fairly uniform terms of employment, and quickly realized that they would be whipsawed by the unions in separate negotiations. Several states in the north (British Zone) experimented briefly with joint negotiation of separate agreements but found this to be clumsy. Most of the states attempted joint negotiation with the ÖTV and DAG in February 1949, but reached no conclusion because of the absence of a competent employers association. In March the Council of States decided to try to form an association to conduct negotiations. At a meeting on April 22 the Bargaining Association of German States (Tarifgemeinschaft deutscher Länder or TdL) was established. The first membership assembly was held on May 23, and negotiations began on May 31. Bavaria was not an initial member, but joined soon afterward. Berlin and Saarland joined when they achieved statehood.

The TdL statutes state: "The purpose of the Bargaining Association is the protection of the interests of its members in the uniformity of the terms of employment in the public service. The Bargaining Association pursues this purpose especially through the conclusion of collective agreements." The members of this employers association are the eleven states. West Berlin belongs with reference only to its salaried employees, since most of its wage-earners have functions similar to those of municipalities. The controlling body is the membership assembly. Each state has one vote. Adoption of any measure requires a 60 percent majority. The assembly ratifies the conclusion or cancellation of agreements.

The member states are obligated to pay annual dues, to provide requested information concerning their terms of employment and other relevant matters, to abide by the terms of negotiated agreements, and to conclude no separate collective agreement without the approval of the membership assembly. The TdL has now operated for twenty years with relatively little friction. However, there has been at least one instance in September 1969 in which some individual states made commitments without the required approval. The statutes provide no penalties other than expulsion, which is impractical and has not been seriously considered. There has apparently been no consideration of the possibility of imposing a fine or denying voting rights for a specified period.

The national negotiations on behalf of local governments are conducted by an organization known as the Federation of Local Government Employers Associations (Vereinigung der kommunalen Arbeitgeberverbände or VKA), which was established soon after the TdL. The meeting of April 22, 1949, at which the TdL was founded was attended by representatives of six state associations of local governments. They decided, however, that they would set up their own national federation rather than join with the states. In view of the variety of local government agencies and the complexity of their organizations, it appears that this was a wise decision.

The statutes of the VKA contain the following statement of purpose: "The Federation has the function of protecting the common interests of its members in the labor-law area. It facilitates the exchange of experience between them. It establishes the basic principles of bargaining policy and can serve as a party in concluding collective agreements, if the membership assembly so determines on the basis of the joint interest of all members of the Federation. It can also establish, by agreement with the unions or otherwise, binding guidelines for the conclusion of collective agreements by its individual members."

Members of the Federation are twelve local government employers associations in the states—one for each state, except that Bremen is not a member, belonging only to the TdL, and that Baden-Württemberg, which was formed by the merger of three smaller states, still has three separate associations of local governments, though their merger appears imminent. In the membership assembly, which normally meets annually, each member association has a number of votes proportional to its annual dues, which in turn are based upon the number of its wage-earners and salaried employees. It cannot split its votes. The assembly elects the first and second chairmen of the presidium, the members of the specialty committees, two members of the central committee, and the director and executive director, who head the staff. It also approves the budget, revises the statutes, and passes on the expulsion or fining of members.

The member associations are obligated to adhere to the terms of collective agreements and any guidelines, to avoid the negotiation of any separate agreements concerning matters on which the Federation has negotiated or intends to negotiate, and to provide in their statutes for penalizing any of their members who exceed the terms of agreements. Any member association that violates an agreement or a Federation decision and refuses to terminate such violation immediately may be expelled or fined up to five times its annual dues.

At the state level of negotiations with local government agencies the organizational structure is more complex. It differs considerably from state to state, but the general pattern is fairly clear. In each state except Bremen there is an employers association for cities and one for counties and usually one for each other type of local employer, such as incorporated public utilities, hospitals, and savings and loan associations. These band together in a statewide employers association of all types of local agencies, which in turn is one of the twelve VKA members. In order to avoid undue generalization, the structure of a single general association will be examined. For this purpose, one of the smallest has been selected—one of the three which divide the state of Baden-Württemberg among themselves—the local Labor Law Association in Württemberg-Baden (Kommunale Arbeitsrechtliche Vereinigung in Württemberg-Baden or KAV, with offices in Stuttgart. An analysis of its membership indicates the variety of local governmental employers in Germany. In August 1968 it had a total membership of 212. The principal groups of members were as follows: 109 municipalities; 15 municipal associations, most of which were formed for some specific purpose such as provision of public utility services, sewage disposal, accident insurance, or welfare; 28 counties; 42 public savings and loan societies; 1 association of such societies and 13 establishments with legal personality controlled by local governments, which included electric, gas, and water supply, municipal transit companies, an airport, an industrial park, and a fairground. It may be noted that relatively few towns of less than 10,000 inhabitants belong to the association. Nonmembers frequently adopt the provisions of the agreements applicable to member municipalities, but often provide lower fringe benefits.

The internal structure of the KAV is generally similar to that of the TdL, but the differences are significant. Each member may send one representative to the membership assembly, and each has a vote. But a meeting cannot be arranged as easily and as frequently for 212 members as for the 11 TdL members. Consequently the KAV assembly does not have many functions other than the electing of the executive committee, the approval of the annual budget, and the setting of membership dues. It seldom meets more than once a year. Ratification of agreements is handled by the executive committee, which consists of 26 representatives of the various membership groups.

The obligations of the members are somewhat more stringent than in the TdL. Members shall not exceed the terms of applicable collective agreements directly or indirectly and they shall not conclude any independent agreement. Expulsion is not the only available penalty for violation of obligation. An alternate and more practical penalty is a fine of up to five times the amount of annual dues, which are based on the number of employees. The wide variety in the types of work performed by local government employees and in the resulting negotiation problems leads the association to establish specialty committees for several areas, including counties, public utilities, local transit, hospitals, savings and loan societies, forestry, and theater.

THE PATTERN OF AGREEMENTS

Separate agreements are negotiated for wage-earners and salaried employees. The major negotiations result in a master agreement, which covers the noneconomic issues and usually remains in effect for several years, and a pay agreement, which covers the economic issues and recently has been canceled and renegotiated at the end of each calendar year.

Thus the Postal Ministry from time to time negotiates with the DPG a master agreement for its wage-earners and another for its salaried employees, and annually concludes a pay agreement for each group. The management of the Railway Service does the same with the GdED.

Another master agreement covers nearly all other public salaried employees. It is called the National Master Agreement for Salaried Employees (Bundes-Angestelltentarifvertrag: Bund, Länder, Gemeinden or BAT). The parties to the agreement are the Federal Republic, represented by its Minister of the Interior, the TdL, and the VKA on the one side and the ÖTV and the DAG on the other. This one master agreement obviously covers a vast number of employees at all levels of government. Separate provisions relating to federal-state employees and to local employees are found only in Section 23, on promotion, Sections 26 and 27 on basic pay standards, Sections 28 and 29 concerning the difference in pay groups, and Section 39, which leaves to regional decision the amount of the length-of-service bonus in local agencies. This agreement, which has now undergone 24 amendments, was signed on February 23, 1961, after about nine years of negotiation. Its termination was announced by the unions in 1969, but it will continue in effect until replaced, which may well be at least 1971. In one published form it runs about 65 pages. It is supplemented by another hundred pages of additional provisions relating to 29 special employee groups, such as hospital workers, teachers, librarians, and employees in local transit, public utilities, savings and loan associations, airports, forestry, and foreign service. Although the BAT covers all levels of government, the pay agreement for salaried employees ' in local agencies is separate from the corresponding federal-state agreement.

For wage-earners the basic negotiations are also national, excluding only the postal and railway services and a few others. One difference is that the ÖTV is the sole bargaining agent for the workers, since salaried employees are not involved. The other major difference is that, although most of the negotiations are held jointly with the Interior Ministry, the TdL, and the VKA, the result is three separate master agreements for the wage-earners of the Federal Republic (Manteltarifvertrag für Arbeiter des Bundes or MTB), of the states (Manteltarifvertrag für Arbeiter der Länder or MTL), and of the local governments (Bundesmanteltarifvertrag für Arbeiter gemeindlicher Verwaltungen und Betriebe or BMT-G). These also required several years of negotiation. The MTL I was concluded on April 1, 1959, and replaced by the current MTL II on April 1, 1964. The MTB I was signed on May 25, 1960 (effective July 1) and was replaced by MTB II on April 1, 1964. The BMT-G was terminated by notice from the ÖTV as of April 1, 1969, and is now under renegotiation. The MTL and MTB have been canceled as of July 1, 1969, but it appears unlikely that there will be much negotiation on their replacement until the completion of a new BAT and BMT-G.

The MTB and MTL are very similar. The chief reason for the three separate agreements is that there are such wide differences in the work performed by wage-earners in the local agencies as compared with the state and federal governments.

In addition to the master agreements (and their revisions)

and the pay agreements, there are several others negotiated for the same employees by the same parties. These deal chiefly with the classification of specific positions into the pay categories set forth in the basic agreements. Other subjects covered include piece rates, annual bonus, children's bonus, reimbursement of travel costs, and old age and survivors insurance. In addition, there are agreements covering other groups of workers, such as apprentices and trainees, who are not included in the main categories of wage-earners, salaried employees, or civil servants. In 1970 separate agreements have been concluded regarding the length of vacations and the basic pay ranges of public wage-earners.

One other group of government employees is not covered by the master agreements already mentioned—those who work for a federal organization that has a separate legal personality. Such organizations are referred to in Section 191 of the Federal Civil Servants Act, which states the obligation to negotiate, as "a public law corporation, institution or foundation directly responsible to the Federal Republic." Among the major organizations in this category are the Federal Institute for Employment Service and Unemployment Insurance (Bundesanstalt für Arbeit), the German Federal Reserve Bank, and the federal institutes for various types of social insurance funds. The agreements covering these employees are similar to those applicable to other federal employees, but in this case the unions negotiate with the management of the particular organization rather than with the Ministry of the Interior.

Since the ÖTV is a party to nearly all public collective agreements except those of the postal and railway services, a good impression of the scope of government negotiations can be obtained from a study of its annual volumes containing all agreements in both the public and private sectors concluded by its national staff in each calendar year. The high degree of centralization of public employee bargaining in Germany is illustrated by the fact that even a general employers association of local governments and agencies in one state such as the KAV negotiates relatively few agreements. Most of the significant negotiations applicable to local governments are conducted on a nationwide basis by the VKA as the federation representing the various state associations of local government employers.

THE CONTENT OF AGREEMENTS

There is a broad similarity between German and American labor agreements, but some contrasts may be noted. The German agreements do not contain union security provisions. A union shop provision would be considered unconstitutional. The German concept of freedom of association places equal emphasis on the freedom not to join. There is typically no grievance procedure set forth, since that channel is provided by law. Arbitration of grievances is not mentioned, since such disputes go to the tripartite labor courts or, in the case of civil servants, to the administrative courts. There is little reference to seniority. Length of service is significant in some respects, but is not controlling in layoff or promotion. Legislation on layoff makes individual need a major factor. On the other hand, German agreements usually have more provisions regarding social and welfare payments and the termination of employment.

A summary of the major content of a German agreement in the public sector may be of interest. The BAT, governing most public salaried employees, will be used in its 1970 form for this purpose. This being a master agreement, it does not include the salary schedule. That schedule, together with the rates for overtime and "on call" time, are in a separate agreement. An appendix to the BAT defines the various types of work that are classified in each of the pay groups. Another notable omission from this agreement is a grievance procedure. The channel for a public-employee grievance at the agency level is the staff council, whose membership and operation are covered by legislation (see Chapter IV). One section of the agreement relating to discipline provides that the employee has the right to see, and to copy from, his complete personnel file and that unfavorable items shall not be entered in the file without his being heard and permitted to attach his comments.

In other respects the subjects covered are much like those found in American agreements. The substance of the provisions is, of course, often different. A few illustrations may be mentioned. For example, the probationary period is 6 months. The regular workweek is 43 hours, with the provision that it shall be reduced to 42 hours in January 1971. Full sick pay for 6 weeks increases by degrees up to 26 weeks after 10 years of service. A single-payment length-of-service bonus is granted after 25, 40, and 50 years of service.

Paid vacations are scaled according to pay group and age, rather than length of service. They vary from 3 weeks to an employee age 30 in a low grade up to 6 weeks for one in the top group who is 40 years old. Since the purpose of vacation is shown by its designation as "recuperation leave," pay in lieu of vacation is allowed only in case of termination.

Paid leave for personal reasons is granted under a variety of circumstances. Illustrative are: 4 days for death of spouse, for moving when assigned to a new location, and for a sick wife or child when care is essential and no one else is obtainable; 2 days for marriage, childbirth of wife, and death of close relative; one day for local moving, for marriage of child, for 25th and 50th wedding anniversaries, and for 25th, 40th, and 50th employment anniversaries. Thus it may be seen that a typical German public labor agreement differs from an American one more in detail than in general coverages.

Job security, as in most European countries, is less than provided by American agreements. Normally dismissal and resignation are permissible, provided there is adequate advance notice, varying from 2 weeks for probationary employees up to 6 months after 12 years of service. The BAT provides that after 15 years of service and 40 years of age, dismissal is not allowed unless immediate discharge is justified by the actions or conduct of the employee.

Since most of the agreements for public employees are nearly national in scope, there is relatively little variation in the terms of employment of wage-earners or salaried employees performing similar work for different agencies or in different parts of the country, with the exception of a location bonus. With reference to basic rates, the variations arise largely from the difficulty, and perhaps impossibility, of uniform classification of all jobs into the pay groups established in the agreements. For example, the city-state of Bremen and the state of North Rhine-Westphalia are reputed to have relatively high rates. Also, we exaggerate when we describe the agreements as nationwide. At the federal level we have noted the separate agreements for the railways, the postal service, the Federal Reserve Bank, and the employment service. Some minor variations inevitably result, as well as some exceptions at the state level.

One group of state salaried employees is covered by the BAT, but not by the pay agreement. The latter contains no provisions for school teachers. Nearly all teachers are state civil servants, but a few—chiefly those who are not fully qualified and kindergarten teachers—are salaried employees. Since state and local civil servants are paid according to state law and since there is inevitably some variation in these laws, the states have insisted on statewide, rather than national, pay negotiations for salaried employee teachers, so that their salaries can be closely related to those of their more numerous civil servant colleagues.

Finally, at the local level, we have already noted that variations may exist, because many of the smaller villages are not members of any municipal employers association that is affiliated with the VKA. As previously stated, they tend to conform to the agreement with reference to basic rates, but often not with reference to fringe benefits.

THE NEGOTIATING PROCESS

The first step toward negotiation involves of course the preparations of the separate parties. On the side of the government the federal Interior Ministry takes the lead. For pay negotiations it consults chiefly with the Finance Ministry. For revisions of the basic agreements it may consult with all of the other ministries. In either case the plans and objectives may be discussed in a cabinet meeting. Consultation with the leaders of the TdL and VKA will also be necessary. On the union side, from the point of view of the ÖTV as the chief bargaining agent there must first be an internal decision on tentative objectives. This may be a lengthy process, particularly if negotiation of a basic agreement is involved. For example, the 1969 planning on the demands to be made for revision of the basic agreement for federal wage-earners started with a week-long conference of the twelve regional directors of the union's wage-earner division. After the internal decision comes consultation with the other DGB public service unions and usually an agreement on joint goals. If salaried employees are involved, there may be a consultation with the DAG. These two unions, however, can scarcely be said to be on friendly terms. Their demands are formally set by their respective "large rate commissions" and reveal some differences that are apparently based in part upon competitive membership appeal. Nevertheless, they typically include much less "blue sky" than American union demands and in recent years have not been more than 3 or 4 percent above the anticipated settlement. Even during the negotiations consultation between the two is minimal, but no instance is known in which either has accepted an offer until the other was ready to do so.

Negotiations are usually held either at the Interior Ministry in Bonn or in Stuttgart, where both the ÖTV and the VKA have their headquarters. If agreement cannot be reached within a day or two, the sessions are usually recessed for at least two or three weeks. The annual pay negotiations, since they affect such a large number of unions and government units, are attended by quite a throng of representatives. Only a few of these are in the conference room. The rest are waiting to be consulted during intermissions if their views are wanted or if caucuses are held. Doubtless they also want an immediate first-hand report on any developments. The general climate of such a session can best be described in the words of an official of the Marburger Bund, who reported on his impressions as an observer-in-waiting at a recent pay negotiation:[15]

Before the building in Stuttgart black limousines and bright middle-class autos crowd each other. Three hundred worthy men are streaming to the fourth round of negotiations. They can be distinguished only by their cars. Their suits are gray; their expressions tense. In his hand each holds the obligatory briefcase. It can be sensed that their thoughts involve opposition and the will to combat.

10:00 A.M. Women and men sit in long rows at the long table. It is the large commission [of union representatives]. The leader gives a situation report. Both he and the report are already well known. We are meeting for the fourth time! The discussion goes from one district rep to another, from one craft representative to another. Technicians, foremen, junior managers, doctors, scientists at the research institute, punchcard operators, interpreters, actors all participate in the discussion. All want 8 percent.

11:00 A.M. All want the wage hike because everything costs more and because the insurance contributions have risen. Eight percent on the base pay equals 6.4 percent on the gross; deducting 2 percent insurance equals 4.4 net. We must have 8 percent, not a penny less.

All the arguments have been heard before. Then comes the news that the employers have asked for a one-hour recess. Pause. The large commission breaks up into small groups. The card players, the strollers, the world improvers who can't stop arguing even when no one listens. Others read, write, telephone, or check with other representatives. All are on the hunt for information. "Have you heard that . . . ," "The Interior Minister of Lower Saxony said . . . ," "The Hamburg Senate let us know that . . . ," "The city director is of the opinion. . . ." Nowhere anything concrete. Nowhere a firm clue.

It is certain only that on October 7, 1968, in Stuttgart 3 percent was offered, on November 6 in Stuttgart 4 per-

15. Quoted by permission from H. Trawinski, "Begin 9 Uhr—Ende 4:10 Uhr," in *Der angestellte Arzt,* II (1969), 60 ff.

cent, on December 5 in Bonn 5 percent. Today they will probably offer 6 percent. And then? A joker said, "Then we will begin to think it over."

12:30 P.M. After an hour and a half of waiting, the small commission is called for first consultation. Federal Interior Minister Benda is there. Anticipations are not high. The difficulties of pushing through an improvement of the wage-earners' pay structure become ever clearer. But the workers won't yield. Why should they? All have encouraged the workers in their demands: Schiller, Strauss, Kiesinger, the unions, the TV, the radio, the press. Why should they back down now? In another hour we will know more.

The large commission reconvenes. Reporting. The card games are interrupted; the strollers rounded up. The first report is presented. They have offered 5.5 percent for salaried employees, but no change in the wage-earners' pay structure. TV and radio bring the first news. The reporters swarm around us. Amazing how many there are. Each new announcement always has to be discussed.

1:30 P.M. The big boys invite each other to lunch. Hopefully they will accomplish more over the dining table than they did over the conference table. They were to reconvene at 2 o'clock; they reconvened at 3:30.

Small commission, smaller commission. The employers can't agree among themselves. The unions stand firm. The TV first evening news comes on. "The struggle continues." The struggle? The waiting wears the nerves. General unrest spreads. A crowd of men around me in the canteen. Nine tenths of them should be dieting, but they are drinking and eating out of boredom.

7:00 P.M. Small commission, smallest commission, bargaining commission, the commission of 42, and the latest newscasts. Each reporter always knows more than the others, and the big boys being interviewed take care to give the right impression. "We won't go below 8 percent." "We can't go above 5.5 percent." Each means what he says, but no one believes it.

9:00 P.M., 11:00 P.M., 1:00 A.M., 3:00 A.M. The card players are drowsy. Weary fighters have stretched out on the chairs and await the commission report. Waiting. Some even sleep a little. Most wander about restlessly. Does the negotiation ritual require battling all night long? Is it a necessary part of the script or just a habit? Does the public demand of the 300 negotiators a sleepless night? Or is it just impossible to get used to better working hours? If you ask, each one thinks that the others want it that way.

4:10 A.M. The negotiations are recessed. The commissions can't reach agreement. The salaried employees are offered 6 percent. Changes in the wage-earner pay structure seem to be too involved for the employers to accept directly. Next appointment: January 28 in Stuttgart.

One possible wrong impression should be corrected: the agreed percent will of course go also to the wage-earners. The structural change they sought was not won that year. The following year it was agreed to only in principle, with details still to be ironed out. Final settlement came only on July 10, 1970, in a separate agreement on a "monthly wage," providing that the top of the range for each pay group will be raised each October until in 1972 it will equal the top for comparable salaried employees.

BACKGROUND OF RECENT NEGOTIATIONS

Now that the nature of the agreements, the identity of the participants, and the general atmosphere of the negotiations have been discussed, it may be helpful to analyze two pay negotiations of the autumn of 1969 as a concrete illustration of just how the bargaining process actually operates. This will provide a varied view, because it involved not only a regular negotiation but also a preceding emergency negotiation growing out of a unique wildcat strike wave. Before turning to the actual negotiations, it will be necessary to examine their background in terms of the wage-salary structure, budgeting practices, and the 1969 political and economic conditions.

Pay Structure

There are some differences in the pay structure of the wage-earners and the salaried employees, and in the federal-state structures as compared to those in the local agencies. Section 26 of the BAT provides that the pay of salaried employees shall consist of the base rate, the children's bonus, the location bonus, and the special location bonus. The last three of these will not be involved in the negotiations to be discussed, because the BAT provides that they shall be the same as those provided by law for civil servants. It will be helpful, however, to have some impression of the relative importance of the base and bonus items.

The children's bonus is a flat 50 DM monthly per child, but an increase to 60 DM appears imminent. The special location bonus is 3 percent for employees in Berlin and Hamburg. It has a long historical background. It was originally adopted because these cities had more than a million inhabitants, but Munich was not included when it reached that size.

The other location bonus is rather complex, being scaled according to salary, city, and number of dependents. There are four categories based on salary. All cities are placed in one of two classes. Strangely enough, a bonus is paid for both cases, as a result of the 1964 reduction in the number of classes from three to two. The bonus is about 10 to 20 percent higher for the large metropolitan areas than for the smaller ones. There has been considerable agitation to move to a single class or to terminate the bonus with appropriate adjustments. The Minister of the Interior announced in April 1970 that the government proposed to reduce the bonus differential by one third before the end of the year with the intention of consolidating the two classes within two or three years and perhaps incorporating the bonus into the base pay. The consideration of dependents means that the bonus increases with each child, and at an increasing rate until it reaches 54 DM for each child in excess of five. There is also an increase for an employee who is or has been married or has reached the age of forty. The total location bonus ranged in 1969 from 141 DM for a low-classification bachelor in a small town to 300 DM for a high-classification bachelor in a large city and to 584 DM for a similar husband with five children.

A separate agreement provides for a year-end Christmas bonus of 40 percent of monthly earnings in 1968, 50 percent in 1969 and 1970, and 66⅔ percent thereafter. For all federal employees (including civil servants) the fringe items account for about one fourth of total earnings. About three fourths of the annual federal payroll of 27 billion DM is attributable to the base rates.

The base rate of the municipal salaried employee depends upon his job classification, his age, and his length of service. He is classified in one of 13 pay groups. The starting rate for each group is 10 percent more than for the group below. Thus starting monthly rates for employees at least 21 years old ranged in 1969 from 475 DM to 1493 DM. An automatic length-of-service increase is received every two years until the top rate of the pay group is attained. This is reached in from 16 to 22 years. It exceeds the starting rate by from 28 percent in the lowest group up to 68 percent in the top group, so that top rates range from 610 to 2510 DM. Some agency heads believe that this gives too much weight to length of service, since an employee of 20 years in a low classification may have higher base pay than a beginner who is three or four classifications above him. State and federal salaried employees have a fairly similar overall range, but are divided into 17 pay groups or classifications.

The pay schedule of the wage-earners is less complicated than that of the salaried employees. The location bonus of federal and state workers varies only with location and pay level—not with family situation. It is calculated in with the base rate, with the difference between large and small communities ranging from .09 to .13 DM per hour. There are only nine classification groups, and in each there are but five automatic two-year increases. The 1969 hourly rates ranged from 3.04 to 4.75 DM. Wage-earners also receive the year-end bonus and a special bonus based on family size and composition.

This wage-earner pay structure as it existed prior to the 1969 negotiations was considerably modified by the "monthly wage" agreement of July 10, 1970. In addition to shifting the wage-earners to a monthly salary, it made their rates correspond to those of comparable salaried employees by raising the number of length-of-service increases from five to nine and provided greater uniformity in the pay of municipal and state or federal workers. The adjustments will be made in three stages, to be completed on October 1, 1972.

Budgetary Practices

A close coordination between budgetary planning and pay increases is essential. Normally, the governments are developing their next calendar-year budget during the autumn quarter, and these get final approval by the appropriate legislative body in January or February. Thus there must be some preliminary estimates of probable payroll increase before negotiation begins in November or early December. The budget proposals go to the various legislatures in late autumn, and thus become public. This gives the unions some clues as to what they may hope to win, but does not seriously limit their demands. Negotiations will be concluded before final budget action, so that, if there is agreement for a higher increase than the governments had anticipated, budgetary adjustments can still be made. Wage demands may be rejected on the grounds that the government treasuries cannot meet the strain, but not because the budget has been frozen.

A few years ago the federal government adopted the practice of maintaining a tentative four-year budget plan, which is called "mid-range planning." That plan, in its 1969 form, anticipated a 5.5 percent pay increase for 1970 and the next three years. By early autumn, economic and political conditions had made it clear that this estimate would prove to be unrealistically low.

Political Conditions

Political conditions also affect public service negotiations, and in the second half of 1969 they were relatively tumultuous. Following the establishment of the Federal Republic in 1949, the Christian Democrats and their Bavarian partner, the more conservative Christian Social Party (CDU/CSU), had headed a coalition government that included the small, conservative Free Democratic Party (FDP) under the chancellorship of Adenauer, and later Erhard. In 1966 Erhard's popularity waned, partly as a result of the recession. Toward the end of that year he was replaced by the new CDU leader, Kiesinger, with the support of the Social Democrats (SPD), who had received nearly 40 percent of the votes in 1965. The SPD entered the "grand coalition" over the objections of its left-wing members and of many union leaders, who felt that their party had temporarily sacrificed too many of its long-range objectives. This new coalition had an overwhelming majority in the Bundestag, whose sessions became very peaceful. The major struggles occurred instead in the cabinet meetings. These focused especially on SPD Economics Minister Schiller and CSU Finance Minister Strauss, and peaked in November 1968 and May 1969 when Kiesinger twice sided with Strauss in rejecting Schiller's vigorous recommendation for upward revaluation of the mark. During the summer Schiller continued a public attack on this Kiesinger decision. As the September national election approached, it seemed unlikely that this complex economic issue of revaluation, which threatened financial loss to farmers and some industries, could find wide voter appeal, but Schiller proved to be an effective orator. He had already achieved considerable popularity, because of the widespread belief that his policies were responsible for the brevity of the 1966-67 recession. More and more voters became convinced that revaluation would have restrained the rising cost of living. The decline in the degree of opposition to rapprochement with the East may also have contributed to SPD election gains.

The election resulted in a plurality of the votes for the CDU, but the SPD narrowed the gap. In 1965 the CDU/CSU, SPD, and FDP received respectively 47.6, 39.3, and 9.5 percent of the votes cast. The corresponding figures for 1969 were 46.1, 42.7, and 5.8. It had been widely assumed that the "grand coalition" would be continued, but Kiesinger was shocked to find that the leaders of the SPD and the FDP (which had received little more than the 5 percent necessary to maintain its representation in the Bundestag) were so busy planning a new government that neither had any interest in discussing the possibility of a coalition with the CDU. The SPD and FDP were able to agree on major policies, and formed a new government under the chancellorship of Willy Brandt that had a majority of six to twelve votes in the Bundestag (not counting the Berlin delegation), depending on the doubtful party loyalty of three FDP legislators.

Union leaders viewed the political results with mixed emotions. Many were unhappy that the SPD had found it necessary to promise the FDP it would not press for the major union demand of extension of full codetermination—50 percent labor representation on the board of directors and labor control of the appointment of the personnel manager—from the steel and mining industries to large companies in other fields. On the other hand, most of them welcomed the increase in the number of union members in the Bundestag.

The new cabinet included two former union presidents. The Labor Minister, Walter Arendt, had been president of the DGB Mineworkers. Georg Leber, a carry-over from the previous cabinet as Minister of Transport and an ex-president of the Construction Workers, now served also as Minister for Post and Telecommunication. His deputy (state secretary) in charge of the postal service was vice-president of the DPG.

The consequences of these political changes for public employee negotiations cannot be measured. They should be appreciable, but not great. In general, it can be expected that both the administration and the legislature will be somewhat more receptive to union demands, but there had not been serious dissatisfaction with previous governments on this score. The replacement of Interior Minister Benda (CDU) by Genscher (FDP) will probably have only a subtle effect. The transfer of the Finance Ministry from Strauss (CSU) to Möller (SPD) will probably be more significant. It seems clear that the Bundestag will not have a limiting effect on the negotiations by the Interior Ministry any more in the future than it has in the past. The fact that the new government was not ready to operate until the end of October may have slightly delayed budgetary planning, but presumably the ministry staffs carried on their preparations with little interruption.

Economic Conditions

The economic situation in 1969 was clearly one of industrial boom. A recession starting in 1966 had carried well into 1967. It did not result in serious unemployment for German employees, because the burden of layoff fell partly on the more than a million foreign workers. By mid-1969 the number of foreign workers had increased again from 900,000 to 1,500,000. The number of unemployed had dropped from a peak of almost 700,000 to 100,000, as compared to over 800,000 reported job vacancies. The unemployment rate was about one half of one percent. The annual increase in the cost of living, which had been very slight for several years, was accelerating and had at that time reached nearly 3 percent.[16] Industrial profits were bringing exultant comments in reports to stockholders. And, significantly for the public service, federal tax receipts for the first half-year were an unexpected 17 percent higher than the year before. The yield of the "value added" tax, which is the most lucrative one, was up 32 percent, and the wage and income taxes—the next most significant ones—were up about 20 percent.

A major factor affecting public sector negotiations is of course the current scene in private sector labor relations. For the workers the recession had meant two years of very lean pay gains. Negotiated wage increases in the private sector, after averaging about 7 percent in 1965 and 6 percent in 1966, averaged less than 3 percent in 1967 and less than 4 percent in 1968. By mid-1969 the increases were running around 6 percent, and the agreement signed on August 2 for some 4 million employees in the metal-working industry was estimated at 8 percent and was heralded as a great

16. A year later, in mid-1970, unemployment had declined further to 95,000 and reported vacancies had risen to nearly 900,000. Foreign workers had increased to over 1,800,000. The cost of living had risen roughly 5 percent.

union victory. The whole labor relations scene in Germany appeared to be totally serene and peaceful.

Exactly one month later, it suddenly became chaotic in a manner that for Germany was unprecedented. A wildcat strike in one Ruhr steel plant was based on a demand for higher pay to equal the rates paid in another plant of the same company in the same city. Within 36 hours management had completely capitulated and even paid for time struck. Such instant success led workers in other plants and other industries to try the same new tactic. In most cases they were equally successful, even though their demands were usually not so well justified. The details of this uprising are given in Chapter V. For purposes of its effect on public sector negotiations, it will suffice now to mention briefly the final outcome.

In addition to the concessions granted to wildcat strikers, some industries and many companies hastened to negotiate or grant immediate or retroactive increases without waiting for a strike. It will be remembered that collective agreements for private employees, unlike those for public employees, set only minimum rates, and that private employers may—and customarily do—pay substantially more. Many of the renegotiated rates involved increases of as much as 10 or 11 percent.

On September 16—two weeks after the first wildcat and twelve days before the national election—ÖTV and DAG leaders met with the Minister of the Interior and the heads of the TdL and VKA to demand immediate negotiations for a supplemental increase for public employees. The ÖTV argued that the union could no longer consider itself bound by the current agreement, because it had been made under the false assumptions that wage increases in private industry would be gradual and that the cost of living would remain stable. When this conference ended with the refusal of the government representatives to negotiate until after the formation of the new government, ÖTV president Heinz Kluncker announced to the press that the union could no longer guarantee social peace in the public services under the circumstances. He has said subsequently that he would not have made this statement if the government had promised negotiations immediately after the election instead of a month later when the new government had been formed.

The next day there was a brief strike of the municipal trash collectors in Duisburg. The following seven days witnessed a series of one-day or half-day strikes by trash collectors or local transit employees in at least a dozen of the larger cities. In some instances, these were ended only after negotiations with local ÖTV leaders had resulted in a promise to grant a flat monthly bonus for the remainder of the year or a commitment to take such action if negotiations with the VKA should not yield a similar result.

In these cases there was obviously a violation by some cities of their VKA membership obligation to refrain from negotiating separate agreements. The cities obviously felt themselves to be under great pressure. The strain was very real. So far as can be determined, interruption of municipal public services by strike had occurred since the war only on March 19, 1958. City governments viewed the stoppages as especially serious because of their possible effect on the impending election. Then too there was the immediate precedent of capitulation by private industry to similar action. The cities were also influenced by an inconsistency in the bargaining structure. Some incorporated public utilities do not belong to the VKA but to an Employers Association for Gas, Water, and Electricity. Prompt agreement of this association to union demands for an increase brought additional pressure on the cities. The fact that the municipal government of most of the large cities was under SPD control is perhaps a further factor in understanding why none of the affected cities attempted to hold out against the strikes or even considered taking any legal or disciplinary steps against the strikers for their clear violation of contract and law.

THE 1969 EMERGENCY NEGOTIATIONS

The negotiations related to these strikes are not illustrative of the customary nature of collective bargaining in the public sphere. On the contrary, they were a unique occurrence. They illustrate only how much the customary procedures may be modified when subjected to great stress.

The VKA and its member associations were under great pressure from the larger cities to negotiate immediately. On September 18—the day after the first public service wildcat—the minister presidents of the states of North Rhine-Westphalia and Lower Saxony made a public plea for instant negotiation. On the same day the ÖTV held a meeting of its Large Rate Commission and its executive committee in Berlin, and the DAG announced its demands for a 15 percent increase from September 1, an increase of the year-end bonus to a month's earnings, a reduction of overtime work in hospitals, and a lengthening of vacations by ceasing to count Saturdays as vacation days.[17] At the same time the DAG announced that it could not assure peace unless negotiations should begin the following week, i.e. before the election.

On September 22 the railway management met with GdED leaders. The union asked for immediate negotiations and presented demands for a flat monthly bonus of 100 DM for the last three months of the year and the disregard of Saturdays in measuring vacations. Management said it would be guided by any decisions reached at the cabinet meeting the next day. Similar talks were held between the Postal Ministry and the DPG.

On the same day the VKA held a meeting of its membership assembly in Stuttgart. Representatives of the Interior Ministry and the TdL were present. The ministry urged the states and the VKA to stand firm with the federal government in refusing to negotiate until after the election. The TdL decided to do so, even though at least two state heads had publicly urged immediate negotiations. After a three-hour meeting the

17. This last demand is now current also in private industry. Vacation clauses define the length as a certain number of workdays. This is understood to include Saturdays. As the workweek is being gradually reduced toward 40 hours, most German workers now have a five-day week, even though their workday is somewhat longer than 8 hours—hence the demand that Saturdays no longer be counted as workdays for vacation purposes. By 1969 some private industries had already granted this demand in the form of a series of annual adjustments. The governments subsequently granted it in the summer of 1970.

VKA rejected the federal plea and decided that it could not withstand the pressure for prompt negotiation. It offered to start negotiations with the ÖTV and the DAG on September 24. This decision demonstrates that the three levels of government are not always able to maintain a united front. It also appears to substantiate the charge made by some local government officials that the VKA is dominated by the large cities and that the towns and counties have relatively little impact.

The following day, September 23, the federal cabinet discussed the problem in detail. It decided that it would negotiate with the unions on a revision of the current pay agreement, and instructed its ministers of Interior, Finance, Economics, and Labor to prepare materials that would enable it to determine the details of the federal offer when it met again the following week. It urged the states and communities to join with the Minister of Interior in meeting with the unions two days later for general discussions, with the understanding that no definite conclusions would be reached until after the cabinet meeting on October 1.

On September 24 the VKA again rejected the cabinet's plea, and held to its promise to negotiate at once. Negotiations began at 3:00 P.M. and continued until 5:00 the next morning. It was a hectic session with frequent pauses for the parties to caucus or to confer with their larger committees, which were waiting nearby. As the evening went on the VKA received more and more telegrams from member cities urging an immediate agreement to avoid strikes threatened for the next morning.

One major question was whether the increase would be a flat sum, as asked by the ÖTV, or a percentage, as proposed by the DAG. The outcome on this issue was considerably prejudiced by the fact that most of the cities that had jumped the gun by prior commitments had offered a flat amount. Another issue was the union demand that the increase be considered as a permanent increase in pay rather than just a one-shot bonus. This demand would mean a significant change in relative pay rates, since a flat monthly bonus of 100 DM would mean more than a 15 percent increase for some wage-earners, but less than 5 percent for many salaried employees. The outcome on this issue would obivously have a considerable effect on future negotiations. In the early morning hours the unions agreed to drop the demand for incorporation in order to get the 300 DM for the last three months. The vacation issue was also dropped for the time being, but subsequently granted during the following summer.

The meeting with the unions that the cabinet had proposed was held the next noon by Interior Minister Benda and TdL representatives. There was little to discuss, since Benda could not make any offer until after the next cabinet meeting, and adjournment came within an hour.

The cabinet met as planned five days later, on October 1. After the meeting Benda met with reporters. He said that negotiations would be held on October 3, that the offer would involve a lump sum scaled to family status and rising to at least 300 DM, that some of the increase would be held as capital investment rather than paid in cash, and that it would be regarded as a stop-gap rather than a new agreement. He said he would confer immediately with the states to assure unity. His statement introduced two new elements of family scaling and investment, which could be expected to meet union resistance.

The federal and state negotiators met with the ÖTV and the DAG during the morning of October 3. The offer was a flat bonus of 250 DM plus 30 DM if married and 20 DM for each child, with 104 DM withheld for investment. The family scaling proposal apparently indicated a rather desperate attempt to avoid rubber-stamping the VKA agreement and perhaps an inclination to punish VKA for not waiting. The investment proposal showed the government's concern in minimizing inflationary forces at that time. The unions rejected the offer, and the negotiations were adjourned for six days, so that Benda could seek cabinet approval of a new offer. Two separate negotiations for the railway and postal services were held simultaneously that afternoon with, of course, similar results.

The cabinet meeting October 8 evidently decided that the union demands would be granted if necessary, for some minister told the reporters that an agreement with the unions the next day was almost certain. Intentionally or unintentionally, this indicated to the unions that they could sit tight.

Negotiations resumed on the morning of October 9, with the government changing its previous 250-30-20 offer to 260-25-20. This was more difficult for the unions to reject, since a larger proportion of their members (including those with only one child) would find it more attractive than the VKA agreement. The ÖTV held firm and received a flat 300 DM for salaried employees. It subsequently received some resignations from members with large families.

The settlement for the wage-earners contained an interesting variation. Some of the states had long experienced difficulty in recruiting them in a tight labor market because many cities paid them more. The TdL could find no way of increasing their rates without having the VKA follow suit. It occurred to a TdL official that here was a chance to raise their base rate while granting a lower temporary bonus, so that the unions would have no strong argument for a matching increase from the VKA. The federal government was reluctant to join in this proposal, but finally did so in order to avoid the possibility that the TdL would conclude a separate agreement. The unions accepted for the wage-earners a lump sum bonus of 260 DM plus an increase of .06-.07 DM in the base hourly rate.

The significance of this development is that it shows that the TdL, in its joint bargaining with the federal government, is not dominated by the latter. Its freedom to conclude separate agreements gives it equal "bargaining power" in its separate conferences with its negotiation partner. On the other hand, the outcome of the negotiations appears to lend some support to the ÖTV claim that it has the dominant role on the union side. The DAG had originally demanded a percentage increase. This obviously would have been to its advantage, since its salaried employee members are in general more highly paid than the wage-earners, who constitute more than half of the ÖTV membership. It apparently felt itself obliged to go along with the ÖTV insistence on the flat rate.

Following the morning agreement, separate negotiations were again held for the postal and railway employees. Not surprisingly, they reached the same results. There was, however, a variation in the course of these negotiations that reveals problems the DGB unions occasionally face in coordinating their goals and tactics. The DPG decided, quite naturally, that it would prefer a family-scaled increase if it equaled the 300 DM for a married man without children. It obtained the concurrence of the GdED and notified the ÖTV that they would both accept such an offer. In the earlier postal negotiations, when the 250-30-20 plan was offered, the union told the Postal Minister that it would accept a 280-20-20 offer. But the final offer, instead, was only 260-25-20; and even that offer was not made to the DPG and GdED, after the flat 300 agreement with the ÖTV. The DPG says it is informed that the minister did not even mention its proposal during the cabinet discussions.

This variation indicates that the DGB unions may on occasion go separate ways.[18] One can only surmise some of the motivations in this case. Was not the DPG proposal equally attractive to the ÖTV? Did the ÖTV oppose it only to avoid embarrassing the VKA after the latter had been good enough to yield to its demand for immediate negotiation? And, if the federal government wanted a scaled plan, why did it not offer one that would be acceptable to the DPG and GdED? Was it only because of the additional cost or because it attached more importance to maintaining uniformity or because it did not want to arouse the ire of the ÖTV?

The cabinet had already announced that any bonus agreed to for wage-earners and salaried employees would also be granted to the civil servants. Legislation to this effect could

18. The DPG claims that this has happened in some instances and that its agreements are better than the ones with the ÖTV in a few respects.

not be passed promptly, for the Bundestag was not in session, pending the formation of the new government. Since funds were available without special appropriation, it was decided to pay the civil servants immediately. Retroactive legislative sanction was subsequently obtained on December 5. Thus, in the final analysis, an entire national pattern had been set by a few cities that had capitulated prematurely.

The municipal wildcats and the negotiations resulting from them obviously complicated the problems of negotiating the 1970 increases. Would the strained relationships between some of the negotiating parties have any continuing effect? Would the bonus be incorporated into the new rates? Or would the traditional pay relationships be maintained?

NEGOTIATING THE 1970 PAY INCREASE

Description of the negotiations regarding public employee pay increases for 1970 will focus on formal meetings and official statements. The many informal contacts cannot be recorded. Obviously, government and union officials are almost continuously in touch with each other regarding one problem or another, so that a considerable exchange of views has taken place before formal meetings begin.

Early in November the ÖTV announced cancellation of the 1969 pay agreement at the end of the year. The demands of the DAG for salaried employees were formulated by its Large Rate Commission at a meeting on November 26. The central point was an increase of 15 percent in the base rates, which would mean about a 12 percent rise in total earnings. A further controversial item was a minimum increase of 100 DM, which would mean a somewhat higher percentage for the lower levels. It appeared that the DAG would be willing to accept the payment of part of the increase in some form of investment rather than cash.

During November officials of the Interior Ministry invited the other ministries to submit views on the extent of the future increases, and conferred at length with the Finance Ministry in this respect. Toward the end of the month it was announced that the Interior and Finance ministers had agreed on a firm figure, which would be presented to the cabinet on December 4 for its action. Consultation by the Interior Ministry with the heads of the TdL and VKA, which had undoubtedly begun earlier, was continued at this time.

On December 2 the new Interior Minister Genscher notified the unions that negotiations could start on December 16, that the government was hopeful that an agreement could be reached before the end of the year—about a month earlier than usual—and that it was prepared to offer a "significant increase."

On December 4, while the cabinet was discussing its position, the ÖTV Large Rate Commission (110 members) was formalizing its demands. These were announced as including increases ranging from 12·to 23 percent, which would result from a flat 70 DM for all plus a 6 percent raise and various other adjustments. The following day government negotiators from all three levels conferred in Bonn regarding the ÖTV demands.

In the meantime the situation had been complicated by a quite unusual development. During November there had been considerable discussion about pay increases for the civil servants. The DBB had presented demands to the Interior Ministry and publicized them. The government had indicated its intent to proceed with legislation on this point as soon as the negotiations for the wage-earners and salaried employees were completed. But on December 3 the CDU/CSU opposition party submitted to the Bundestag a bill on this subject, proposing a 12 percent increase with a 100 DM minimum! The advance presentation of an opposition bill on civil servant pay, when it was known that a government proposal would soon be offered, was probably unprecedented. It was apparently an attempt to embarrass the government, because there was no indication that the latter was prepared to offer the wage-earners and salaried employees such a high raise. It was one of several actions that appeared to indicate that the party, in its new opposition role, was suddenly trying to show itself to the electorate as more liberal than the SPD. This is one of the very few instances in which a party has clearly tried to make political capital out of the terms of employment of public employees. The bitter reaction of SPD leaders in denouncing the move as irresponsible showed the extent to which they were embarrassed.

This was further indicated at the first negotiation session on December 16, when the government offer was found to amount to only 9.6 percent, consisting of a basic pay increase of 8 percent and "structural" improvements, such as bonus increases, estimated at 1.6 percent. Under the circumstances, the unions' rejection was not surprising. Their objection, however, at least in the case of the ÖTV, appeared to center more on the absence of a 100 DM minimum than on the size of the total package.[19]

At this point ÖTV took an unusually aggressive stance, and issued on December 19 an "ultimatum" that the government add the minimum 100 DM provision to its offer by January 9. The consequences of an unfavorable response were not spelled out. Until the expiration of the current agreement, the unions were subject to the "peace obligation," which forbids not only use of force but also threats to use force.

There followed two weeks of arm's-length negotiation by press release and interview. Government spokesmen told reporters that the current offer would bring a monthly increase of at least 100 DM to the great majority of the employees, that the addition of a minimum would threaten efficiency by narrowing the pay relationship between skilled and unskilled, and that the federal budget for 1970 was already stretched to its limits. The unions countered with the contentions that the minimum would be a help to many who were most in need, that a slight narrowing of pay ratios could do no harm because they had been widened by the past practice of granting only percentage increases, and that in any case a union that had won for the workers a 100 DM increase for the past three months could not now agree to a reduction of income for any of them.

19. At the same time the parties in the postal and railway services were conducting their futile ritual of separate negotiations—a strange sight in this age of realism.

As the peace obligation ended with the new year, strike hints grew stronger. It was suggested that the strike would be selective, focusing on services such as trash collection, local transit, and utilities, where it would be most noticed by the public. Army civilian employees were mentioned as another likely participant group. On January 5 the ÖTV executive committee set the date for a strike vote as January 21-22, and called a planning meeting of its officials for January 11. DAG officials indicated, however, that they thought a strike vote on behalf of the salaried employees would not be justified, since relatively few of them would be affected by a 100 DM minimum.

At this time Interior Minister Genscher wrote to ÖTV president Kluncker that the government would not be able to make a new offer by January 9, since the cabinet would not meet again until January 16.

The parties continued to use the press for tactics that had often been used before. The newspapers reported that informed sources in Bonn were convinced that the government would not raise its offer even in case of a strike. On the other hand, an ÖTV spokesman suggested that, if it came to a strike, the union's demands would undoubtedly be raised. Reference was made especially to a long-standing goal of monthly salaries for wage-earners.

Genscher then invited Kluncker to meet with him on the ultimatum date of January 9. They apparently had a heart-to-heart talk "under four eyes." It is probable that the minister told the union leader of his intention to seek cabinet approval to increase the past offer by adding for all employees with gross monthly earnings up to 1000 DM an extra 13 DM monthly in the form of investment funds rather than cash, so as to encourage employee capital accumulation and avoid inflationary impact. These capital-saving benefits are exempt from income and social security taxes and are frozen for six years. Each employee has his choice of one among several investment plans and of the bank or savings and loan association he will use. It was probably suggested that this additional offer would mean a total increase of at least 100 DM for nearly all employees. In any case, at the conclusion of the conference it was announced that both participants were seeking to cool the tensions of these sharp negotiations, and the ÖTV president stated that plans for a strike vote would be canceled.

The agenda for the conference of ÖTV officials on January 11 had to be changed. Instead of laying strike plans, they presumably discussed details of a possible settlement. They learned that the Interior Minister would meet with TdL and VKA representatives on January 13 and that negotiations would be resumed on January 14.

The negotiations continued for thirteen hours into the early morning of January 15, when agreement was finally reached along the lines just mentioned. Presumably most of the time was spent in debate regarding the details for managing the investment funds, since this was a provision that had little precedent in German labor relations. It took only one hour that afternoon to reach a similar agreement with the GdED for the railway system. The DPG, however, tried unsuccessfully to obtain a restructuring of pay schedules for salaried employees of the postal service, and delayed its concurrence until January 20.

At the time of the negotiations on the flat 300 DM bonus in the autumn of 1969, there was much questioning regarding the probable long-run influence of that action on the public employee pay structure. Now conclusions on this point were possible. It appears likely that the autumn negotiations and the wildcat strikes that led to them had little effect other than to win for the public employees three months earlier all or part of the raise that they would have received anyhow on January 1. There seems to be no reason to believe that the offer of 9.6 percent would have been any lower if the 1969 agreement had been allowed to run to its end without disturbance. Moreover, the new aspect of a substantial flat grant has largely disappeared as it has been reduced from 100 to 13 DM a month. It remains only to be seen whether the concept of a part-payment in investment funds rather than cash will develop in the future into a practice of significant proportions, for this is the one real consequence of the autumn turmoil. It appears that it will be an important innovation. The government and some employers have long expressed interest in encouraging capital accumulation by employees. Unions have also looked on it with favor, but not at the expense of lesser gains in cash pay. There will probably be future increases in the volume of the accumulation beyond its present modest 13 DM level. The government action quickly gave new impetus to negotiation of similar plans in the private sector. One of the earliest investment programs was negotiated in the construction industry several years ago. Because of its contributory feature, it was used by only half of the employees. In May 1970 a monthly savings grant of 26 DM was negotiated for the steel and metal-fabricating industries under the Act to Promote Employee Capital Formation. Such programs now cover about half of the employed labor force. A doubling of the grant to public employees from 13 DM to 26 DM is forecast for 1971.

This account of these two negotiations depicts, better than can any generalizations, the nature of German public bargaining: the timing of meetings, the variety of tactics, the variations in motivation, and the relationships between the unions, between the governments, between the parties, between the organizations and their members. It has shown that meetings are spaced far apart to allow full consultation by each party with the many groups it represents, that full use is made of the news media to influence public opinion, that there is often advance information on government offers, that significant negotiating takes place outside the formal sessions, that brief stoppages in municipal services are a stronger union weapon in Germany than in some other countries, and that the threat to take a strike vote can itself be an effective weapon. It has given two of the rare instances in which political motivation has appeared—the surprise pay bill submitted by the CDU/CSU and the public plea of two state heads for immediate negotiations under circumstances where the plea, if sincere, could probably have been made more effectively in private. It has shown some of the problems of interunion relations, such as the two unsuccessful efforts of the DPG for variation in settlement, the differences in the demands of the ÖTV and DAG and the degree of conflict in their interests. It has revealed some of the problems of intergovernment relations, such as the efforts of the Interior Minister to hold the states and cities in line, his attempt to reach a settlement different from the VKA emergency agreement (and the union's refusal, even when it involved rejection of a very attractive offer), the ability of the TdL to get federal acceptance of its desire for a variation in the wage offer, and the rare occurrence of a VKA breakaway.[20] It has also shown some of the problems of the relationship between the organizations and their members, such as the inability of the VKA to prevent some of its members from concluding separate agreements in violation of their membership obligations and the apparent firm control of the ÖTV over its members in staging a wildcat that was not really a wildcat.

It has given some indication also of the degree of authority possessed by the negotiators for the government agencies on the one hand and the public wage-earners and salaried employees on the other hand. As has been noted, the principal negotiators for the governments are the Interior Ministry, the Postal Ministry, the Federal Railways management, the TdL and the VKA, while the negotiators for the employees are in most instances top officials of the ÖTV, the DPG, the GdED, and the DAG. None of these negotiators has complete and final authority to approve the terms of a settlement.

20. There have been at least five earlier instances of similar disunity. In 1962 the VKA negotiated a general increase for local wage-earners and salaried employees at a time when the federal and state governments were refusing to act. In 1964 it granted wage-earners six weeks of sick pay (which all salaried employees already had), while wage-earners of the federal and state governments—and private industry—obtained this benefit only by legislation effective January 1, 1970. During the 1955 negotiations on evaluation of salaried employee positions, the VKA refused to concur in the results approved by the federal and state governments. This happened again in March 1966 regarding an agreement on the introduction of trial promotions. Negotiations with the VKA then continued for six months before a somewhat different agreement was reached. There is also a separate travel reimbursement agreement.

In the case of the federal government, a representative of the Finance Ministry attends all negotiations as an observer, and approval by the ministry will normally be needed, unless it is replaced by approval of the federal cabinet. With reference to the state and local governments, agreements require ratification by the membership assembly of the TdL and the central committee of the VKA. The members of these two groups will of course want to keep in close touch with those whom they represent.

Also on the side of the unions, the negotiators do not have personally the authority to commit their organizations and members. The practices of the various unions are not identical, but all require approval of agreements by some particular committee. Ratification by the membership is not required. The membership is polled only in case the executive committee considers that a deadlock has been reached and has decided to take a strike vote. The statutes of most of the unions require a three-fourths majority of the members affected to authorize a strike.

Although the negotiators on both sides lack final authority, their lines of communication within their organizations are so open and so direct that they know how far they can go. If the unions reject a federal offer, the Interior Minister may adjourn negotiations until he can confer with the Chancellor or the cabinet. When an agreement is thought to be imminent, the unions and the TdL and VKA have their appropriate committees waiting in the wings near the conference room. In fact the committees are likely to be consulted throughout the negotiations. Thus when agreement is reached it is in effect final and is promptly announced to the press. Agreements in the public service are not tentative, and there is no waiting for final approval.

Finally, this account has revealed something of the tenor of the relationship between the parties. On the basis of these and the many other negotiations, the bargaining relationship may be characterized as tough but seldom bitterly antagonistic. The unions have had to put up a strong argument for every gain they have won, but the governments have

PUBLIC SECTOR NEGOTIATION

not been reluctant to grant occasional concessions that led the way to private industry, such as in the 1970 agreements on capital-saving benefits and longer vacations. And the unions have never acted irresponsibly in their regular negotiations. Perhaps such a lack of antagonism might be expected in the public sector (even though the situation in some countries makes this doubtful).

The employees, of course, want a square deal just as much as do their counterparts in the private sector; but they do not have the feeling that every demand they lose merely increases the funds flowing as profits into the pockets of private stockholders. Similarly as to the government representatives, they want to keep within their budgets and avoid adding to inflationary pressures, but they do not feel that every concession they grant is decreasing the value of their stock options and perhaps endangering their job security.

As might therefore be expected, the personal relationships between the negotiators usually are relatively cordial. The situation will vary somewhat depending on the personalities involved. There is rarely a change in the unions' representatives, but there have been several changes during the last decade in the identity of the Minister of the Interior and his state secretary.

Fairly close personal relationships are likely to develop, because of the frequency of contact. It seems that there is always some negotiation in process. Wage and salary bargaining is mostly confined to December and January, but minor revisions in the basic agreements are negotiated fairly frequently, and a total renegotiation of each occurs every three or four years and usually takes a year or two.

In addition to the formal negotiations, there are frequent informal conferences. In these the Interior Ministry is usually represented by a department head rather than the minister or state secretary. The subject matter of these conferences is sometimes the details of a particular union demand, but frequently it is rather a problem that has been encountered by one side or the other. It is in these sessions that the problem-solving approach is most often used. After a problem has been analyzed and a solution found, the subsequent negotiation may be very simple.

In view of our analysis of public employee negotiations, it is not surprising that settlements have been achieved without deadlock or other crisis. The right to strike has never been exercised in connection with the negotiation of any of the regular agreements since a one-day stoppage by municipal wage-earners on March 19, 1958, and a brief strike of air traffic control personnel in 1962. The nearest that the parties have come to an exception in this respect was the setting of a date for a strike vote by the ÖTV in June 1962 and January 1970, but on each occasion the action was rescinded and a settlement was reached.

The detailed analysis of strike history in Chapter V shows a recent increase in strike frequency, but these instances were not related to regular negotiations. Such a history leads to the conclusions that negotiators for both parties have almost invariably acted in a responsible manner and that the employees and their unions thus far have not abused their right to strike in connection with regular negotiations for public wage-earners and salaried employees.

IMPACT OF FINANCIAL LIMITATIONS

The account of the two negotiations did not reveal anything about the degree to which pay levels are limited by budgetary considerations. Since this is one of the most important differences between various public employee relations systems, it deserves special attention here. At the one extreme are situations in which employee salaries are set with little or no regard to the financial position of the employing agency, and the agency has to adjust to an increase in the price of its labor just as it does to an increase in the price of coal or any other supplies. At the other extreme may be situations in which public employees tend to be regarded almost as residual claimants, whose salary increases may depend chiefly on the amount of funds that are estimated to be available after all other costs have been met. Where on the continuum between these two extremes do the major German negotiations fall? And what adjustments can be made by an agency that finds its payroll increased without regard to its financial resources?

Timing of Negotiations and Budget-Making

The customary timing of negotiations has gradually come to be such as to permit a maximum interaction between salary-setting and budget-making. As mentioned earlier, budget-planning at all levels of government takes place during the last quarter of each year and usually becomes definitive in late January or February. The unions have come to adapt to this situation by regularly terminating their pay agreements as of year-end, which is likely to result in a January settlement. Prior to 1965 the government's fiscal year began on April 1, and negotiated wage increases were often effective as of that date.

Economic gains are not always effective at the start of the fiscal year. The pay agreements permit termination at the end of twelve months or of any calendar quarter thereafter. Sometimes it may have appeared to the unions that the end of the budget year was, from a cyclical point of view, not the most favorable time for new negotiations. And even a December 31 termination does not assure a January settlement. For example, in 1962 local employees obtained a raise on April 1 (the cancellation date), while state and federal employee increases were effective as of July 1. Timing such as that requires adjustment by supplemental budget. The same is true in the case of new benefits occasionally negotiated during the year, such as the lengthening of vacations agreed to in the summer of 1970.

Present practice, on the other hand, now permits wage and salary increases to be included in the initial budgets. It is, however, impossible to include payroll increases in early budget planning, and only a rough estimate is possible until the budgets are practically ready for enactment. It is probably impossible to conclude negotiations much earlier, for the governments are not likely to be willing to reach a settlement until they see how their budgets are shaping up. For example, in 1969 the federal government announced its intention of seeking to reach a settlement in December, so that employees would know in advance what they could expect to be paid in January. But even then agreement was not obtained until January 15.

One can only conclude that in Germany the dovetailing of negotiations and budget-making is now optimal and is scarcely subject to further improvement.

Relations between Fiscal and Negotiating Authorities

At the federal and state levels the negotiators are well informed regarding the general financial position of the governments they represent. As has been noted, the key federal negotiations are conducted by the Interior Ministry, but a Finance Ministry representative is present at all formal bargaining sessions. The relationship between bargaining and purse strings formerly was closer, when the Finance Ministry was the Federal Republic's primary negotiator, but this procedure was discontinued in 1960.

Thus at the federal level, it has been concluded that the relationship between fiscal and negotiating authorities can be too close, and that it is preferable to avoid an identity between the two. It is believed that a fairer settlement will generally result when the negotiators do not have fiscal responsibilities and can evaluate the validity of the union demands without primary concern for availability of funds. After one ministry has decided to what extent the union demands are justified, it can confer with the Finance Ministry with regard to fiscal feasibility. Then, if the two ministries are unable to reach agreement with each other on the size of the government offer and the issue is referred to the cabinet for resolution, a protagonist is present to support each point of view. The cabinet members are thus assured of a well-balanced presentation of the arguments before reaching a decision. Such assurance is impossible when the same agency decides on both the reasonableness of the demands and the feasibility of granting them.

At the state level the practice regarding the assignment of the negotiating function is not uniform. Some states still continue to use their Finance Ministry, while others have followed the lead of the federal government by transferring the function to their Interior Ministry. The separation of functions is perhaps less important at the state than at the federal level, because the federal government exercises a good deal of leadership in negotiations. The actual negotiators are, to be sure, acting as officers of the TdL rather than as state officials. Nevertheless, the identity of the responsible state officials is important, since, with only eleven members in the association, each state has a rather direct impact on negotiation policies.

At the level of local government, on the other hand, the impact of any one agency on negotiation policies is so negligible that the relationship between negotiation and budget-making authority becomes practically immaterial. The local agency officials who vote in the selection of officers of their employers association are presumably ones who have also a major voice in the formulation of the agency budget, but this does not mean that the financial condition of the agency will receive any consideration at the bargaining table. When the line of a town's influence passes, for example, through the state association of towns and then the state association of all local agencies before reaching the VKA, it is obviously impossible that there remains any consideration for the fiscal condition of that town. It is not surprising, but perhaps inevitable under centralized negotiation, that most of the thousands of local agencies feel they have no influence on negotiations regarding their employees. Those who contend that VKA policymaking is largely dominated by the large cities may· well be correct. How could it be otherwise under the circumstances?

The lack of influence by the individual local agency does not mean that the condition of fiscal resources is ignored in VKA negotiations. The government representatives at the bargaining table will have a good knowledge of the general status of municipal finances. They will know whether tax receipts have been running behind or ahead of expectations. They may even have data on the number of local agencies that were unable to balance their budgets during the past year. The general financial condition will be considered, but there can scarcely be any consideration for the way in which any specific local budget is shaping up for the year ahead, except in the major cities. Thus while there is an interaction between salaries and budgets at the federal and state levels, the relationship at the local level is largely one way—the budgets have to adjust to the pay rates.

Prevailing Rates vs. Ability to Pay

Can the German public servant expect to receive each year the full increase to which he is reasonably entitled or does emphasis on ability to pay make him the residual claimant? Although it was noted that the impact of ability to pay is less immediate at the local than at the state and federal levels, that fact may not have much bearing on an answer to this question. One reason is the strong tendency for similar pay adjustments at all levels. There is little difference between increases at the local and higher levels. There was the 1962 instance when local employees received an increase three months earlier than state and federal employees, but the latter obtained a flat lump-sum bonus to compensate on the average for the delay. And in the emergency negotiations of 1969, when local employees received a flat 300 DM bonus, state and federal wage-earners got a smaller bonus plus an increase in their rates; but the increase merely served to bring their key rates (*Ecklohn*) more nearly in line with those of the municipal wage-earners. Realistically we must consider that negotiations are held jointly for the three levels of government, even though the results are technically embodied in separate agreements.

Another reason why a single answer to our question may be sought, rather than three separate ones, is the strong tendency for financial stringency to be about the same at each level of government. There is in Germany a notable inclination to share government obligations and government resources among the levels of government, with the result that the degree of fiscal adequacy tends to be fairly uniform. A sharing of obligations occurred, for example, in 1970 when an exceptional need for the rapid construction of additional university facilities led the federal government to budget substantial grants to the states for this purpose, although such expenditures had previously been considered as exclusively a state obligation. Another illustration of this attitude is the sizable grants made by each state annually to local agencies for special purposes. For example, the state of Baden-Württemberg in 1970 budgeted nearly 700 million DM for this purpose. Part went to support the police forces of the few large cities that have their separate police. Some went for the construction of county or municipal hospitals and homes for the aged. Other grants were for such purposes as school construction, sewage disposal construction, subsidization of municipal theaters, and special aid to university towns. Thus the state shares the obligation for many projects that are primarily a responsibility of the communities.

The sharing of resources may be seen also in the occasional revision of the way in which tax receipts are divided between federal, state, and local governments. For example, major changes took effect at the start of 1970, in accordance with the Financial Equalization Act of August 28, 1969. Formerly, the municipalities were financed chiefly by the business earnings tax, with the result that they were rich or poor in proportion to the amount of industry they contained. Now they receive about 60 percent of the proceeds of this tax, with the remainder divided equally between the federal and state governments. On the other hand, the municipalities now receive 14 percent of the revenue from the income and wage taxes. There were also major changes in the way in which four other taxes are shared by the federal and state governments. In other words, although some taxes are considered as allocated to a particular level of government, there is a remarkable readiness to modify the sharing of several taxes in accordance with changes in relative need, even though the process involves difficult and sometimes bitter negotiation between federal and state officials.

The ability to pay does sometimes play a role in the outcome of negotiations, it appears. Without tracing back through the history of negotiations, it may be noted that the 1970 settlement might well have been slightly higher if the other demands on the federal budget had been less urgent. Increased expenditures were needed for many purposes, including school and highway construction. On the other hand, higher taxes, which would have yielded needed revenue and also helped to combat inflationary pressures, were politically impractical, because the Social Democrats, in their exuberance at becoming the senior governing partner rather than the junior partner after the 1969 election, had made rash promises of tax reductions, which they were unable to fulfill.

Although limited ability to pay has undoubtedly acted as a restraint on pay increases in a few cases, public employees have by no means been relegated to the position of residual claimants. One reason is that during the past twenty years national income has been rising rapidly and government budgets have rarely been under serious pressure. More importantly, public employees are highly organized. Their unions are strong and wield considerable bargaining power. These unions—and presumably their members—have been fairly well satisfied with the gains achieved. They have accepted the negotiated terms without invoking their right to strike—except for a one-day stoppage of municipal employees in March 1958. (The wildcats of 1969 are not included here, because they did not result from deadlocked negotiation of a terminated agreement.) Such acceptance would certainly not have been forthcoming if the unions had believed that their members were being denied reasonable increases because of budgetary shortages.

If ability to pay has seldom been a limiting factor, what is the criterion of reasonableness in judging union demands? It is clearly not a matter of matching "prevailing rates," as this term is applied to the wage-setting of some American public employees. This term refers to the comparison of public and private rates for comparable tasks or classifications. Such detailed comparison can find little place in German negotiations. Since the major settlements generally apply equally to all classifications, comparisons must usually be on a much broader basis.[21]

Reasonableness is thus judged not so much by prevailing rates as by prevailing wage levels—the extent of changes in the average earnings of certain large groups. An extensive study along this line, ordered by the federal government in April 1970, will be mentioned later in connection with civil servant pay.

Methods of Meeting Financial Shortages

The federal government has not faced any serious problem of meeting shortages as a result of pay increases for its employees. Its leadership role in negotiations concerning public wage-earners and salaried employees, its legislative control over the terms of employment of civil servants at all levels, and the close relationship of the negotiating and drafting authorities with the financial authorities all combine to produce assurance that any increase in personnel costs can be met by the federal government without financial embarrassment.

Similarly, the state governments as a whole are unlikely to face difficulty in meeting increased payroll obligations. They participate through their TdL in the negotiations concerning their wage-earners and salaried employees; they are consulted by the federal government in the drafting of legislation affecting their civil servants; and the resulting bills are subject to review by their representatives who constitute the Bundesrat. The fiscal problem for the states is that the percentage increase in their payroll costs is the same for all of them, while some of the states are appreciably poorer than others. States with a high concentration of industry such as Hamburg, North Rhine-Westphalia, and more recently Baden-Württemberg have in general faced less serious budgetary problems than those that are predominantly rural, such as Schleswig-Holstein.

This problem of unequal resources is largely met by a program of state financial equalization. This program has two parts, dealing with the distribution and redistribution of tax revenues. The sales tax can illustrate the manner of distribution.

21. Detailed comparisons may occasionally be used in an effort to get a certain position moved to a higher classification.

Prior to 1970 all of the proceeds of this tax went to the federal government; now 30 percent goes to the states. Its distribution among the states does not depend on where the tax was collected; rather, the total share of the states is pooled. Three fourths of this fund is divided on the basis of population; the remainder is distributed in such a way as to reduce state differences in the per capita receipts from all taxes.

It is at the local agency level that budget limitations may cause the greatest problems in adjusting to increases in payroll costs, and it is there that methods of financial aid are most needed. This need is met by a considerable variety of revenue adjustments.

Further adjustment to individual need of the municipalities takes place through the counties.[22] The county in Hesse collects few taxes. It is largely dependent for revenue upon its municipalities. Although the situation varies to some extent from state to state, the county normally obtains its revenue by assessing its municipalities a percentage—often 30 to 40—of the revenue they would receive if their tax rate were the same as the average rate set by towns in that county. (Increase in the assessment beyond a certain level requires state approval.) It usually obtains in this way considerably more revenue than it needs for its own purposes and allocates the rest back to the communities for special purposes on the basis of their needs.

In spite of these equalization measures, a municipality may find itself in financial straits. In such a case it may seek relief in any of several ways. It might reduce its expenditures by reducing its services and its staff. It might increase the rate at which it levies its business earnings tax. It might operate at a deficit for a year or two, if it thinks that its problems are only temporary. It might apply to the county for a special relief grant. If the county is unable or unwilling to offer further aid, application could be made to the state. In this case, a state financial inspector would study its operations

22. This does not apply to the larger cities that are "county free" or not a part of any county.

and its books. He would submit his recommendations for increasing the efficiency or reducing the scope of the town's operations. If he should conclude that the community is in real need in spite of reasonable efforts, he would authorize a supplemental grant.

A county that finds itself with insufficient funds has similar alternatives. It may curtail its operations, reduce its grants to its municipalities, raise its levy on them, run at a temporary deficit in the hope of soon improving its position, or apply for a deficiency grant from the state.

As a result of these various means of fiscal problem-solving, local government agencies need not hesitate to commit themselves to meet the terms of employment negotiated on their behalf by the VKA. They can adjust to a rise in their personnel costs just as they do to an increase in any of their other costs; and their employees need not be the ones to bear the brunt of fiscal stringency by accepting employment on substandard terms.

IMPACT OF NATIONAL ECONOMIC POLICY

National economic policies inevitably have some effect on the federal government's negotiations with its wage-earners and salaried employees and on its enactment of terms of employment for its civil servants. This influence is exercised both directly and indirectly. It is necessarily closely related to public policy regarding terms of employment in private industry, since a substantial difference in these terms in the public and private sectors cannot be long maintained. The influence of national policy in the public sector is direct when changes in the terms of the public employees are made in the expectation that they will lead to similar changes for private employees. The impact is indirect when its effect in the private sector subsequently carries over into the public area.

There is little indication that the government has used its influence on the public terms of employment to pioneer in setting a pattern for improvement of the terms in private industry. Perhaps the final addition of 13 DM a month in investment funds to the 1970 offer may have resulted from such motivation. The government had long favored steps by industry to promote employee stock ownership, but the unions had been unable to make significant progress in winning such provisions in their industrial negotiations until after this government action.

The indirect impact of national policy on negotiations and legislation in the public area has probably been at least as great as the direct one. The government has sought in general to be a pattern follower more than a pattern setter. A major consideration in the negotiations and legislative decisions regarding the pay of public employees has long been the facts on how well private employees had fared during the previous year. The government's impact on the private sector is thus indirectly an important factor in the public settlements.

The influence of the federal government on the general wage level is exerted by means of a program called "concerted action." It was introduced by Karl Schiller when he became Economics Minister with the formation of the grand coalition in late 1966. He adopted a general goal of "social symmetry," or a reduction of the inequalities in the distribution of income. The concerted action program was supposed to be a means of working toward this objective. It is the German counterpart of the former American wage-price guidelines, but quite different in its operation. It involves extensive annual conferences of the minister with the negotiating parties (the "social partners") in private industry and other major economic interest groups in the hope of achieving some degree of consensus regarding wage-price-employment developments for the coming year. Major objectives are maximum growth with full employment and stable prices.

The conferences are usually held near the end of the calendar year. The annual report of the Council of Experts on Economic Development (see p. 116) is normally released in early November. After studying the report on the cyclical situation and the economic prospects for the coming year and discussing it with the Council members, the minister then confers separately with the leading officials of the major unions and employers associations. At these sessions the officials set forth their current plans and objectives, and the minister emphasizes whatever aspects of the economic picture he considers relevant. Then follows a joint session with a free exchange of views regarding probable future developments and the possibility of increasing wages without a significant increase in prices. One end result is likely to be a statement by the minister as to his conclusion regarding the amount of general wage rise that he believes can be achieved without endangering economic stability. The program is explained by the federal Press and Information Office as follows:[23]

> The "Konzertierte Aktion" deals not only with wages policy. Questions involving the formation of wealth, policy on competition, fiscal and social policy are decisive for further economic development and social equilibrium.
>
> The "Konzertierte Aktion" can be understood as a comprehensive exchange of information, which provides all those participating in the economy with an insight into the process as a whole.
>
> In theory, and to a degree in practice, this insight can persuade each group in turn to "concert" its actions with those of other groups.

It is obvious that this program is quite different from the American wage-price guideline policy, even though it is similar in objective. It does not involve the application of any fixed formula but is highly flexible. It involves a great deal of input from union and industry leaders. Their plans, their views, and their attitudes have an appreciable influence on its outcome. It covers a broader range of the whole area of national economic planning. Even some aspects of government fiscal and monetary policy are often included in the discussions.

Union and industry leaders have not been reluctant to participate. In general they appear to have welcomed the opportunity to present their problems and urge acceptance of their views. Union officials have emphasized their refusal to be bound by any conclusions in setting their wage goals.

23. *The Bulletin,* Feb. 3, 1970.

Nevertheless, the outcome of subsequent negotiations has generally been in line with the minister's final proposal. In fact, it might not be too far from the truth to characterize the wage aspects of the discussions as a heretofore unknown form of labor dispute settlement—prenegotiation mediation.

There is some difference of opinion as to how successful this program of concerted action has been. At the time of the wildcat explosion in August 1969, many commentators concluded that the resultant widespread and unexpected wage increases signified the failure of the concerted-action procedure. This erroneous conclusion resulted from the belief that the strike wave was the result of a general economic imbalance of wage, price, and profit levels rather than of local grievances and their mishandling by management. Actually, the concerted-action procedure has continued in use in modified form. During late 1969 and early 1970 the discussions appear to have had a more general content and to have resulted in less guidance, perhaps as a result of the greater influence of most unions on government policy under the SPD-FDP coalition. Schiller may have done more listening and less talking in the spring of 1970 than on previous occasions. Nevertheless, it is reported that the final session ended with his statement of his anticipations regarding the percentage increases in wages, prices, and profits for the year ahead. It seems reasonable in any case to accord this program a share of the credit for the rapid cyclical recovery, the substantial wage increases, the high level of employment, and the relative price stability of the late 1960s.

·III·

Civil Servant Legislation
and Its Enactment

WHILE legislation has relatively little effect on the terms of employment of public wage-earners and salaried employees, it is all-important for the civil servants. Their terms and conditions of work are set exclusively by law and by ordinances authorized by law. Unions, in representing them, are denied a negotiating function and must rely entirely on their efforts to persuade the government officials who draft the bills and the legislators who enact them. An analysis of the nature and effectiveness of the procedure will indicate that the unions have a considerable impact, even though they criticize the process and seek to change it.

THE CONTENT OF CIVIL SERVICE LAWS

The Federal Constitution guarantees the existence and status of the civil service.[1] Two provisions of Article 33 are relevant:

4. The exercise of sovereign authority shall as a rule be assigned as a permanent duty to members of the public service, who stand in a public law relationship of service and loyalty.
5. The law regarding public service shall be determined with due regard to the traditional principles of the professional civil service.

These traditional principles, which have already been briefly discussed in Chapter I, are generally considered to include a number of points: (1) a public-law relationship of service and loyalty, in contrast to a labor-law contractual relationship; (2) lifetime appointment, except for occasional appointments that are probationary, revocable, or for a limited period; (3)

---

1. It will be remembered that the meaning of the term "civil service" with reference to Germany is not synonymous with its meaning elsewhere.

termination only by resignation or for legally specified reasons and after thorough procedure; (4) the "alimentation principle" that compensation and emergency grants are not for job performance but as a guarantee of an appropriate standard of living, and consequently are not subject to negotiation; and (5) responsibility to the state and the public—not to any political party.[2]

A case involving this provision was decided by the Federal Constitutional Court in June 1958.[3] It was actually a joint decision of two cases. A retired mayor and a retired army officer had both complained that, since they belonged to a particular group of retired civil servants whose pensions were not increased (as were all others) by the Pay Revision Act of 1951, their pensions during the subsequent year had been less than required under the traditional principles of the professional civil service. (This group had not been granted the increase until a year later, on the grounds that the federal budget in 1951 could not bear the extra charge.) The court held that adequate salaries and pensions were among the most important of the traditional principles, and that their adequacy could be determined by comparison with the increase in the general standard of living. It stated that it would ordinarily be difficult for a court to determine the appropriate amount, but that in this case the government had indicated the appropriate change by the increase that it granted to all other active and retired civil servants. It concluded that the legislators had violated the constitutional rights of this particular group and should therefore take steps to reimburse them.

The federal government, in its statement to the Bundestag supporting its draft of a pay increase bill in the autumn of 1960, accepted the court's view that appropriate compensation for civil servants involves their sharing the gains of any general increase in productivity. In spite of general ac-

2. W. Fürst, *Beamtenrecht* (Division II, Vol. 30, in the series Schaeffers Grundriss des Rechts und der Wirtschaft). Stuttgart: W. Kohlhammer Verlag, 1968, pp. 30–33.
3. Bundesverfassungsgericht, *Entscheidungen*, VIII, 1.

ceptance of this guideline, there continues to be much debate regarding the details of its application, and it is widely conceded that the remuneration of civil servants has not entirely kept pace during the last decade with the earnings of nongovernment employees.

The other reference to the civil service in the Constitution is found in Article 75, concerning the relative scope of federal and state legislation. "The Federal Republic has the right, under the conditions of Article 72, to issue limiting regulations (*Rahmenvorschriften*) concerning: (1) the legal relationships of persons in the public service of the states, local governments and other public-law corporations." In other words, while the states have the basic authority to regulate the terms of employment of state and local employees, federal law can set certain general standards to which state laws on this subject must conform.

This constitutional provision still permitted very considerable variations between states and between them and the federal government in salaries and other terms. In order to obtain greater uniformity, an amendment of May 12, 1969, added the following statement: "Limiting regulations (in this sense) may, with the approval of the Bundesrat [the second house of parliament, consisting exclusively of official representatives of the several states], provide also for uniform standards for the structure and measurement of compensation, including the evaluation of positions as well as the minimum and maximum amounts."

The federal government immediately exercised this new authority. In fact, the Bundestag tentatively passed the new legislation even before the amendment had become effective. This revision of the Federal Pay Act provided that the state laws cannot set a top rate for any pay group higher than the federal rate and imposed certain other limitations. Thus the state and local pay schedules should conform closely to the federal schedule. It further provided that any state which already exceeded the federal standards could grant only two thirds of future pay increases until such time as it was in conformance. As a result of these provisions it appeared that differences

in civil servant remuneration would largely vanish with the enactment of the 1970 pay increase. This expectation, however, soon proved to be short-lived. On March 4, 1970, the Hesse legislature passed an act to increase the salary scales of judges and states attorneys, in spite of a warning from the federal Interior Minister that it would conflict with federal law. On April 28 the federal government requested the Federal Constitutional Court to declare the Hesse act invalid as contrary to federal pay guideline legislation and the constitutional principle of loyalty to the Federal Republic.

Another blow to the principle of uniformity came with the passage on May 21 of a new civil servant pay bill for the state of North ·Rhine-Westphalia. The act provided for the wholesale granting of position supplements to teachers. The state Interior Minister (an FDP member) claimed that the bill would violate federal guideline legislation in eight respects, which was denied by its SPD and CDU supporters. The act was adopted under pressure of an impending state election and teacher protest. This protest took the form of a three-week refusal to perform overtime teaching, which was in widespread use as a result of the teacher shortage.

A third instance of breaking ranks occurred on July 8 as Schleswig-Holstein adopted a new civil servant pay law. It raised the 14,000 teachers a half or a full grade and granted a position bonus to certain other groups. In this case the measure was supported by the CDU-FDP coalition and opposed by the SPD.

In the meantime the federal government had decided that the 1969 constitutional revision and the ensuing guideline legislation were still inadequate to prevent growing disparity in the pay structures of the states. It therefore proposed a further constitutional revision, which was under consideration in mid-1970. It involved the insertion in the constitution of a new Article 74a, which would give federal legislation priority over state legislation in matters relating to the remuneration of all active and retired civil servants. In its supporting statement the government argued that the change was necessary because

some states were disrupting the uniformity of civil servant compensation by such methods as the excessive use of position supplements, promotion without a change in position, the granting of entrance to certain positions without certification of competence, the granting of length-of-service credit for non-government experience, and the transfer of certain positions to higher pay groups. The North Rhine-Westphalia cabinet announced its decision to support the federal proposal in the Bundesrat. Presumably, the ministers concluded that it would be preferable to place decision-making on civil servant pay at a level less susceptible to local pressures. Adoption of this proposal would presumably assure a higher degree of uniformity in the payment of civil servants at all levels of government, provided state legislatures can be required to conform. It would not affect the system of negotiation on the terms of employment of public wage-earners and salaried employees.

The most basic of the federal laws of interest to this study is the Federal Civil Servants Act of July 14, 1953.[4] A general indication of the scope of this act and of the content of the most important of its sections will be helpful to subsequent discussion.

The first main section deals with the position of the civil servant—the nature and conditions of appointments to the civil service, the limitations on transfer, and the forms and conditions of termination of the relationship. The four types of appointment are probationary, revocable, limited time, and lifetime. The probationary period may not exceed six years (three states say five years). The revocable appointment applies primarily to persons serving an internship. A lifetime appointment cannot be obtained before age twenty-seven. Several of the state laws specify a maximum age limit for entry.

All appointments are made at one of four career levels, depending largely on the extent of the person's education. The "simple service" normally requires only a grade-school (*Hauptschule*) education and a half-year internship (two and a half years in the postal service). The "middle service"

4. *BGBl.*, 1965, I, 1776 (revised form.)

requires completion of grade school and at least one year of internship (two years in the postal service). The "elevated service" requires secondary-school (*Realschule*) graduation, three years of internship, and the subsequent passing of an examination. The "higher service" requires a university degree and the passing of the first and second "state examinations," separated by an internship of two and a half years.[5]

Transfer from the wage-earner or salaried employee status to the civil servant status is possible when the entry requirements have been met. Such transfer occurs frequently to the lower levels of the civil service, as in the case of postmen, postal clerks, streetcar conductors, and stenographers (if they are interested in a permanent career) after a certain length of service and the passing of a test. Such transfer usually involves a reduction in current income but a net gain in better fringes, pensions, and promotion opportunities.

Advancement of civil servants from one career level to a higher one is difficult, since it usually requires the obtaining of additional education, the passing of a promotion test, and, after an internship, a career test. The opportunity has been limited further to persons within a certain range of age and length of service, but these latter requirements have recently been dropped by Berlin and Hesse. In the federal service advancement to the top level was available only to those who had reached the age of forty-five, who had had fifteen years of service, and who were at the top of the elevated service. The Federal Career Ordinance of April 27, 1970,[6] removed the age and seniority requirements and introduced greater flexibility in a number of respects.

The widespread dissatisfaction with the rigidity of the career levels has been moderated as a result of this ordinance. All of the unions with civil servant members, including the DBB, had been advocating some modification of the structure that

5. The postal service presently has higher educational requirements for the middle and elevated services and compensates for this to some extent by facilitating advancement to the next career level. For example, it currently undertakes to fill half of the vacancies in the middle service by advancement and half by new entrants.

6. *BGBl.*, 1970, I, 442.

would facilitate advancement, and they will doubtless continue to press for further changes. One proposal is a merging or abolition of the levels with reference to promotion, and retention of them only in the form of four different entry levels.

The next section of the Civil Servants Act concerns the obligations of the civil servant. It covers such matters as the administration of the oath, avoidance of conflict of interest, nondisclosure of confidential information, limitation on secondary employment, and moderation in private political activity. This last point does not preclude candidacy for public office. In fact, civil servants who run for election may obtain two months of paid leave for campaigning and unpaid leave while in office, which may help to explain why civil servants constitute nearly a third of the membership of the Bundestag.

The first-mentioned among the rights of the civil servant is the right to care and protection. The general statement in Section 79 sets forth this special aspect of the status of the German civil servant: "The employer, within the framework of the relationship of service and loyalty, shall provide for the well-being of the civil servant and his family, including the time after the ending of the civil servant relationship. It protects him in his official activity and in his position as a civil servant." The Baden-Württemberg law is a bit more specific in providing that the state shall protect him against any exterior political influence that might affect the performance of his duties. Several of the state laws mention the special grants that may be made in case of any emergency, such as births, deaths, and illness. The federal act specifies also the right to take an annual vacation, to examine his personnel file, to engage in union activity without discrimination, and to be represented by his union.

The key provision on union activity regarding terms of employment is found in Section 94: "The federations of the appropriate unions shall participate in the preparation of general regulations of the legal civil servant relationship." It is this provision that gives the unions their role in the preparation of laws and decrees governing the terms of employment of civil servants, replacing their role of negotiation on behalf of public wage-earners and salaried employees.

There is room for some difference of opinion as to precisely what is required in a right to participate (*beteiligen*) in this connection. A guide to interpretation is found in the legislative history. The government's original bill called for a right to be heard. It is clear that the Bundestag, in revising this proposal, intended to strengthen the role of the unions. Presumably the distinction is that the unions, instead of being entitled to a single hearing on a measure, can expect to be informed and consulted more than once, as the draft is modified.

The unions have complained to the Minister of the Interior of inadequate opportunity for participation in certain instances. As a result of one such complaint, the Ministry on July 20, 1963, sent to the other ministries the following statement of its interpretation of the right to participate:

> In the preparation of regulations of major significance, the federations shall be given the opportunity, even before the start of interagency dealings, to discuss at least the basic questions that are likely to arise during the drafting of the proposal.
>
> In case new basic questions arise in the course of the dealings with the ministries, the federations shall be informed of them.
>
> If a bill or proposal is modified on a matter of basic significance after the formal participation of the federations in accordance with Section 94 of the Federal Civil Servants Act, the federations shall be given again the opportunity to state their position.

Though there has been but one court case on the nature of the unions' role, the failure to involve them has twice been successfully challenged. On September 29, 1966, the administration presented to the Bundestag the draft of a Finance Planning Act to place federal budgetary planning on a more than one-year basis. The bill included the proposed 1967 budget, which contained—as a. recession measure—provisions that would in several respects reduce the benefits of retired civil servants and their widows. The unions had issued press releases in opposition to the measure, but had not been called in for consultation. The DGB on October 7 submitted a protest to Chancellor Erhard and indicated its intention to bring suit. On October 14 the Minister of the Interior invited the union to a consultation on October 25, explaining that the stringent time pressure on the preparation of the bill and the need to consult all other ministries had precluded the usual union consultation at an earlier date. The union brought suit before the administrative court, but withdrew it after receiving from the Chancellor an admission of error and a promise of future observance of the unions' right to participate.[7] In a similar case an administrative court in June 1968 directed the state administration of Rhineland-Palatinate to consult in the preliminary stages and to inform the state cabinet of the content of the discussion.[8]

The Federal Civil Servants Act also contains several sections under the heading of personnel management. These provide for the establishment of a permanent, independent Federal Personnel Committee of seven members. The chairman is the president of the Federal Accounting Office (*Bundesrechnungshof*). A second *ex officio* member is the head of the Personnel Legislation Department of the Ministry of the Interior. The other five members are named for four-year terms by the federal President on the recommendation of the Minister of the Interior. They include the head of the Personnel Department in another ministry and four other civil servants, three of whom are selected from the nominees of the appropriate union federations. The state laws are similar, except that many provide for a larger membership with a smaller proportion of union nominees.

The committee has the right and duty to cooperate (*mitwirken*) in the preparation of provisions concerning the training and testing of civil servants and of general regulations regarding the legal civil service relationship. It shall take a position

7. DGB, *Geschäftsbericht, 1965–68*, pp. 632–33.
8. DBB, *Geschäftsbericht der Bundesleitung, 1969*, p. 25.

on grievances of basic importance submitted by civil servants or rejected applicants. It also has the function of providing flexibility in the administration of civil service laws as a result of its right to approve exceptions to them in individual cases with reference to waiving entrance requirements, reducing the length of the probationary period, setting a salary in excess of the basic schedule, and postponing retirement beyond the age of sixty-five.

The act further contains "maintenance" provisions. Noncontributory pensions are scaled from 35 percent of earnings after ten years of service to 65 percent after twenty-five years and a maximum of 75 percent after thirty-five years. Comparable assistance grants may be made to persons who do not qualify for pensions. There is also provision for dependents' benefits, accident compensation, and termination grants of up to six months' salary.

The act states that grievances may be presented and advanced up to the head of the agency. No mention is made of the staff council as a grievance channel, because it is covered by a separate act. A civil servant who wishes to bring suit regarding his employment shall take it to the administrative court. This is in contrast to the situation for wage-earners and salaried employees, whose suits go to the labor court. This distinction was hotly debated in the Bundestag, where a strong effort was made by the SPD to use the labor courts also for civil servants. The outcome illustrates the widespread view of the special relationship of the civil servant.

Four years after the passage of this act, the federal government took advantage of its constitutional right to enact limiting regulations governing the corresponding state laws. The Civil Service Legislation Framework Act (*Beamtenrechtsrahmengesetz*) of July 1, 1957,[9] provided that state laws should be brought into conformity with it within three years. As might be expected, it contained most of the more basic provisions of the 1953 federal act (as revised up to that time). Some provisions were stated in general terms, so that they could be adapted to the structural variations of the several

9. *BGBl.*, 1957, I, 667.

states, and others were stated broadly enough to allow some options. Many details of the earlier act were omitted. On the other hand, there were additions regarding special provisions for some types of state or local employees that are not used by the federal government. For example, the general career levels and the corresponding requirements need not be applied to the police, and an earlier retirement age may be set for them. Professors are exempt from the general provisions regarding career levels, probationary periods, transfer, and hours of work. Upon reaching age sixty-eight they are not retired, but rather are "relieved of their obligations."

The Federal Civil Servants Act contains a number of provisions regarding the performance and conduct of the civil servant that indicate various kinds of action or inaction that would justify discipline. Most of these cover situations that are universally considered a violation of duty—insubordination, dishonesty, disclosure of confidential information, unapproved acceptance of gifts, etc. There is, however, one obligation that is unusual in its scope and is indicative of the special position of the German civil servant, namely the requirement that his conduct off the job must be appropriate to the respect and trust that his profession requires. Since the civil servant is an embodiment of the state, he must avoid actions that would injure trust in his office or respect for the professional civil service. This applies during retirement as well as during active service. Possible infractions would be habitual drunkenness, violation of generally accepted moral standards, frequent association with persons of bad reputation, to say nothing of treason.

The disciplinary procedure that applies only to civil servants is set forth in the Federal Disciplinary Ordinance, most recently amended by the Act for the Revision of Federal Disciplinary Laws of July 20, 1967. The general policy is that everything possible should be done to correct and counsel a civil servant, with discipline imposed only as a last resort.[10] In its latest

10. As one union official complained: "If a wage-earner or salaried employee on official travel goes second class and tries to collect for first class, he will probably be discharged; whereas a civil servant might well get off with a written reprimand in his file."

revision, the ordinance speaks only of disciplinary measures rather than penalties and takes care not to refer to the individual as "the accused." It is emphasized that the official who investigates the incident and the one who may represent the agency in formal proceedings are not hostile to the employee or acting as a prosecuting attorney, but are equally concerned with the employee's interest and mitigating circumstances. It may well be said that this should be equally true in any disciplinary procedure, but to Germans it seems to have a special significance in the case of civil servants.

The possible disciplinary measures are (1) a reprimand, (2) a fine of no more than one month's pay, (3) a reduction in pay of no more than one fifth for no more than five years, (4) demotion to an office in a lower pay group of the same career group, without repromotion until after at least five years, (5) removal from the service, and (6) in the case of retirees, reduction or cancellation of pension. Since this revision, a written warning is no longer considered a disciplinary action. At the same time two other measures were discontinued: denial of the next length-of-service increase and transfer to a lower length-of-service level in his current pay group. The immediate superior has authority only to issue a reprimand. Only the head of an agency can impose the maximum fine. The second in command can impose a fine up to half that amount, and the third in command up to a fourth.

If the agency concludes that a penalty more serious than a fine is called for, it appoints an independent investigator (a civil servant with judicial qualifications). At this point the employee is entitled to name a defender. For this purpose he may use an attorney, a law professor, an active or retired civil servant, or a union representative. The report of the investigator to the agency is entirely factual, without recommendation. If the agency decides to pursue the case, it forwards the report and all relevant documents to the federal disciplinary attorney, who draws up a statement of charges and refers the case to the local chamber of the Federal Disciplinary Court. The chamber consists of a member of that court and two civil servants—at least one of whom must have judicial qualifications—selected from an area panel established by the Minister of the Interior. Either the employee or the federal attorney may require that the court take testimony anew rather than relying on the investigator's report.

A provision indicating the special position of German civil servants permits the court, in case of a verdict of removal from service or cancellation of pension, to grant for a specified time a maintenance allowance of up to 75 percent of the pension. It may direct that the allowance be paid in whole or in part to specified dependents of the employee.

The employee may appeal from disciplinary action taken within the agency—reprimand or fine—by presenting a grievance, which, if not settled within the agency, may be taken to the Federal Disciplinary Court for final determination. In the case of more serious penalties—set in the first instance by a local chamber of the Disciplinary Court—appeal may be taken to the Federal Administrative Court. Records of reprimands or fines shall be removed from personnel files after three years of good behavior. Similar action in the case of reduction of salary shall be taken after five years.

The state laws on disciplinary procedure for civil servants are in general quite similar to the federal provisions, except that the two state courts involved are the disciplinary chambers of the administrative court and the Superior Administrative Court. Further appeal to the Federal Administrative Court is permissible on major issues.

The Federal Pay Act of July 27, 1957 (revised most recently on April 15, 1970), contains the provisions regarding remuneration of civil servants, including the structure and level of basic salaries. It also covers the various bonuses. A permanent position bonus and a temporary assignment bonus are provided to permit flexibility in situations that otherwise cannot equitably be fitted into the regular schedule. Several other bonuses are applicable only to foreign service.

The base salary of the civil servant, like that of the salaried employee, depends upon his pay group and his length of service. Civil servants—other than university academic employees, who have their separate "H" groups—are assigned to one of twenty-seven pay groups, designated as A 1 to A 16 and B 1 to B 11. The vast majority of them are in one of the A groups. Grades A 1 and A 2 are the entrance grades for the simple service. Grade A 1 covers very few classifications other than office helper. Grade A 2 includes, for example, railway guards and postmen. Grade A 5 is the top grade of the simple service and also the entrance grade for the middle service.[11] Many of its classifications carry the title of assistant, e.g. tax assistant, customs assistant, and management assistant. A 9 is the entry grade for the elevated service. Most of its classification titles include the designation of inspector. The entry level of the higher service, A 13, includes consuls, high school teachers, and army majors.[12] The B groups cover most of the department heads in the federal ministries and other high positions ranging from the director of the Federal Office for Foreign Trade Information to the state secretaries (deputy ministers). For each of the A pay groups there is a series of from nine to fifteen specified rates, starting at the beginning rate at age 21 and providing for an automatic increase after each two years of service until the top rate is reached.[13] The higher B groups carry only single rates. Advancement to a higher pay group normally comes only with promotion and a change of assignment.

Our analysis of the pay schedule is based on the provisions of the Seventh Act to Revise the Federal Pay Act, effective

11. It is reported that the entrance grade for each of the career levels may be raised in 1971 by one grade, thus ending this overlap.

12. This study does not deal with members of the armed services unless specially noted. It also excludes judges, who technically are not civil servants, although their position is in most respects very similar. It may be of interest to note that of all federal civil servants about 5 percent are in the simple service, 45 percent in the middle service, 35 percent in the elevated service, and 15 percent in the higher service.

13. Persons entering before age 21 do not accumulate length of service until they have reached that age. Those entering at a later age may count as service a variety of activities such as study and military service. Time spent after age 21 in nongovernment activity is counted at half value, i.e. one increase for each four years. It is reported that the government may change in 1971 from a length of service differential to an age differential, thus making transfer from the private to the public sector more attractive.

January 1, 1970.[14] The schedule, though it had been restructured in 1969, is still much less symmetrical than the one for salaried employees (page 61). The A 1 pay group starts at 430.20 DM and reaches, after 16 years of service, a top of 585.40 DM. Grade A 16 begins at 1662.40 DM and peaks after 28 years at 3007.80 DM. This schedule is roughly similar to the salaried employee schedule in the upper groups, but at the lower levels the fifth civil servant group equates with the second salaried employee group. This indicates that the lowest civil servant groups correspond rather to wage-earner groups, which is consistent with earlier comments regarding the overlapping of assignments to all three types of government employees. The civil servant rates as a whole go far beyond the salaried employee rates, when we include the B 1 to B 11 groups, for which there are no corresponding salaried employee classifications. They carry single rates that range from 2659 DM to 6231.60 DM.

The act formerly provided that promotion to the next group within a career level could be made only when the employee was assigned to an appropriately higher position. In 1965 some states, in one of the few instances in which they have taken the initiative and thus got out of line with federal provisions, introduced one automatic promotion at each level. The federal government has reluctantly adapted to this situation by permitting advancement from the entry group to the next group without change of function after special knowledge or experience has been gained by two to five years of satisfactory performance in the entry group.

The act seeks to control the volume of promotions by providing that the job table of nearly all agencies shall not place more than a specified percentage of the members of any one career level in the upper groups of that level. For example, of the agency jobs classified in the middle service, not more than 40 percent may be in the A 7 group, not more than 25 percent in A 8, and not more than 5 percent in A 9.

The act has several appendices that go into considerable

14. *BGBI.*, 1970, I, 339.

detail. There is, for example, for each pay group a listing of the position titles that are included in it—in most instances some thirty to fifty titles. In the higher pay groups with a single rate many of the titles apply only to a single individual, such as the head of a particular agency or government institute. Adjustments are occasionally made in the allocation of particular positions to the various pay groups to meet changing conditions. Thus teachers were raised in 1969, with grade-school teachers, for example, moving from A 9 to A 11. It has been noted that at least two states attempted to raise them higher in 1970. These shifts were presumably occasioned by the teacher shortage, though they were justified on the grounds of increased training requirements.

Other federal civil service legislation includes the Staff Representation Act (see Chapter IV), the Federal Moving Cost Act of April 8, 1964, the Federal Travel Cost Reimbursement Act of March 20, 1965, and ordinances on work hours, mother protection, vacations, and leaves of absence.

DEVELOPMENT OF CIVIL SERVICE COMPENSATION

Adjustments in the pay level of civil servants have been less frequent than in the case of the negotiated increases for wage-earners and salaried employees, but it is generally agreed that the overall increase during the past decade has been comparable. Following a general increase in 1953, the basic Federal Pay Act was adopted on July 27, 1957, effective April 1 of that year. Since that time there have been ten increases as indicated in Table II.

A brief review of some of the related developments during these years will give more meaning to Table II and will illustrate the procedure of union impact on enactment. There is general agreement that the rates set in 1957 were appropriate and placed the civil servants in a satisfactory relationship to private employees.

In June 1958 came the Constitutional Court decision that recognized a constitutional obligation of government to see that civil servants share fully in improvements in the general

TABLE II
Increases in Federal Civil Servants' Basic Pay

Enactment date	Effective date	Months since previous increase	Percentage increase
June 8, 1960	June 1, 1960	38	7
Dec. 23, 1960	Jan. 1, 1961	7	8
Feb. 21, 1963	Jan. 1, 1963	24	6
Feb. 21, 1963	Mar. 1, 1963	2	1.5–12
Aug. 13, 1964	Oct. 1, 1964	19	8
Dec. 23, 1965	Jan. 1, 1966	15	4
Dec. 23, 1965	Oct. 1, 1966	9	4
July 19, 1968	July 1, 1968	21	4
May 14, 1969	Apr. 1, 1969	9	2.5–8
Apr. 15, 1970	Jan. 1, 1970	9	8+2

standard of living. But more than three years passed between the 1957 adjustment and the next one. The legislative history leading to the raise on June 1, 1960, witnessed an unusually wide difference of opinion. The Finance Minister persuaded the cabinet that the federal budget could not stand more than a 4 percent increase, and that was the amount recommended to the parliament. There was wide dissatisfaction, because of the long period of economic improvement since the previous raise. The unions lobbied vigorously. The Interior Committee of the Bundestag recommended 9 percent, but government forces rallied to reduce this to 7 percent in the final action.

Criticism of the inadequacy of this action was so strong that the government soon had a change of heart. Major responsibility for the drafting of civil service legislation was shifted from the Finance Ministry to the Interior Ministry, and in seven months (January 1, 1961) the civil servants received a further 8 percent. It was during the enactment of this measure that government officials and party spokesmen endorsed the reasoning of the 1958 Constitutional Court ruling. These endorsements delighted the DBB officials, who had long sought to establish some kind of a formula for civil service pay increases that would make them less vulnerable to the whims of the budgetmakers and less susceptible to claims of fiscal inability. They rejoiced that in the future they could base their arguments on data regarding changes not only in the cost of living but also in the standard of living and the gross national product. They thought that the civil servants would no longer have to follow in the wake of the government wage-earners and salaried employees, but could now make their own case independently. The DGB officials have been less concerned with efforts to "objectify" civil servant pay increases, since they are more inclined to base their arguments on the raises that their constituent unions have negotiated for other government employees.

The hopes of the DBB officials proved to be short-lived, as their vigorous efforts to win a 1962 revision in the federal schedule were unavailing. It is illuminating to study an unsuccessful campaign, as well as the successful ones. In the national election of September 1961, the CDU/CSU lost its absolute majority in the Bundestag, and formed a coalition government with the FDP. It is not clear, however, that this change of government had any significant impact on the civil servant pay issue, since FDP leaders had spoken as favorably as others on this point. Nevertheless, friction between government and union leaders quickly intensified as the DBB campaigned unsuccessfully in an effort to win for civil servants a year-end "Christmas" bonus, such as had long been granted to public salaried employees.

On November 10, 1961, the national executive committee of the DBB demanded a new civil servant salary adjustment. A week later DBB President Krause met with the Minister of the Interior and was informed that the cabinet had decided to present a pay increase bill to the Bundestag in the spring of 1962. On December 19 the Interior Minister met with union leaders and explained plans to submit a bill to "harmonize" pay provisions of the state and the federal governments. The DBB officers took the position that a pay increase should come first, because they correctly anticipated that the drafting and enactment of the harmonization law would be a lengthy process.

On February 3, 1962, the DBB executive committee formulated its specific demands, the chief of which was an increase of 7.7 percent in the base rates, effective retroactively to January 1. This decision was based on government estimates that 1961 had witnessed increases of 2.5 percent in cost of living, 4 percent in national productivity, 7.7 percent in per capita income, 9.8 percent in average earnings of employees other than civil servants, and 9.9 percent in gross national product. Thus while the Interior Minister was arguing that national productivity should be the determining consideration, the DBB was pinning its case on per capita income. On February 21 the DBB again wrote to the Interior Minister, urging that the pay raise issue be separated from the harmonization bill to permit prompt action. At the same time DBB officials met with the Bundestag's SPD members to urge their support for this demand.

Since the government seemed determined to defer any pay increase until adoption of the harmonization law, the DBB turned its attention to the 1962 federal budget. It found that the tentative draft made no provision for raises to any federal employees. It wrote to the Finance Minister on January 16, urging that provision for higher pay be included in the budget proposal that would soon go to the Bundestag. Since this request was not granted, it then urged all members of the Bundestag Budget Committee to insert such an item. In the budget debates the government did not argue that a pay increase was unwarranted, but rather that it could not be afforded this year, since the budget already foresaw expenditures 15 percent greater than in 1961. The budget adopted on April 12 made no provision for a raise.

Another complicating factor was the negotiation of pay increases for the government wage-earners and salaried employees. In mid-February the DGB unions announced cancellation of the current agreements as of April 1 and demanded an increase of about 9 percent. The prospect of these negotiations was for a time cited by government officials as a reason for postponing a decision regarding the civil servants. The DBB argued vigorously that the facts were now available to permit an independent decision. Its failure to win on this issue was probably due in part to lack of support from the DGB, which was well satisfied to base its case for the civil servants on what it could win in its negotiations for the other government employees, who were legally free to strike for their demands.

The negotiations proved to be difficult and lasted for several weeks. Finally on May 11 the VKA, representing the local governments, broke ranks with the TdL and the federal government and reached separate agreement on a 6 percent raise as of April 1. The federal and state governments held fast for a time, in spite of some talk of a strike vote. Finally on May 30 the cabinet authorized the Interior Minister to resume negotiations. On June 7 he and the TdL agreed with the ÖTV and DAG on a 6 percent raise as of July 1, with a flat grant of a 50 DM payment to the wage-earners and salaried employees in the lower pay groups in lieu of retroactivity to April 1.

The DBB and DGB then urged immediate enactment of a similar increase for civil servants, but to no avail. Not even the unusual DBB tactic of holding mass protest meetings in some dozen cities during June could modify the government's resolve to defer a civil servant raise until 1963 by including it in the harmonization bill. The Bundestag refused to consider an SPD proposal that civil servants be given a half-month's pay as a carryover to 1963. Seldom has the federal government allowed such a clear indication that the legal inability of the civil servants to strike may cost them a delay, if not a denial, of comparable increase.

As a last resort, the DBB shifted its attack from the federal to the state level. On June 14 DBB President Krause met with the chairman of the Conference of State Finance Ministers; and on June 28 the executive committee called on the states to take direct action as independent employers to correct the "injustice." The DGB also contacted state officials through its state branches. These efforts met with rather surprising immediate success. On July 3 the government of North Rhine-Westphalia decided to grant its civil servants a 6 percent increase as of July 1; and the following day a law to this effect was passed by the state legislature in emergency action. Since this occurred just two or three days before a statewide election, there were immediate accusations of an "election present." This is one of the few instances in which it seems clear that political considerations have influenced the timing, if not the substance, of legislation regarding public employees. On the other hand, it must be recognized that there was strong factual justification for the raise.

Two other states had taken similar action by July 5, when the federal Interior Minister met' with the state finance ministers to urge that they stand firm with the federal government on this issue. He was able to obtain only a resolution supporting the general principle of unity of state and federal action on pay policies. Within a week of this meeting all of the other eight states had followed the lead of North Rhine-Westphalia, Hesse, and Saarland.

This action of the states demonstrated the strength of the argument in favor of a raise, after all public wage-earners and salaried employees had received an increase. The obstinacy of the federal government in this matter had resulted temporarily in a complete collapse of the usual unity of action. First the local governments had broken away by negotiating in May an increase for the wage-earners and salaried employees. Now the states had broken away by legislating similar results for state and local civil servants.

The federal government at last felt obliged to modify its position. On July 12 the Interior Minister called in the federation heads to review with them the proposed terms of a bill to grant federal civil servants the same 6 percent increase that was already being paid to all other public employees. He stated that this raise should take effect the day after enactment of this measure. The unions took strong exception to this effective date and insisted that it should be no later than July 1, when state action became effective. This proved in the long run to be an unfortunate decision. The final result was that the federal government reverted to its original position. The pay increase together with the harmonization measures finally became law on February 21, 1963. The general 6 percent increase carried an effective date of January 1. The equalization provisions, which involved varying increases with a minimum of 1.5 percent, took effect on March 1.

Further progress toward similarity of state and federal laws was achieved by an act adopted on December 18 of the same year, which contained many minor revisions and increased the location and children's bonuses, but not the basic pay schedule.

The revision of August 13, 1964, brought an 8 percent increase as of October 1. It also raised the children's bonus to a uniform 50 DM and simplified the location bonus by reducing the number of classifications from three to two.

Before continuing our survey of the chronological development of civil servant pay, we must pause to consider a statistical report published at this time, which has considerably influenced subsequent pay discussions, particularly with reference to the application of the standards suggested in the Constitutional Court decision of 1958. The relevant data are contained in a section on "Payment in the Civil Service" in the first Annual Report (1964-65) of the Council of Experts on Economic Development, entitled *Stable Money— Steady Growth.*[15] The members of this Council of Experts were appointed by the President in accordance with an act of August 14, 1963. The Council has the duty of describing the current and prospective situation of the national economy and investigating the possibilities of safeguarding the stability of the price level, a high rate of employment, an equilibrium in international payments, and a steady economic growth. It is somewhat analogous to the President's Council of Economic Advisors in the United States, with the major exception that it shall not make any policy recommendations. It is an independent group and is not considered as a part of the governmental structure.

In its first report it analyzed the increase in the pay of civil servants and of various other groups of income recipients. For the civil servants it began with the fundamental pay revision of 1957. Since this law did not have its full effect in the state and local governments until the following year, the adopted base was the average annual basic pay of all civil servants for the years 1957-58. Their estimate of the cumulative increase over this base for the subsequent years

15. Stuttgart: W. Kohlhammer, 1964.

was 2.6 percent for 1959, 9.1 for 1960, 20.9 for 1961, 24.0 for 1962, and 32.9 for 1963.

In comparing these estimates of increase in average pay with the general increases that were enacted during this period, it is obvious that the former were appreciably larger than the latter and that there was some increase in pay received even in years when the schedule remained unchanged. These contrasts indicate that there was a steady increase in the percentage of public servants in the higher pay groups. This could result both from a growing need for more highly trained employees and from a shifting of some positions to higher groups. Another factor may have been an increase in the average length of service, placing a larger proportion of the employees in any one group at the higher steps in that group.

The Council of Experts also estimated the change in average pay for civil servants other than those engaged in defense-related activities. They cited an increase of 35.6 percent for the restricted group, as compared to 32.9 percent for all. There had been little employment in defense at the start of the period and a large expansion during the second half. One reason why the inclusion of the defense group brings down the total average is presumably that it had in 1963 a very short average length of service. Another reason may be that perhaps it consists largely of persons in the lower groups, with the higher supervision supplied chiefly by military officers. In any case, it seems clear that the 35.6 percent increase for the restricted group gives the fairer picture of how civil servants had fared during the total period.

For purposes of comparison, the council presented estimates of the change in average income since 1957 for certain other groups. They concluded, for example, that by 1963 the national income per economically active person had risen by 52.4 percent, the gross total of wages and salaries per employed person (excluding civil servants and professional soldiers) by 58.4 percent, and the gross total of wages and salaries per employed person (excluding all government employees) by 60.8 percent.

The council was careful to avoid making any prohibited recommendations. The DBB welcomed these quasi-official data as providing a basis for implementing the standards mentioned in the 1958 Constitutional Court decision, and proceeded to draw its own conclusions. For this purpose it might with some justification have taken the 60.8 figure for nongovernment employees, but was content to use the 52.4 figure for national income per economically active person as being more relevant to the Constitutional Court's reference to general economic improvement. Comparing this with the 35.6 percent gain for nondefense civil servants, it concluded that a further increase of at least 12 percent of the 1963 schedule for civil servants was needed as a "catch-up" to eliminate the lag that had developed during the six-year period. It has updated the council's estimates each year and contended that by November 1969 the lag had grown to 19 percent.

The DGB and DAG do not join with the DBB in its emphasis on this line of argument. They do say that, if the civil servants are given any special increase, the public wage-earners and salaried employees should receive similar treatment. It appears that, except for brief temporary periods, the three groups of government employees have been treated equally. The argument made by the DBB is therefore somewhat embarrassing to the others, since it implies that they have been too easily satisfied in their negotiations with the Interior Ministry.

It is generally admitted that a lag exists and that some catch-up would be equitable, but there is considerable disagreement as to its exact amount. It is argued by some on behalf of the government that it is really less than might appear, because advancing industrial technology has resulted in a greater increase in average skill in the private than in the public sector. On the other hand, it might be argued, without much possibility of proof, that there has been a corresponding increase in the skills needed in government service. In any case, this issue of lag has played a role in all discussion of pay increases since the publication of the council's report at the end of 1964 and is now again under discussion.

The next pay increase was voted on December 23, 1965.

Since some signs of an impending recession were beginning to show, it took the unique form of providing for a two-stage raise—4 percent on January 1, 1966, and another 4 percent the following October 1.

As a result of the recession of 1966-67, nearly two years passed before the next increase of only 4 percent was enacted on July 19, 1968, effective July 1. Nine months later a further increase was granted in conjunction with an extensive revision of the pay schedule and the enactment of limiting measures intended to assure conformity by the state and local governments, as permitted by the May 1969 constitutional revision. The increases ranged from 2.5 to 8 percent, with an average of about 5 percent.

The next pay act for civil servants was the one previously mentioned that brought them a single 300 DM payment on November 1, 1969, although the legislation sanctioning it was not passed until December 5. This was the action taken following the wildcat strikes of September and the resulting payment of the lump sum to public wage-earners and salaried employees. This time, unlike the discussions of 1962, the government made it very plain that the civil servants would promptly receive any payment made to the other two groups.

It is interesting to note the tactics used by the DBB at the time of the September work interruptions. Although there was no threat of strike by any civil servants, the organization was pressing for additional pay from the outset. On the same day (September 16) when DGB and DAG officials first met with representatives of the VKA, TdL, and federal government to present their unsuccessful demand for immediate negotiations, DBB President Krause met with Interior Minister Benda to urge that the prospective budget surplus for 1969 be used to give civil servants a single bonus for the remainder of the year. Two days later the DBB publicized its demand that the federal government act promptly to narrow the growing gap between pay in the public and private sectors. Four days after that it sent a telegram to the Chancellor urging the need for immediate pay action and arguing that the granting of such well justified demands could not possibly be interpreted as an election present.

On the next day (September 23) the cabinet met to discuss the pay problem. It announced that negotiations with the ÖTV and DAG would be opened as soon as the cabinet could decide on the terms of its offer at its next meeting the following week—after the national election. The cabinet further indicated that it recognized that all public employees must participate in the fruits of the national economic growth and pledged that the civil servants would receive the same increases as negotiated for the other two groups.

The DBB immediately issued a sharp criticism of the decision to delay negotiations. It stated that this action would not check the growing unrest in the public service. It also specified its demands as involving a bonus of one month's pay for 1969 and a 13 percent increase in basic pay, effective January 1, 1970.

On September 25 (some twelve hours after the VKA had negotiated a 300 DM bonus for local wage-earners and salaried employees and two weeks before the federal and state governments took similar action) the state secretary of the Interior Ministry conferred with the DBB president and stated that a civil servant pay bill would be ready for discussion by mid-October. The following day he held a similar conference with Waldemar Reuter, the head of the DGB Civil Servant Department. On October 9 the bonus for state and federal wage-earners and salaried employees was negotiated, and the civil servants received a similar bonus with their next pay checks.

In the meantime, discussion had begun concerning the 1970 increase for civil servants, paralleling the increase eventually negotiated on January 15 for the wage-earners and salaried employees. When the DBB indicated in late September its goal of a 13 percent increase on January 1, it suggested that 8 percent was for participation in the growth of national income and 5 percent, which might be paid in noninflationary investment funds, was for reduction of the lag in civil servant pay. On November 12 the DBB released a letter sent to the Finance Minister, taking strong objection to his criticism of DBB demands and to his indication that he envisaged the civil servant pay increase as taking effect on April 1. It suggested that he should not publicly attack its proposals without first having held a conference with its officers. It said his suggestions would tend to keep the civil servants in the position of suppliants and to defeat DBB efforts to make their pay determinations more objective.

Nevertheless, the cabinet on November 20 decided to defer drafting of the new pay bill until midrange budget planning for 1970-73 could be worked out. The DGB said that at least the lower ranks should receive 100 DM a month, starting January 1. The DBB said that an effective date of January 1 was essential, even if enactment were somewhat delayed for development of the 1970 budget.

On December 3 came the surprise introduction of the CDU/CSU bill for a 12 percent raise for civil servants. These opposition parties also asked the government to determine the amount of the lag in civil service pay and to propose methods for eliminating it, a rather strange request to be coming from the parties that had been in control of the government from the birth of the Federal Republic until just two months earlier, but nevertheless a request that was acted on by the government.

During the next five weeks the spotlight centered on the negotiations for the wage-earners and salaried employees, as plans for a strike vote were announced and finally cancelled. On January 11 the government announced its willingness to grant an 8 percent increase in basic pay plus 2 percent in "structural improvements" effective January 1 to civil servants (and to judges, soldiers, and retirees, who normally receive similar treatment). The newspapers spoke of an "agreement" between the Interior Ministry and the DBB that, in view of the retroactivity, the latter would not press any additional pay demands for 1970. This suggests the possibility, considered later, that the unions' right to participate in the drafting of civil servant legislation involves some aspects of negotiation.

On January 23, eight days after the conclusion of negotiations for the wage-earners and salaried employees, the Bundesrat approved the bill to raise civil servant pay and referred it for enactment by the Bundestag. The Interior Minister explained to the Bundesrat that a separate bill would soon be presented providing for a "capital savings" grant of 13 DM a month to civil servants in the lower grades. That bill, applicable to those in pay groups A 1 to A 8, whose base pay did not exceed 811 DM, was enacted on June 4. It approximated the additional offer made to the wage-earners and salaried employees in their final negotiations. The Minister expressed the intention of the government to extend this provision in 1971 to the rest of the civil servants and to double the amount of the grant.

Final enactment of the basic pay increase by the Bundestag came on April 15 with a retroactive date of January 1. It remained to be seen whether the CDU/CSU would be able to make any political capital out of its earlier proposal for a 12 percent increase. Under all the circumstances it seemed likely that most public employees would agree with the view expressed by an SPD spokesman that the CDU/CSU proposal was "not serious."

THE UNION ROLE IN THE ENACTMENT PROCEDURE

The usual sequence of procedures and the variety of tactics of the unions in the enactment of all types of civil servant legislation will be reviewed now that various individual instances with reference to pay laws have been described. The two unions that play the leading roles in this respect are the DBB and the DGB. Thus it will be noted that there are significant differences in the unions that are involved in the negotiating and legislating processes. The DAG representing salaried employees has no role in civil servant legislation. The DBB representing primarily civil servants has a major role in the legislative process, though almost none in negotiations. As for the DGB, the negotiating function is in the hands of the constituent unions such as the ÖTV, whereas the legislative function is largely centered in the parent federation and is conducted by its Civil Servant Department, which maintains liaison with the individual unions through an advisory committee consisting of two representatives each of the ÖTV, the DPG, the GdED and the GEW. This centralization of DGB activity results from the law which grants participation in legislative drafting to the federations rather than the separate unions, but it also serves to coordinate legislative demands.

The first task of the unions is to keep the top officials and the appropriate department heads of the Interior Ministry thoroughly informed regarding union legislative goals. Thus when the new SPD/FDP government was installed in October 1969, the new Interior Minister Genscher was asked to meet promptly with the DGB Civil Servant Advisory Committee. The committee outlined its legislative objectives, placing major emphasis on pay revision. It stated that the DGB demand of the previous June for 8 percent across the board and 5 percent in structural improvements would now have to be increased due to subsequent economic developments. It urged the abolition of the location bonus, the introduction of employee capital-saving grants, and a special increase at the lower levels. It also stressed proposals for revision of other laws to give the civil servants and their unions a greater voice in setting their terms of employment, to provide more flexibility in promotion and movement between career levels, to increase the role of the unions in the staff councils, and to expand the rights of the councils. Normally there is frequent and friendly contact between the federation officials and the department heads, so that discussion covers also matters of lesser import, such as the request for an increase in the lunch allowance from 60 pf. to 1 DM.

Another standard method of exerting influence is to invite government officials to address union conventions or conferences. Such meetings may have a twofold impact. In the first place, the official is inevitably under considerable pressure on such occasions to say some nice things about civil servants, the reasonableness of some of their demands, or government plans to improve their position. No matter how cautiously such remarks are phrased, they are likely to include some comments that can well be quoted back effectively at a later date. Second, since the official is not the only speaker on the program, these meetings give union officers an opportunity to press various union demands and dissatisfactions before an enthusiastic supporting audience. The sessions usually take place in a relatively friendly atmosphere. There was, however, the famous occasion at the 1966 triennial congress of the DBB when Chancellor Erhard walked out in the middle of a meeting when he took offense at the charges of the DBB president that the government had not kept its promises and was being unfair to its civil servants. Since many DBB members come from the higher and more conservative ranks of the civil service, it is not surprising that some of them resigned in protest over their president's remarks.

Some of the staff of the Interior Ministry's Department of Civil Servant Law are constantly working on possible legislative revisions. When it is decided to move ahead on some particular measure, a staff draft is first prepared. It is then checked with some other departments and top officials in the Ministry. Then follows a check with the other federal ministries. The conference with the Finance Ministry regarding availability of funds is likely to be the point at which reconciliation of conflicting points of view is most difficult. Conferences with the state governments is the next step. Revisions usually occur at each stage of consultation. In most cases—particularly if there remains any disagreement among the ministries—approval by the cabinet will be needed prior to presentation to the parliament.

It is during this process of drafting and redrafting that the federations have their legal right of participation. There is much difference of opinion and considerable variation in practice regarding the exact point or points at which this consultation should take place. The unions, of course, wish to be consulted regarding the original staff draft. There are likely to be early informal conferences with union leaders on some of the major questions involved, but the staff is reluctant to submit the entire draft at this stage. It is said that so many revisions will surely be made during subsequent checks with ministries and states that the unions are likely to think that their arguments have been given little consideration and that the revised bill is worse, instead of better, than the one they first saw.

The unions usually cannot expect to see a complete draft until it has the tentative approval of the Interior Minister and perhaps not until it has been checked with the other ministries. They can expect to see it before it is finally checked with the states, because they may, in some instances, want to have their state bodies confer with state officials before the latter submit their comments. They can, however, expect to be consulted orally on major issues while the first draft is being formulated.

The procedure regarding union comments depends on whether or not the issues raised in the draft are ones on which union policy has already been coordinated and crystallized. There is always some immediate discussion, and, if the issue is considered very important, written comments will be submitted subsequently. If the federation representatives have any doubt regarding the union position on any details of the proposal, they will want time to consult with their constituent unions. These unions will then call together their appropriate committees, such as the ones on career levels, pay, welfare, or staff representation. The positions of the individual unions will then be coordinated into a single federation policy. Sometimes it is decided that the individual unions will seek conferences with other federal ministries. This will apply particularly to the railroad and postal unions. The purpose will be to influence both the comments from these ministries to the Interior Ministry and the position taken by the various ministers when the matter comes before the cabinet.

Another channel of influence is the Federal Personnel Committee. One of its functions is to comment on proposed changes in civil servant legislation. Three of its seven members have been nominated by the unions. The federations therefore contact these members to make sure that they are thoroughly informed on the union position.

The conferences at the Interior Ministry are rather similar

to collective bargaining sessions. The Ministry certainly wants to satisfy the civil servants and their unions insofar as it considers this to be reasonably possible. Both sides will do their best to persuade by presentation of facts and appeal to reason. The chief difference from negotiations is the absence of the strike threat. Lesser threats are possible, though they are seldom used. Protest meetings and demonstrations can be held, as they were by the DBB in June 1962. And a modified strike, such as a slow-down, is not entirely unknown (as will be noted later).

It appears probable that agreement is reached on most matters submitted to parliament, even though the unions sought many revisions that were not incorporated. On the other hand, there is rarely agreement on pay increases. The unions naturally always want more. Instances of union agreement on an increase are very rare.

When the federations are not satisfied with a bill that goes to parliament, they then switch to a lobbying role. The lobbying function being informal, it will be carried on as much by the individual unions as by their federations. Here they have several channels. Since the bill goes first to Bundesrat, they have their state organizations contact state officials in the hope that the members of the Bundesrat, all of whom represent their respective states, may be persuaded to support the desired amendments.

In the meantime, statements of the union position and supporting arguments have been sent to the party organizations of the Bundestag members. In the Bundestag the bill will be referred to committee. This is usually the Interior Committee, with sometimes a secondary referral to some other committee, such as the one on budget or justice, depending on the subject matter. The federations then contact the committee and request the opportunity to appear at the committee hearing. This is normally their last chance for formal participation.

Informal contacts with individual legislators will of course continue until action has been completed with the third reading of the bill. There are usually many sympathetic ears, since nearly a third of the legislators are present or former civil servants and well over a half are members of some union. It is therefore not surprising that the unions are usually able to obtain at this stage some of the revisions they have sought, even though they cannot expect any such gain as they won with the change from 4 to 7 percent in the 1960 pay bill. A detailed analysis of union lobbying activities as applied to a bill of special interest to this study is included in Chapter VII.

The unions complain that denial of the right to negotiate and to strike places civil servants in a disadvantaged position. It seems reasonable to conclude, however, that present procedures regarding the enactment of civil servant legislation usually give the unions an ample opportunity to present their views and arguments at a number of different levels and that they have been able to make very effective use of these opportunities. Civil servants have also the assurance that their terms of employment will parallel closely those of public wage-earners and salaried employees, who do have the right to negotiate and to strike.

·IV·

Employee Representation
at the Workplace

FOR the implementation and protection of employee rights
the federal and state parliaments have enacted laws
that set forth the organizational structure and operational procedures of employee representation at the workplace. These
laws provide for the election of a staff council by all of
the employees at each unit (workplace) in the public service.
The composition of these councils is roughly similar to that
of the works councils in private plants, but their authority
is somewhat more limited. To understand the basis for these
staff councils, it will be necessary to review briefly the history
of the works council system in private industry.

Local employee representation in Germany is entirely different
than in the United States. Germany has no real counterpart
of the American local union in the individual plant. The
DPG is exceptional in providing for a union organization at
each "office." But even here the function is different. A
local membership meeting is held annually. It elects delegates
to the district annual meeting and the members of its own
executive committee. Most national unions have only regional
and district substructures. In the larger industrial centers
the district office may serve its members only in the local
metropolitan area, while elsewhere it may cover several counties.

The district office normally counsels and advises members
on their individual problems and provides them with representation when they carry an unsettled grievance to the labor court.
It seeks to enlist new members, conducts the local worker
education program, and supervises the activities of the shop
stewards. The district officers of the ÖTV, for example, are
elected by a district delegate conference that is held every
four years. Thus the district office usually is not intimately
involved in the labor relations of any particular plant or
agency. That function belongs to the works council or, in

the public sector, to the staff council, which is entirely outside the union structure.

Toward the end of World War I there was a strong movement in Germany toward Communist revolution. Beginning with the mutiny of sailors in Kiel a week before the armistice, there was rapid formation of soldiers councils and workers councils throughout the nation. The situation became highly chaotic, but in most instances the councils were unable to seize the control and power they sought. The opposition of the trade unions was one of the major factors in the failure of the "November Revolution"; but the radical movement retained considerable strength. The formulation of the Constitution and subsequent legislation involved bitter strife and significant compromise.

It was clear from the earliest debates on the Weimar Constitution that provision would be made for some form of employee councils. Indeed, the government had already established a council system during the war. A major issue before the National Assembly, which was drafting the Constitution, was whether civil servants would be covered by the same council legislation that would apply to the wage-earners and salaried employees in both the private and public sectors. The ultimate decision (Art. 130, par. 3) was that "Civil servants shall receive separate representation in accordance with the provisions of national legislation."

The legislation for the private sector was embodied in the Works Councils Act of February 4, 1920.[1] It applied also to public wage-earners and salaried employees, but not the civil servants. It gave the workers in all plants normally employing at least twenty persons the right to elect annually a works council of from three to thirty members. Any three employees could nominate a list of candidates. Votes would be cast for a list rather than for individuals, with election governed by the principles of proportional representation. Separate group councils could deal with matters concerning only the wage-earners or only the salaried employees.

1. I.L.O., *Legislative Series,* 1920, Germany 1 and 2. C. W. Guillebaud, *The Works Council.* Cambridge: Cambridge University Press, 1928.

It was the right and duty of the councils to supervise the enforcement of labor laws and collective agreements, to receive grievances and seek their settlement, to promote safety, to participate in the administration of plant welfare programs, to aid management in fulfilling the aims of the enterprise by offering suggestions and promoting the introduction of new labor methods, and to negotiate supplemental plant agreements on hours, vacations, piece rates, etc., insofar as these matters were not covered by collective agreement. In most companies the council could elect two of its members to serve on the board of directors.

The councils could not invoke measures of labor strife nor collect any dues. The employer must meet all necessary expenses, such as making available an office with equipment and supplies and granting reasonable time off to one or more members.

The unions were at first deeply concerned lest the councils prove to be a serious threat to their leadership of the labor movement. There was good reason for such fears. The unions had no official role in the works council system; and many union members at that time were severely critical of the relatively conservative role of their leaders. Neither the right to vote nor to run for election was limited to union members. There was real doubt that the unions could control the councils or at least coordinate employee representation at the plant level with policies and programs at the union level. On the other hand, the act gave some protection to the unions. It gave union collective agreements precedence over plant agreements. It prohibited use of force by the works councils; and it denied them any separate funds. It also permitted a representative of each pertinent union to attend council meetings in an advisory capacity at the request of only one fourth of the council members.

The unions did have a real struggle for control of the councils, but after two or three years they had clearly won out. At the council elections each of the major unions could find some employees to submit its list of nominees, and the union lists were usually the winners. Thus there was usually a close personal relationship between nearly all of the council members and the district officials of one or another of the unions. The union influence was further strengthened by the training courses conducted by the unions for council members. The Reichstag then turned to the enactment of corresponding legislation for civil servants, as envisaged in the Constitution. In 1921 and 1930 government bills were introduced and hotly debated, but enactment was still unachieved at the time of the Nazi takeover in 1933.[2] There were several reasons for this failure: the conflicting views of the various civil servant unions, the gradual polarization of positions, the large number of political parties, the frequent changes of the national government, and preoccupation with more serious and more pressing problems of extensive unemployment, runaway inflation, and political upheaval.

In the absence of national legislation, civil servant committees were established in nearly all federal and state agencies by administrative order. In most instances these committees were granted the right to express an opinion on most internal operational matters and to represent group and individual civil servant interests within the agency. In the early 1920s, while the revolutionary spirit remained high, these committees were quite active, but their significance subsequently declined. They were particularly effective in the railway and postal services.

In the postal service, for example, there were in 1929 nearly 2,000 local civil servant committees and 45 district committees.[3] Among the matters on which they had the right to cooperate were the formulation of work rules, of the work schedule, and of the vacation schedule, and the establishment and operation of welfare services. At the request of a civil servant, a committee could represent his interests with respect to a number of personnel actions, such as classification, retirement,

2. Werner Potthoff, *Die Mitbestimmung der Beamten im öffentlichen Dienst*. Doctoral dissertation, University of Münster, 1965, pp. 91–108. An excellent analysis of the operation of the council system in the postal service. Apparently the only study of this kind to be found in German literature.
3. Ibid., p. 139.

dismissal, and denial of leave. Cooperation involved the right of the local committee, in case of disagreement, to be told the reasons for rejection of its position and to appeal the matter to the district administrator. This official then had to seek agreement with the district committee. Failing this, he made the decision. If the disagreement was based on differing interpretations of regulations rather than on the facts of the case, the matter could be appealed to the Postal Ministry, whose decision was final, if agreement could not be reached with the central committee.

During the Hitler era the works councils and civil servant committees were abolished. Under the "leadership principle" applied to labor relations, each elected council was replaced by an appointed trustee.

At the end of World War II the allied occupation powers adopted the policy of decartelization of the iron and steel industry. This industry, largely located in the Ruhr in the British zone of occupation, was in a chaotic condition. Many of its plants had suffered severe war damage; others were being dismantled and moved as reparations payment; and most of its previous managerial talent was unavailable. Prominent owners and managers of the industry had been among the most influential of Hitler's early supporters. Many of them were on trial for war crimes, and others were in bad repute.

The British military government established the North German Iron and Steel Control, which in turn created a German-manned Steel Trusteeship Administration to supervise the decentralization and operation of the industry. Its chairman and other industrialists felt that union support was essential in dealing with the occupation authorities. The reviving union leadership, anticipating eventual socialization of the industry, held out for strong union participation in the new steel companies. Agreement was eventually reached that the boards of directors would consist of an equal number of stockholder and labor representatives plus one neutral member and the management committees would consist of a production manager, a business manager, and a personnel manager (or "labor director")—with the last one being named in effect by the union.[4]

Soon after the creation of the Federal Republic in 1949, several bills on the establishment of works councils and tneir rights of codetermination were introduced in the Bundestag. Progress was slow, due to the wide difference in views. It appeared very doubtful that the unions could win throughout industry the same degree of codetermination they had already achieved in steel. It was not even certain that they could retain their position in the steel industry, since the dissolution of the Trusteeship Administration and the return of the industry to German rule was imminent. They, therefore, turned their efforts toward obtaining legislation that would continue the existing degree of employee participation in the steel industry and extend it only to mining. The unions of both the metal workers and the mine workers threatened to strike if necessary to obtain this goal. Chancellor Adenauer then conducted joint meetings of management and union leaders, where agreement on the terms of a bill was finally hammered out. This bill, after only two major changes during the legislative process, became the Codetermination Act of May 21, 1951. It provides that the board of directors shall consist of an equal number of stockholder and labor representatives plus a jointly selected "neutral" member. The board normally has eleven members. The works council names one wage-earner and one salaried employee, and the national union names the other three labor representatives, one of whom has had no recent connection with the union. This law further provides that in these two industries the appointment or dismissal of the personnel manager requires the concurrence of a majority of the labor representatives on the board of directors. The other two members of

4. For the early experience under this system see W. M. Blumenthal, *Codetermination in the German Steel Industry*. Princeton: Industrial Relations Section, 1956; Abraham Shuchman, *Codetermination*. Washington: Public Affairs Press, 1957; Herbert J. Spiro, *The Politics of German Codetermination*. Cambridge: Harvard University Press, 1958; W. H. McPherson, "Codetermination in Practice," *Industrial and Labor Relations Review*, July 1955; Panel discussion, "German Experience with Codetermination," Industrial Relations Research Association, *Proceedings of the Eighth Annual Meeting* (1955).

the management committee—the production and business managers—are elected by simple majority vote of all board members. Legislation covering the rest of private industry was subsequently adopted after bitter debate as the Works Councils Act of October 11, 1952.[5] This law provides for the election of a works council by the employees. Council membership may range from one to thirty-five, depending on the size of the work force. It includes representatives of both the wage-earners and the salaried employees. The council handles employee grievances and in general assures employer compliance with labor agreements and labor laws. It may negotiate supplemental plant agreements within the limits allowed by the master agreement negotiated by the union. These works agreements normally deal with such items as piece rates, starting and ending hours of the shifts, time and place of wage payment, and matters affecting the operation of the works council as, for example, the provision of office and meeting rooms and the extent to which council members are excused from their occupational duties. However, since works councils are not authorized by law to engage in collective bargaining, benefits negotiated by the council supplementary to those established under collective agreement are not legally binding.

The council has the right of codetermination or joint decision with management on matters such as those just mentioned and in the management of plant welfare programs and the classification and transfer of employees. If on these matters agreement negotiated by the union. These works agreements either party may request formation of an arbitration board consisting of an equal number of members appointed by each party and a jointly selected impartial chairman. On a number of other matters the council has the right of prior consultation. In multiplant companies a central works council may also be elected.

The provisions regarding the structure of the works councils and their rights of joint decision apply also to the steel and mining industries. Instead of equal representation of labor and ownership on the board of directors, employee representa-

5. *BGBl.*, 1952, I, 681; I.L.O., *Legislative Series*, 1952, Ger. F. R. 6.

tives in other industries constitute only a third of the membership. They are elected by the employees, rather than appointed by the union and works council. They have no special voice in the selection of the personnel manager. One of the most sharply contested issues was whether the legislation should apply also to the public service. The ultimate decision favored separate legislation regarding employee representation in the public sector. Not only the civil servants but also the public wage-earners and salaried employees would be covered by a separate law. There were some strong arguments in support of this determination. One was the need to take account of the special situation of the civil servants. Another was the widely held view that there was less justification for joint decision where management consisted of officials elected or appointed to represent the public interest, rather than to represent ownership in institutions operated for private profit.

Here there was no Weimar legislation to serve as a model. Instead, the problem was to adapt the Works Councils Act of 1952 to fit the special aspects of government employment. Legislative debate was lengthy and often heated. The ultimate result was the Staff Representation Act of August 5, 1955,[6] which governs only federal employment. Each state has enacted more or less similar legislation governing state and local public service.

THE FEDERAL ACT

The staff council is the public service counterpart of the works council in private industry. A council shall be established in each unit (agency office or workplace) that normally employs at least five persons entitled to vote in a council election (persons at least eighteen years of age, whose civil rights have not been withdrawen by a court as a penalty for illegal action), three of whom are eligible for election (have reached the age of twenty-one, have been in public service a year and at the unit a half-year, are not authorized to make independent personnel decisions, and have gained the right to vote in national elections). A council consists of from one

6. *BGBl.*, 1955, I, 477; I.L.O., *Legislative Series*, 1955, Ger. F. R. 1.

to twenty-five members. If it has at least three members, membership is divided among wage-earners, salaried employees, and civil servants in proportion to their number employed in the unit. Members have special protection against discrimination.

The representatives of each group are normally elected by the members of that group for a three-year term—originally two years. Election is by proportional representation. A list of nominees to represent one of the three groups may be submitted by 10 percent of the voting members of that group. In matters concerning only one of the three groups, decision is by vote of the representatives of that group, after discussion by the full council. The full council elects its chairman. The representatives of each group elect one of their number to an executive committee. If the council has more than ten members, it elects two additional committee members.

If an agency has several administrative levels, its employees elect not only a local staff council but also a district staff council at the middle level and a central staff council at the all-agency level.

Council meetings are held in private—normally during working hours. The unit director may attend any meeting called at his request and any other to which he is invited. The council may, by majority vote, also invite the attendance at a particular meeting of a representative of each union that has a member on the council.

The duties and rights of the staff council are similar to those of a works council, but somewhat more limited. It shall assure administrative compliance with relevant labor legislation and with the terms of collective agreements applicable to the wage-earners and salaried employees. It may receive and seek settlement of employee grievances. An unsettled grievance may be taken by a wage-earner or salaried employee to the labor court or by a civil servant to the administrative court. In either case a union may provide for his representation and cover his moderate court costs. The functions of unions and employers associations in negotiating agreements and consulting on the drafting of legislation are not affected by this law.

The council has two special types of rights regarding its participation in the making of certain administrative decisions. These are designated as "cooperation" (*Mitwirkung*) and "codetermination" (*Mitbestimmung*).

In matters subject to cooperation, any proposed action shall be presented to the council in advance and an opportunity afforded for full discussion in an effort to reach agreement. The proposal is considered to be approved if the council does not raise objection within one week or if it fails to support its objection or proposal. If objection is raised and agreement cannot be reached, the unit administrator shall present a written statement of his reasons for rejecting the council position. The council may then appeal the issue within three days to the next administrative level, which, after consultation with the district staff council, makes a final decision. Similarly, matters arising at the district level may be appealed to the agency head, who confers with the central staff council. In case of appeal, implementation of the proposal shall, if possible, be deferred pending final decision.

In matters subject to codetermination, there is the same requirement of advance information and efforts to reach agreement. In the absence of agreement, however, the appeal may be carried beyond the district level to the head of the agency—usually a cabinet minister—and the central staff council. If agreement is still unachieved, the issue may be taken to an *ad hoc* "conciliation committee"—actually a board of arbitration. The agency head and the central council each name three members and jointly select a neutral chairman. In case of deadlock, the chairman is chosen by the president of the Federal Administrative Court. There is no legal restriction on the selection of the six representative members, except the requirement that, if the matter concerns both civil servants and salaried employees or wage-earners, the members selected by the council shall include one agency employee from each of these two groups. The majority decision of the board is binding.

Most of the matters subject to cooperation or codetermination are classified as social or staff matters. The latter differ somewhat depending on whether or not the employees concerned are civil servants.

The principal social matters concerning which a council has the right of cooperation include the granting of welfare benefits (but only with the approval of the applicant), measures for increasing productivity or easing the work task, appointment of staff doctors, the allocation of employee housing at the agency's disposal, health and safety measures, the formulation of work rules and conduct regulations, and questions of further training to facilitate the promotion of employees.

Social matters subject to council codetermination include the timing of the beginning and end of the workday and the pauses, the time and place of payment of remuneration, the preparation of vacation schedules, the carrying out of basic vocational training, the establishment and administration of employee social services, and the formulation of principles of remuneration and the fixing of piece rates. Since these are subject to codetermination, it logically follows, and is specifically provided, that the council and the administration may enter into supplemental agreements on these topics, insofar as they are not already covered by law or collective agreement. The council has the right to submit suggestions. If the proposal concerns a social matter subject to codetermination, it may be carried, failing agreement, to arbitration.

On staff matters the right of codetermination is very limited. There is no such right regarding civil servants. Concerning wage-earners and salaried employees the right applies only to questions of promotion, demotion, and transfer to another unit. It is still more limited in that consent to such actions may be refused only on the grounds that (1) the proposed action would be in violation of law, collective agreement, regulation, or court decision, (2) that it would represent personal favoritism to an unsuitable employee, (3) that it would involve discrimination against other suitable employees because of race, sex, religion, nationality, origin, or political or union activity, or (4) that the employee would cause trouble in the unit by antisocial or unlawful conduct.

The right of cooperation on staff matters varies as between civil servants and other employees. It does not apply to civil servants in pay group A 16 and above. Nor does it apply to the unit administrator and to scientific and artistic employees except at their individual request. For the vast majority of civil servants it covers appointment and promotion (with objection limited to the four grounds listed in the preceding paragraph), transfer to another unit, premature pensioning (provided the employee requests council involvement), dismissal of a civil servant on probationary or revocable appointment, and limitation on the freedom of choice of residence. The right of cooperation on staff matters for wage-earners and salaried employees covers much the same points, with modification appropriate to the difference in status. It does not cover promotion, which for them is subject to limited codetermination. It does additionally cover continuance of employment beyond retirement age and denial of approval of secondary employment. Cooperation also applies to certain organizational matters, such as the introduction of new work methods and the discontinuance, contraction, transfer, or merger of sections of the agency.

There is no provision for cooperation or codetermination on economic matters in public service, such as exists in the private sector. Mention should be made, however, of an influence by the unions or staff councils in the management of certain government services that arises quite independently of the Staff Representation Act. This is true of the postal and railway services at the federal level and of public utility services that have a separate legal identity at the municipal level. For example, the Postal Management Act of July 24, 1953,[7] provides for a management board of 24 members, 7 of whom are appointed by the government from twice that number of nominees named by the postal unions. The bill for reorganization of the postal service now before the parliament in the fall of 1970 provides that employee representatives shall constitute a third of the membership of the new

7. *BGBl.*, 1953, I, 676.

board, while the unions are requesting one half. Another example is one of the West Berlin utilities. The Berlin law on government enterprises provides for a management board of 12 members, with one third named each by the state parliament, the administration, and the central staff council. Since two of those named by the parliament are union officials, employee representatives may be said to constitute one half of the board.

All disputes regarding the election or operation of the staff councils go to the administrative court, with appeal to the state and federal levels. In the first and second instances they shall be handled by special chambers consisting of a chairman, two federal employees nominated by the agency administration, and one civil servant and one public wage-earner or salaried employee nominated by the unions. The appointments are made by the state government. The court may remove council members from office or dissolve a council for grave negligence or grave dereliction of duty at the request of the council, one fourth of the eligible voters, a union that has members in the unit, or the director of the unit.

Sections 82 to 94 specify certain provisions to be included in corresponding state legislation. Most of these relate to the structure and operation of the staff councils. Section 90, dealing with the rights of the councils, states: "The staff representation bodies shall be granted participation in internal social and staff matters. In so doing, a regulation shall be sought similar to that accorded in this law to the staff representation bodies in federal agencies." It will be noted that this actually allows the state legislators considerable leeway. It is therefore not surprising that there is in the various states much similarity in the structure of the councils, but considerable variation in the nature and form of their participation.

THE STATE LAWS

The states enacted laws in accordance with the federal instructions from 1957 to 1961.[8] Several of the states revised their

8. For a comparative analysis of the provisions of the first nine laws

laws in 1968 to 1970, but the 1957-61 laws will be considered first.[9]

A comparison of those laws shows that the limiting provisions of the federal act were decidedly minimal. It also shows that some of the state legislatures apparently flaunted even those few restrictions in certain respects, though no effort has' been made to enforce the federal provisions by court action. There is even strong doubt of their enforceability.

The state provisions, in their variety, indicate a number of the alternatives that are available in the area of this unique German policy of codetermination for public employees. We may regard this legislation—at least from the point of view of other countries—as experimental; and this experiment is made much more useful by the variety of provisions. This situation cries aloud for research in the form of a comparative analysis of the operational experience under the different state laws; but it appears that no such analysis has yet been made, and it is unfortunately quite beyond the feasible scope of this present study. Here we shall pass over the variations in structure and conduct of the councils, and focus on the extent and nature of their participation.

In general, the three city-states gave the councils more authority than the larger states. This is presumably because their more urban and industrial population tends to be more liberal than in the states with a substantial rural and more conservative population. The three city-states granted participation rights on a somewhat wider range of matters than does the federal government. In Baden-Württemberg and North Rhine-Westphalia the scope was roughly the same as is specified in the federal law, while in the remaining states it was narrower.

The participation varied even more in its nature than its extent. Most of the state laws used the federal terminology of "cooperation" and "codetermination," but defined them in

see W. Grabendorff, "Die Personalvertretungsgestze der Länder," *Zeitschrift für Beamtenrecht,* 7 (1959), 105–09, 140–47, 179–83.

9. The past tense will be used in discussing them, even though some of them had not been revised as of early 1970.

different ways as they spelled out the procedure. The right of cooperation was weakest in Rhineland-Palatinate, Schleswig-Holstein, and Berlin, where it amounted to no more than the right to be notified of proposed actions and to be heard or to comment on them—the right of consultation without appeal. At the other extreme, in Bremen and Hamburg, there was no provision for cooperation, and all matters covered were subject to the stronger right of codetermination.

Codetermination had many different meanings. Only Bremen, Berlin, and Baden-Württemberg followed the federal act in providing an arbitration board as the final step in the process. In Berlin this step was not applicable to civil servants. Hesse provided in the case of local governments for a "mediation committee," which might issue a decision as a final step. It was not a tripartite body, but consisted rather of the head of the municipal or county government and two members elected by the city or county council. At the other extreme, Rhineland-Palatinate and Schleswig-Holstein had no codetermination, but did permit a one-step appeal to a decision of the minister or mayor on a very few matters. The same was true of Bavaria, except that the council had the right to be heard by the authority making the final decision. In Saarland and North Rhine-Westphalia the final decision was made for state agencies by the "state government" (cabinet) and for local agencies by their "top organ." In Hamburg the arbitration board was replaced by the "senate" or municipal cabinet of department heads, which could act after failure of a mediation effort by the immediate department head.

The Bremen law was in a class by itself. It made no provision for cooperation, but subjected to codetermination all social and staff matters that were subject to either form of participation in the federal act. Moreover, codetermination also applied to staff matters concerning civil servants just as much as to those regarding other public employees. And finally, the council, as well as the administration, had the right of initiative in all listed matters. Thus a council might propose a personnel action and, if it were not accepted in full, carry the matter to arbitration. Thus it is not surprising that the law provided for a standing board of arbitration in each agency rather than for *ad hoc* boards. The chairman of each board was to be the President of the Bremen legislature or his representative drawn from the executive committee of that legislature or the Bremerhaven city council, and thus might very well be a union official.

On appeal by the Bremen administration, the provisions of this statute granting full codetermination on staff actions concerning civil servants were invalidated by the Federal Constitutional Court on April 27, 1959.[10] The court said in part:

> Staff sovereignty over civil servants is an essential part of governmental power, and the decision on staff actions concerning civil servants must thus be considered in general as a function of government. If the government should have to bow in cases of disagreement to the decision of an independent arbitration board, an essential governmental function would in reality be granted to this other appelate body and the government would be denied the power of decision and the responsibility that belong to it in a democratic state.
>
> The general transfer of the power of decision in all staff questions concerning civil servants to a board, whose members are not responsible to the government, is thus inconsistent with the principle of the democratic state within the meaning of article 28, paragraph 1, sentence 1 of the Constitution.
>
> In spite of the intermingling of sovereign and non-sovereign administrative acts, the functions of the salaried employees and the wage-earners have nevertheless a narrower political significance than those of the civil servants, since the continual exercise of sovereign authority is to be assigned as a rule to civil servants and not to salaried employees or wage-earners in the public service. . . .
>
> Codetermination by the staff council and the decision-making authority of the arbitration board in personnel matters concerning civil servants would basically change the

10. Bundesverfassungsgericht, *Entscheidungen*, IX, 268.

prevailing public-law relationship of service and loyalty of the civil servant.

This statement serves to emphasize again the special status of the German civil servant.

The Bremen Staff Representation Act was revised on January 25, 1966, and October 14, 1969.[11] Its codetermination procedure now contains a mediation step. In case of disagreement on a matter subject to codetermination, the department head sets up an *ad hoc* mediation committee, consisting of himself as chairman, two other administration representatives, and three named by the council. If mediation fails, an arbitration board is established, composed of three selected by each side and an impartial chairman, named, if necessary, by the President of the Bremen legislature. If the subject is a staff matter involving a state civil servant, the administration 'appointees shall be three department heads who are members of the Personnel Commission, and the chairman shall be the chairman of that commission. If a civil servant is involved, the board shall attempt mediation; and its decision is not binding, but serves only as a recommendation to the administration (advisory arbitration). Thus the Bremen legislature has kept well within the limits set by the opinion of the Constitutional Court.

The Berlin law was extensively revised on July 22, 1968, effective August 30. From the trade union point of view it was much improved, and is now considered one of the strongest of the state laws. The impartial chairman of the arbitration board is now selected by the "senator" (or state minister) for the Interior in agreement with the central council for a four-year term, though the six representative members are still named on an *ad hoc* basis. While the previous law allowed only cases involving wage-earners or salaried employees to be appealed to the board, appeal is now permitted also in civil servant cases. Unconstitutionality of this provision is avoided by allowing decisions in such cases to be appealed by the agency to the state cabinet or "senate." Thus we have here a particularly strong form of advisory arbitration

11. Gesetzblatt der Freien Hansestadt Bremen, 1969, p. 143.

in that the award is binding unless vetoed by the top executive authority.

As of early 1970 two other states had significantly revised their staff representation laws, and more (Baden-Württemberg and Rhineland-Palatinate) were considering revision. Schleswig-Holstein's new law of November 14, 1969,[12] elaborates considerably on the matters subject to cooperation or codetermination by the full staff council or its group subcouncils. It also introduces in this state full codetermination by providing for the use of arbitration boards along the lines of the federal act.

Hesse, which contains the commercial metropolis of Frankfort and has a Social Democrat cabinet, revised its law on February 19, 1970.[13] This new act ranks, along with Berlin's, as the strongest of all the staff representation laws from an employee point of view.

The right of cooperation is stronger than usual in that a local matter, in the absence of agreement, may be appealed not only to the intermediate level, but on to the head of the agency, who makes the final decision after consultation with the central staff council.

The right of codetermination is appreciably expanded as to both its nature and scope. Whereas Hesse formerly provided for a final administrative decision, it now provides for the creation of *ad hoc* arbitration boards at the top level in all local and state agencies. A minor difference from similar laws is that, in case of deadlock, the seventh (neutral) member is named by the President of the State Personnel Commission rather than the President of the State Administrative Court.

The scope of the matters subject to codetermination appears now to be even greater in Hesse than in Bremen. In Bremen cooperation is not recognized as a form of council participation, and the stronger form of codetermination is applied to practically all matters subject to participation. In Hesse cooperation still exists, but it applies almost exclusively to a few matters, such as the formulation of job tables,

12. Gestez- und Verordnungsblatt für Schleswig-Holstein, 1969, p. 225.
13. Gesetz- und Verordnungsblatt für das Land Hessen, 1970, I, 161.

that in nearly all other states are excluded from council participation. Codetermination applies to all of the matters that in the federal law are subject either to codetermination or cooperation, and to a few more. In granting councils a right to initiate proposals in all matters subject to codetermination, this law has granted a much broader power than the other laws, as a result of the wider scope of codetermination. It also grants a broader area for supplemental local agreements when it permits these in any social matter subject to codetermination.

Another innovation is the granting of participation in certain matters characterized as "organizational and economic." In this category cooperation is permitted in the formulation of organizational and staffing plans and in the disbanding, curtailment, transfer, or merging of offices or major parts thereof; and codetermination applies to the introduction of new work methods and the formulation of general principles for the measurement of personnel needs.

We must conclude that the recent revisions of state laws indicate a strong tendency toward extending and strengthening the rights of the staff councils.

EXPERIENCE UNDER THE STAFF REPRESENTATION LAWS

An analysis of the provisions of laws such as these on staff representation tells little or nothing about how they operate in practice. In an effort to appraise the actual functioning of the councils, interviews were held with government and union officials at the federal, state, and local levels and with a few council members. Since the coverage could not be extensive, the conclusions must be qualified. Use is also made of the single pertinent German study—an excellent and thorough analysis of the early experience in the postal service.[14]

In the private sector, due to low employee interest or high employer opposition, works councils are lacking in many plants—especially the smaller ones—where their creation is

14. See Potthoff, *Die Mitbestimmung der Beamten im öffentlichen Dienst.*

permitted by law. In the public sector, on the other hand, it is probable that a staff council exists at every place where one is supposed to be. This is largely because the laws make their establishment mandatory rather than permissible.They even provide that, if the employees fail to take the initiative in naming an election committee, the director of the unit shall do so.

The total number of staff councils is not known. The Postal Ministry, in 1966 had 982 local councils, including separate ones for postal service and for telephone and telegraph service in the larger communities. It also had 23 district or regional councils and a central council of 25 members—15 civil servants, 3 salaried employees, and 7 wage-earners. The central council has an executive committee of 5 members, all of whom are relieved of duty in order to devote full time to representation matters. At the other extreme, a small town is likely to have one council for its administrative staff and one for its utility employees. A county may have one for its hospital and one for its police. Since the latter are state employees, their local council has the possibility of appeal to a regional and a central council. (Most states have separate statutory provisions for police and teachers; and the federal government has different laws for judges, soldiers, border patrol, and intelligence agencies.) As an illustration of the number of councils in a large city-state, West Berlin has about 230.

Some of the bitterest debate at the time of the enactment of the federal statute centered on the issue of the protection of "minority groups" in the council structure, as between the three main types of public employees. In general, the DBB (representing primarily civil servants) favored such protection, while the DGB unions opposed it. The civil servants constitute the largest of the three groups in many agencies and a majority of all employees in some, but the DBB feared that on many issues the wage-earners and salaried employees might combine forces against the interests of the civil servants.

One aspect of the minority-protection issue was the question of election of council members at large or separately by the three groups. The final decision was that elections would be held separately unless otherwise decided in any unit by a majority of the eligible voters in each of the three groups. It is not known how many instances there have been of such decision, but it is clear that the condition is so difficult of achievement that there have been very few, if any, exceptions to the general rule of separate election. Hesse, in its revised statute, has somewhat reduced the condition by requiring only a majority of those voting on the issue in each group, rather than of those eligible to vote.

It is doubtful that the employees as a whole have any particular interest in joint voting. While the three groups occasionally have a conflict of interest, their members usually work very well together. In fact the members of one group sometimes elect someone from another group as one of their representatives. This usually takes the form of a civil servant being chosen among the representatives of one of the other groups. This results from respect for his experience, ability, and higher education. In the Postal Ministry in 1960, when there were 8,724 members in some 1,280 local councils, they included at least 41 civil servants elected by salaried employees and 109 by wage-earners.[15]

Another aspect of minority protection is the question as to whether council decisions concerning only one group should be made by the full council or by only the members representing that group. The final compromise was that the decision should be made by the group representatives after discussion by all members. This appears to have worked very satisfactorily in practice. It is said that in some instances the members of the concerned group feel that others—particularly civil servants —have presented very helpful arguments. It seemed possible that there might be frequent conflict of views in a council as to whether a particular matter was of concern to more than one group. The council chairmen interviewed indicated, however, that they had encountered no such difficulty. In the rare instances when the question had arisen, the members had been well satisfied to vote as a whole.

Another of the most controversial provisions of the federal

15. Ibid., pp. 289–93.

act was that relating to the extent of union participation in the council system. One aspect of this issue relates to the nomination of council candidates. The act does not permit the unions to submit nominee lists directly. Nomination is on petition by one tenth of the eligible voters in the group. The larger unions have no problem—but only a nuisance—in getting enough members to sign a union list, but the smaller ones often find it difficult, and advocate direct union nomination. They now sometimes meet the problem by combining with another small union to present a joint list.

North Rhine-Westphalia has long allowed nominations by unions, and Hesse has done so since 1970. It may be expected that other states will soon follow suit. It is difficult to think of any good reason for denying this right. Practically all nominee lists are presented on behalf of unions, and the sponsorship of each list is well known to the voters. It seems probable that the unions would want to consult with the employees in drawing up their lists to be sure of including the most popular candidates, even if they did not have to get individual signatures to their petitions. Independent lists are a great rarity, but could still be permitted along with union nominations.

Another aspect of participation that is of even greater concern to the unions is the right to have a staff member attend in an advisory capacity meetings of staff councils and of the staff assemblies, which are to be held semiannually to permit a report to the entire staff on council activities and a voicing of employee desires to the council. The administrator of the unit is normally invited to the assemblies and usually makes some comments after the report of the council chairman. He may also convene an assembly, but this is a very rare occurrence.

The federal act permits the attendance of a union representative only at those individual meetings to which he is invited by majority vote of the council (or assembly). If an invitation to a council meeting is offered, it must apply to all unions that have a member on the council. The invitation to an assembly must go to all unions having members in the unit. Berlin makes the meetings more accessible to the unions.

It permits those with members on the council to attend council meetings at the request of only a fourth of the membership. The same unions may send a representative to a staff assembly without invitation, though in practice they are inclined to wait for an invitation. Hesse, in its 1970 revision, is the first state to allow union representation in all council meetings and assemblies without invitation.

There is no comprehensive information regarding the frequency of union representation at council meetings. It is said that union interest in obtaining invitations decreased after the first year or two of operation under the act. There is a general impression that invitations are seldom extended. The several council chairmen interviewed stated that their councils had never considered such invitations and that their members definitely preferred to meet alone. It appears probable, however, that district and central councils invite union participation somewhat more frequently than local councils, because they are dealing largely with more important issues. In the Postal Ministry during the two-year period 1960-62, 6 of 21 district councils and 90 of 468 local councils invited unions to one or more meetings.[16]

The opening of council meetings and assemblies to union representatives without invitation is one of the strongest of union demands for revision of the staff representation laws. Most union officials feel that they can be of considerable help to council members, who they think are generally not well informed on legal, contractual, and technical matters concerning employee rights or on the methods used by other councils in meeting certain problems. They feel that many council members do not consider an invitation because they are unaware of their own limitations and handicaps. And finally, they believe that their attendance would give them more assurance that competing unions are not obtaining any unfair advantage through council actions.

On the other hand, there are some union officers who do not concur in this union demand. One has pointed out that the union staffs are quite inadequate to permit representation

16. Ibid., p. 370.

at more than a small proportion of council meetings. He feels it is likely to be embarrassing, and frequently counter-productive, to attend a meeting when he is not welcomed by at least a majority of those present. He thinks that if he attended many meetings of different councils, he would find it difficult to maintain his legal obligation of secrecy concerning all confidential matters discussed there. He usually has little interest in attending an assembly. On such occasions he is often asked to state the union's bargaining plans and its prospective demands in the next negotiations. This is a matter that he would rather discuss only with members of his union and not with the whole work force. Another official has suggested that a union representative should usually be able to obtain an invitation to attend a meeting if he takes the initiative in a tactful way. The infrequency of invitations shows clearly that most council members feel them-selves capable of handling nearly all of their problems and usually prefer to meet by themselves.

It seems to this author that the arguments favoring retention of the present federal provisions outweigh those of the unions for revision. Surely the preference of the council members deserves considerable weight. It is difficult to believe that council action can be disadvantageous to one union and favorable to its competitor so long as neither is represented. Council members are not antiunion and are seldom unorganized. Nearly all are strong union members, whom a union has chosen to nominate. Nor are they lacking in union counsel, even in the absence of a union representative. Each union has several lines of contact for informing and advising its council members. Most important are the training courses specifically structured for them. In addition there are instruction manuals and monthly publications to keep them informed on significant developments, whether these be new agreements, new laws, court decisions, or the experience of other councils. Finally, the present provi-sions are probably fairer in that the several unions are all notified when a meeting is open to their representatives, whereas when all meetings are open it is probable that one union often will be represented when the others are not.

A first-hand appraisal of the significance of the work of the councils to the employees and the agencies is beyond the possibilities of this present study. A perusal of the minutes of the local councils at the head offices of two federal ministries yielded some general impressions that are valid for administrative offices but probably not for service operations. Local councils normally meet weekly, whereas district and central councils usually meet monthly. It is clear that agreement with the administration is almost always reached on all matters that require agreement, though some matters may be the subject of consultations over a period of several weeks before they are finally resolved. With regard to staff actions, there appears to be an emphasis on appointments and promotions, with the council urging promotion from within and frequently making an alternative proposal with reference to promotions. Among the various social matters handled by the councils, housing has high priority. With housing still rather tight in the Bonn area, there is obviously much employee concern and council attention to the allocation of residential units at the disposal of the agency. The councils are much concerned with the award of hardship grants to meet special emergencies. They fear that the granting of such requests may involve favoritism or that their denial may constitute discrimination. Council action in this area is limited by the law's concern for protecting the confidential character of the plights of individual employees. Among the items subject to codetermination, the setting of the scheduled workweek has occasionally been of deep concern. In particular, as the length of the workweek has been gradually reduced, there has been a strong effort to obtain free Saturdays. This is again a matter of much discussion in the autumn of 1970 as preparations are made to move from a 43-hour to a 42-hour workweek at the end of the year. It is reported that many councils are urging that the shortening apply only to Friday rather than be distributed throughout the week to move closer to an 8-hour day. During 1970 there has been much attention to another of the work-hours questions, in which the council has an equal voice. Several of the federal ministries, following the lead of a few private companies, have begun to experiment with the use of a "sliding work-day." This system allows each employee to report for work at any time during a period of about two hours and to adjust his quitting time accordingly. It is hoped that this will increase convenience to the employee and reduce traffic congestion, while maintaining a period of about six hours when all employees will be present. Participation in the plans for manning irregular shifts and standby services is highly valued.

Among other items handled by one council in the course of a year were the following: transfers, dismissals, quits, leaves of absence, continuation after age 65, shifts from wage-earner to salaried employee status, agency reorganization, performance evaluation, sport and child-care facilities, and canteen hours.

The effectiveness of cooperation is difficult to judge. On the face of it, it is not a forceful procedure, since it permits a final decision by the administration upon appeal to the next higher step. In actual practice it appears to be more significant than might be expected. All administrators and council members interviewed stated that both sides usually make a good-faith effort to reach an agreement. When neither side can convince the other of the merits of its position, they generally seek, and usually find, an acceptable compromise position. For example, when the administrator sticks by his selection of an individual for promotion but the council makes a strong case for an alternative, there may be an understanding that the council's candidate will receive the next subsequent promotion. Council members believe that the chances for agreement at the initial step are considerably increased by the legal requirement that rejection of the council position must be accompanied by a written statement of the reasons. They think that this makes rejection difficult if the council has a valid point.

There is, on the other hand, some definite evidence concerning the effectiveness of codetermination. It is clear that in the federal service agreement is almost always reached on matters subject to this procedure. The total number of instances of the use of an arbitration board is not known, but it has been learned that in nearly fifteen years of experience since the passage of the federal act in August 1955, a board has been used not more than once in the Interior and Postal Ministries! That is a remarkable record in view of the employment of several hundred thousand employees in these two agencies; and there is no reason to believe that the experience has been different in the rest of the federal service.

Thus the provision of arbitration as a final step for settlement of differences regarding certain "social matters" concerning any employees and a few "staff matters" affecting other than civil servants is important not because of its use and the arbitral decisions issued, but because the availability of arbitration serves as a strong incentive to achieve agreement. Administrators make every effort to reach an acceptable solution rather than risk a decision by a neutral chairman; and the central staff councils, on their part, appear to act in a responsible manner and avoid ready resort to arbitration.

When use of arbitration is so very rare, one wonders what kinds of issues have actually been carried to the final step. The one case in the Interior Ministry occurred in the late 1950s in connection with a general one-hour reduction in the federal workweek. The ministry proposed a slight reduction in the length of each workday. The central council preferred a lengthening of the workday in order to obtain at least an occasional free Saturday. The ministry thought that the arrangements for a staggered free Saturday would be too complicated. The board ruled that each employee should have at least one free Saturday per month.

The case that has given the most trouble in the Postal Ministry arose in 1967 and involved a technical matter. The ministry operates its own office canteens under a rule that the income from the prices charged shall cover the direct costs, including employee payroll. The specific question was whether the special emergency welfare grants occasionally awarded to canteen employees are a part of payroll costs. The ministry had not so considered them, but was instructed by the Federal Accounting Office (*Bundesrechnungshof*) to change its policy. The central staff council objected on the grounds that welfare grants of canteen workers should come out of the ministry budget just like its grants to any of its other employees and that the grants awarded under the new policy would be lower than otherwise, because of the inadequacy of canteen funds to finance such irregular but substantial payments. The issue appeared to be headed for arbitration, but the ministry denied that it was subject to codetermination. It therefore was taken to the administrative courts on this latter question. The local court ruled in favor of the agency, and the district court in favor of the council. As of December 1969 the federal court had not issued its decision, though it had just ruled in favor of a government agency in a similar case. In the meantime the parties had worked out some kind of a compromise settlement on their basic problem. Perhaps it would therefore be more accurate to say that the Postal Ministry has never used an arbitration board.

An issue may be headed for arbitration in the Defense Ministry. The Federal Accounting Office has ruled that a number of salaried employees are overclassified and must be reduced to a lower pay group. The central council claimed that the matter involved a downgrading or demotion and hence was subject to codetermination. The ministry took the position that it was merely the correction of an error. It wished to make the change and let the employees take their grievance to the labor courts. It was relying on a decision by the Federal Labor Court of July 26, 1966, which held on a minor point that the transfer of a salaried employee to a higher or lower position .was subject to codetermination, but not a reduction in pay for the same work when that pay had been in excess of the contractual amount. The council, however, took the matter to the administrative courts on the direct issue of the applicability of codetermination. The Federal Administrative Court ruled on April 17, 1970, that the downgrading of salaried employees who had mistakenly been overclassified is subject to codetermination.[17] Thus, unless the ministry and central council reach agreement on the reclassification, it will presumably be taken to arbitration.

17. Bundesverwaltungsgericht, *Entscheidungen*, VII, 69.

A disagreement that arose in a federal agency that has recently been renamed as the Ministry of Intra-German Relations (i.e. relations with East Germany) shows that there is at least one alternative to appeal to the courts or arbitration in case of a deadlock regarding interpretation of law or regulations. A relatively small, independent agency was being merged into the ministry. The latter proposed to bring in a certain person for a leading position in the new group. The central council urged a promotion from within. Although this matter, since it involved a civil servant, was subject only to cooperation rather than codetermination, the ministry did not simply reject the council's position but instead questioned whether the council had the right of cooperation with respect to this new group while it was still in a transitional stage. Instead of going to the administrative courts, the parties agreed to seek an opinion from the Interior Ministry. This instance also serves to support our earlier conclusion that cooperation is in practice a fairly strong right and that the administration normally does make a real effort to achieve an agreement where this right exists.

There has been little experience with arbitration on social and staff matters at the state and local levels, because so few states have provided for any full codetermination. The experience of West Berlin is of interest, since it has allowed arbitration from the outset. Under its original staff representation law there was on the average approximately one arbitration per year. During the first year of operation under the new law (1969) the office of the board's chairman received seven appeals. Three of these were withdrawn before a hearing date had been set. One was still pending at the end of February 1970. The decision in one of the remaining three, involving the dismissal of a school teacher, upheld the council's position. Its position was rejected in the other two cases, which concerned an appointment to a trainee position and the Saturday opening of a branch of the municipal book store. The increase in the number of arbitrations was presumably due in part to the newness of the revised law and also to the expanded scope of codetermination. There is as yet no experience under the provision permitting a cabinet veto of an award in cases on staff matters affecting a civil servant, since the only award in favor of the council involved a salaried employee. It has been noted that until recently the state of Hesse has had at the local level a final step misleadingly called a "mediation committee," which should perhaps be considered as a special type of final administrative decision, since the committee members are the major or county superintendent and two elected by the city or county council from its own membership. In any case, a survey of the experience with these committees was made by the state's Interior Ministry. In nearly ten years of experience up to October 1969, committees received 68 cases in the 9 largest cities, 48 in the other cities, one in a village, 60 in the counties, and 78 in public corporations, institutions, and foundations (mostly public utilities). Of these 255 cases, 57 (22 percent) were settled by agreement or withdrawal, and three were pending. Of the 195 decisions, 53 (27 percent) upheld the council position. It may be noted that an average of 20 decisions a year for all local agencies in this populous state is rather low and supports the conclusion that the parties usually make a sincere effort to reach agreement. The fact that the councils were upheld in more than a fourth of their appeals further shows that this unique type of final step, which was criticized by the unions as inadequate, was far from ineffective.

The significance of the staff assemblies is difficult to judge, since their main function is to facilitate the exchange of information and views between the staff and its council and between the staff and the administration. It is a significant function and doubtless serves a useful purpose. There is often not careful observance of the legal requirement that the assemblies be held semiannually. Many councils call a meeting only once a year. This appears to be the optimum frequency. Interruption of the work of the unit for two or three hours for regular meetings oftener than annually seems unnecessary, especially since a special assembly can always be called if needed.

The act states that the head of the unit shall attend

157

any assembly that is convened at his request and any to which he is expressly invited. The councils almost always extend such invitations. Indeed, from their point of view the major purposes of an assembly are to give any dissatisfied employee an opportunity to voice his views directly to the unit head, and to show the latter that the dissatisfactions that have been presented to him in council meetings are but a true reflection of employee attitudes.

It is probable that many, if not most, supervisors welcome the opportunity to participate occasionally in an assembly. They usually take advantage of these sessions to express their major policies and their views on significant problems. They know that they will probably be subject to some criticism, but many think that such an exchange may be constructive. One federal minister several years ago told an assembly that these meetings always seemed to put the supervisor "in the defendant's seat." The council chairman regretted this attitude and suggested that some criticism must be expected under even the best of relationships.

A questionnaire answered in 1963 by about 450 local staff councils in the Postal Ministry indicated that in 86 percent of their units the supervisor always attended the assemblies and that in 80 percent of the units he "as a rule" addressed them.[18]

Of major importance in appraising the actual operation of a staff representation system is an impression of its general climate or the nature of the reciprocal attitudes. Judging just from the few interviews with administrators and council members, the relationship in their units appears to be cooperative and mutually satisfactory. There was no indication of hostility, resentment, impatience, or serious criticism on either side. There is some reason to believe that this is the prevailing situation throughout most of the public sector. For one thing, the unions, though seeking revision of the laws to expand participation rights and increase the union role, do not complain of any general attitude of rejection on the part of administrators

18. Potthoff, *Die Mitbestimmung der Beamten im öffentlichen Dienst,* p. 351.

or of any general difficulties in enforcing the legal rights of the councils. Another bit of evidence is that the cases concerning staff representation that go to the administrative courts deal more frequently with matters of union rivalry in the election and operation of the councils than with disputes between the councils and the agencies.

The relationship between the staff councils and the administration in the public sector seems definitely more cordial than that between the works councils and management in private industry. As might be expected, the difference appears to be greatest in agencies that are under the supervision of members of the Social Democratic Party. One might perhaps anticipate that administrators would be more cooperative where they are working only under budgetary limitations rather than under the private-profit system, and that employee representatives would be more cooperative where the function of the institution is serving the general public rather than providing earnings for private investors. Indeed, this seems to be the case in Germany, even though we may find little indication of it in certain other countries.

The administrators interviewed generally indicated that they try to go beyond the letter of the law to observe its spirit. They are strict in granting the right of codetermination only on matters that are prescribed by law, but they are usually willing to discuss with the council, and seek its agreement on, a wider range of matters than those that are subject to the right of consultation.

Given the cooperative attitude of most government administrators, it is not surprising that the councils generally reflect this in a spirit of reasonableness and a problem-solving approach to their duties. To be sure, administrators can easily be found who believe that some council members occasionally try to use their position to promote their own job interests or those of their friends, or to recruit members for their union. It has been said that staff representation has faced particularly serious problems in the railroad service, where technological change and reduction of schedules have brought a steady decline in the size of the work force, but even here there have been no indications of serious administrative dissatisfaction or substantial resort to arbitration. It is possible that the climate may be less cooperative in the public utilities, where the work is more industrial in character and the proportion of wage-earners is higher. This present study has not included any survey of this section of local government service, but no particular complaints have come to light. It seems unlikely that several states would recently have expanded council rights of codetermination if there had been any widespread dissatisfaction of government officials with the staff representation system.

Another reason for the cooperative attitude on the part of council members may be the tendency to elect relatively high-ranking civil servants to these positions. It has already been noted that wage-earners and salaried employees sometimes elect civil servants as their representatives. There is evidently a similar tendency within the various ranks of the civil servants.

When it comes to a general evaluation of the significance of the staff representation system for the resolution of internal administrative differences, the evidence of a cooperative climate and good morale points toward a favorable conclusion. The reaching of agreement on nearly all matters subject to codetermination and on a large proportion of those subject to cooperation proves that the system has thus far worked well to assure the public employees of effective protection of their interests. That this has been accomplished without serious dissatisfaction or complaint from administrators speaks very well for those who drafted the legislation and those who are involved in its operation. The German "experiment" with codetermination in the public sector has thus far been a success. This conclusion, however, has no applicability to other countries that have not had a similar long history of experience with this unusual form of administrative employee participation.

It must be emphasized that these conclusions apply only to the federal legislation and to similar state laws. There has not yet been enough experience to permit evaluation of the results of the new laws of Berlin and Hesse, which substantially expand the scope of matters subject to codetermination. There is a real possibility, but no certainty, that such legislative modification may result in increasing both the delay in administrative decision-making and the amount of work time devoted to this process to the extent that government operations may become less efficient without any offsetting gain in employee protection.

The unions are pressing strongly for revision of the federal and other state laws on staff representation. Each union of public employees has its own list of desired changes (see pp. 193-95). Work on the drafting of possible federal revisions began in the Interior Ministry before the end of 1969. At least two states are seriously considering changes in their laws. It remains to be seen whether the agencies and the legislatures involved will defer action until the recent experience in Berlin and Hesse can be evaluated. The present probability is that they will not.

There is room for serious question as to whether the more extensive form of codetermination is appropriate for the public sector. Codetermination has become a very popular slogan in the unions and, probably to a lesser extent, in the total work force. By the same token, there is a clear tendency to undervalue the effectiveness of the cooperation procedure for the employees. Since the evidence shows that most administrators make a serious effort to reach agreement with the councils on matters subject to cooperation, there is perhaps no real justification for moving increasingly from cooperation toward codetermination in the public sector, where administrators are working in the interests of the general public rather than those of private stockholders and where there is a special need to maintain the authority and responsibility of administrators acting on behalf of a democratically constituted government.

· V ·

Labor Disputes
and Their Settlement

FACILITATING PROCEDURES

THE German public employee negotiation system has in general worked so well during the postwar period that there is no apparent need for any special facilitating procedures for resolving deadlocks.

There is no federal mediation agency. Each of the states has a mediation officer, but he operates only in the private sector (p. 11). Use of mediation or fact-finding in the public sector is unknown. So far as can be determined, no consideration has been given to the possibility of introducing such procedures, except perhaps as a strike substitute for civil servants. Such an arrangement would be difficult, since their terms of employment are legislated rather than negotiated.

There are several reasons for the success of the present system. First is the high degree of centralization of bargaining, which places all major negotiations at a very high level. If there were separate negotiations for each village or county or school district, facilitating procedures would probably become necessary.

Second, negotiations have been eased by the recent practice of timing the pay negotiations to coincide with budget-making. This results in a degree of flexibility that usually permits a reasonable settlement.

Third, the general willingness to deal with pay increases on a similar across-the-board basis for all public employees is a very important aid. The extent of friction is greatly reduced by the acceptance of the appropriateness of existing occupational wage differentials and the focusing of attention on the extent of the overall increase. Modification of the differentials is not excluded, but it occurs largely in the form of individual exceptions to the general rule, which are occasionally necessary to adjust to changing job requirements or to variations in labor market conditions. The constant jockeying of each group to improve its position relative to all others is avoided.

Finally, the ease of settlement has been promoted during nearly all of the postwar period by the rapid rise in real wages and the standard of living. Almost every year has witnessed, in both the public and private sectors, substantial wage increases that have regularly exceeded the fairly rapid rise in productivity without causing significant price increases. The rather amazing ability of the German economy to avoid substantial increases in the cost of living in the face of appreciable wage increases—at least up through 1969—is surely a major reason for the absence of serious labor conflict in both the private and public sectors.

STRIKES IN THE PUBLIC SERVICE

Legality of Strikes

The Constitution and laws of the Federal Republic contain no specific provision regarding the legality or illegality of strikes in the public sector.[1] A provision guaranteeing the strike right was considered by the Parliamentary Council (which drafted the Constitution), but was deleted when the unions wanted it limited to strikes called by them, and others were unwilling to accept this limitation. Thus the Constitution in its original form left the matter up to the legislators. It has occasionally been claimed that freedom of association includes freedom to strike. This is a very doubtful view, but a recent addition to Article 9 (3), providing that police and military actions permissible in times of serious danger shall not be invoked against strikes called by a union to protect the terms of employment, seems to introduce an implication that public wage-earners and salaried employees have the right to strike. In any case, their right to strike after reaching a deadlock in negotiations is unquestioned.

In the absence of specific federal legislation on this subject,

1. Even in the private sector, the only provision is a prohibition on strikes led by a works council.

there was until 1970 almost universal agreement that civil servants do not share this right to strike. An express denial of this right was considered during the enactment of the Federal Civil Servants Act of 1953. The original bill submitted by the government contained the following statement: "Withholding of service and cessation of work, even for the purpose of safeguarding the terms of employment, are not permissible." There was objection to this from the DGB unions. The Bundestag committee then decided to drop the proposal. Such a decision would normally give a presumption of upholding the strike right, but in this case the opposite was true, because the committee explicitly stated in its report to the Bundestag that, in suggesting the deletion, it had no intention of changing the existing law on this subject. Rather, it considered any new provision unnecessary, because the incompatibility of withholding of services with the duty of the civil servant was already so clear and so firmly fixed in the minds of the civil servants and citizens in general. Because of this legislative history, it has been almost universally recognized that civil servants cannot legally strike.[2] A decision by the Federal Constitutional Court on October 30, 1922, remains controlling on this point.[3] At least three of the states specifically prohibit civil servant strikes in their constitution or legislation.

Some questioning of the illegality of civil servant strikes began to appear in 1970. Three unions commissioned legal opinions on the subject, and two of the resulting analyses affirmed a limited right to strike. Dr. Ingo von Munch, in his opinion prepared at the request of the GdP,[4] concluded that civil servant strikes are illegal. He rejected some of the arguments frequently presented in support of this conclusion, but upheld the views that such a strike would be inconsistent with the special civil servant relationship of service and loyalty and contrary to the traditional principles of the civil service. He argued that it is further impermissible in that it would

2. DBB, *Die Beamten und das Streikrecht* (DBB Dokumente No. 4), 1969, p. 30.
3. Ibid., p. 19.
4. *Rechtsgutachten zur Frage des Streikrechts der Beamten.* Hilden-Düsseldorf: Verlag Deutsche Polizei, 1970.

prevent the state from executing the laws and from carrying out its constitutional duties to the citizens.

Wolfgang Däubler, in a lengthy analysis prepared for the ÖTV,[5] presented thirteen arguments in support of the alleged legality of a civil servant strike, going even so far as to claim that it is sanctioned by the European Convention on Human Rights and the European Social Charter.[6] He claimed that the constitutional provision that "the law regarding public service shall be determined with due regard to the traditional principles of the professional civil service" (Article 33, Section 4) is no more than a guideline for legislators. He urged that a strike to influence civil servant legislation is not a political strike because it is directed against the state in its function as employer rather than as the incorporation of the public will. Court vacations, it is suggested, prove that an interruption of governmental functions is not contrary to the public interest. Yet even Däubler granted that civil servant strikes are illegal under many circumstances, depending primarily on the essentiality of the services.

A third opinion on this subject was prepared by Professor Thilo Ramm for the DGB.[7] He came to much the same conclusion as Däubler that civil servants are subject not to any special strike prohibition but to the same limitations that apply also to public wage-earners and salaried employees. These limits were seen as based on the principles that a strike should not infringe upon the rights of others nor transgress the constitutional order or the moral code. He suggested that some strike alternative such as arbitration should be made available to the persons performing functions the discontinuance of which would be illegal under these principles.

In view of these last two publications, it can no longer be said, as of the autumn of 1970, that the complete illegality of a civil servant strike is almost universally recognized. It can only be said that it is generally recognized, but increasingly questioned. On the other hand, it is universally recognized

5. *Der Streik im öffentlichen Dienst.* Tübingen: J. C. B. Mohr, 1970.
6. Ibid., pp. 172, 177.
7. *Das Koalitions- und Streikrecht der Beamten.* Cologne: Bund-Verlag, 1970.

that public wage-earners and salaried employees do have a very broad, though not unlimited, right to strike in case of deadlock regarding the terms of a new agreement. Their employment relations are governed by private law rather than public law. For them there is no difference between the public and private sectors with reference to the right to strike. Here again there is no specific federal legislation, but there is general recognition of the legal situation. This recognition is supported by a considerable number of decisions of the National Labor Court from the time of the Weimar Republic.

For wage-earners and salaried employees it is held that the very existence of a collective agreement implies a "relative peace obligation," but not an "absolute peace obligation." The former forbids during the life of the agreement the use of any weapon in a dispute regarding the contents of the agreement. This outlaws a strike or even a threat of strike regarding the interpretation of the agreement. Such disputes—grievances —should be taken to the labor courts. It also outlaws action to force a change in any of the terms of an existing agreement or in the terms of a new agreement until the old one has expired. But the mere existence of an agreement in no way implies illegality of a strike concerning matters that are not covered by the agreement. Such action is illegal only in case the agreement itself so provides.[8]

A strike in either the private or public sector may further be illegal because of its aims or methods. Since the aim must be to influence the terms of employment, a strike for political aims is illegal. A strike to inflict damage disproportionate to the possible gains might be considered contrary to public morals. Thus in some cases the provision of essential services may be crucial to the legality of a strike. Objectionable methods that might result in the illegality of a strike include the sanctioning of property damage, sabotage, or assault by the sponsoring party or the timing of the strike so as to

8. A. Hueck, H. C. Nipperday, E. Stahlhacke, *Tarifvertragsgestez,* pp. 94–101.

affect seriously the public interest or cause irreparable loss.[9] It will be noted that illegality of a strike because of objectionable aims or methods will be a very rare occurrence, but the limitations are more likely to be applicable in the public than in the private sector. Nevertheless, the right to strike of the public wage-earner and salaried employee is relatively unlimited as compared with the complete prohibition that presumably applies to the civil servant.

If a strike by civil servants is indeed still illegal, it is reasonable to assume that this is equally true of a slowdown or other strikelike pressure. Such actions are similar to the strike in their purpose and—with some difference in degree—in their effect. They are equally inconsistent with the principles of the civil service. Däubler and Ramm disagree with this view.

The differences between civil servants and other public employees in their right to strike are nationwide. They do not vary from state to state, as they may in the United States and Canada. Nor are they based on a judgment regarding the essentiality of the work performed. We have already noted that civil servants are engaged in a wide variety of tasks of all degrees of essentiality, and that often the same task is performed both by civil servants and by wage-earners or salaried employees. The differences depend strictly on the legal basis of the employment relationship. The rationale for the distinction is the theory of the special mutual relationship of the civil servant and the state as lying quite outside the employer-employee relationship.

Whether or not the actual results of the distinction happen to coordinate to some extent with the degree of essentiality depends on how one defines or interprets "essentiality." There seems to be general agreement that the continuous service of policemen, firemen, and prison guards is essential. These employees in Germany are civil servants. When we go beyond these groups there is no unanimity on the criteria of essentiality.

9. Hans Reichel and Hanns Zschocher, *Conciliation and Arbitration and the Law as Applied to Labor Disputes.* Bonn: Federal Ministry of Labor and the Social Structure, 1963, pp. 10–14.

Many believe that the uninterrupted operation of government administrative offices is essential to the concept of state sovereignty. Nearly all members of the professional staff of the ministries are civil servants; but their effectiveness would be handicapped without the services of the secretarial and communications employees, most of whom are salaried employees unless they have served for four or five years.

If essentiality is considered, on the other hand, from the point of view of the public as "consumer" of government services, it seems probable that there would be relatively little concern if some of the ministries were closed for a week or two and much more if there were interruption to some services less related to state sovereignty, such as local transit and trash collection. These services are staffed largely by wage-earners and salaried employees, and are thus subject to interruption under certain circumstances. The postal and railroad services are also of great concern to the public. Here we find a large proportion of civil servants, but it is doubtful that they could maintain a high level of service in the absence of the wage-earners and salaried employees.

Essentiality of services does not always depend solely on the nature of the service. In many cases it will vary with the conditions or timing. Thus the public feels the need of railroad service more acutely during the vacation and holiday seasons than at other times. It resents a break in postal service particularly during the pre-Christmas period. Some services, such as trash collection, may not be truly essential in terms of an interruption of a week or two, but become increasingly so if nonperformance continues.

In view of these various considerations, we must conclude that German law regarding which employees may and may not strike does not have the effect of differentiating on the basis of essentiality of service, even though the employees who are denied the right to strike include many whose services are clearly vital.

Union Attitudes

There is a considerable difference in the attitudes of the

DBB, the DAG, and the DGB unions concerning the use of the strike. This is a natural result of the difference in their membership.

The DBB, whose membership consists overwhelmingly of civil servants, is aggressive but nonmilitant in its tactics. It places considerable emphasis on the special relationship of the civil servant to his government. It seeks to modify the career structure of the civil servants to increase flexibility and permit easier promotion of qualified persons, but it strongly favors retaining the special status of the members of this group. It would vigorously oppose transferring their relationship from one of public to private law and regarding it as an employer-employee relationship. Thus it has consistently opposed any strike action or slowdown by civil servants and would strongly oppose any steps toward legalizing such action.

The most serious strain on the self-control of the DBB came during its unsuccessful efforts to win a pay increase for the civil servants in 1962 after raises for public wage-earners and salaried employees had been gained by strike threat. Mention has been made of the protest meetings that it held in major cities during June of that year. At the Hamburg session a resolution was adopted stating: "The traditional view, not set forth in any law, that the civil servant has no right to strike because of his duty of loyalty to the government, necessarily needs reexamination now that breach of trust by the government has become the rule. We demand that our union officers take immediate steps to make it constitutionally possible for the civil servant also to make use of the single means that the government respects—namely the strike."

The Interior Minister then wrote to the head of the DBB expressing his surprise and concern. He stated his view that any claim of the right to strike for civil servants endangers the justification for their special status, and invited the leadership to inform him of its disapproval of the resolution.

He should not have been surprised at the reply he received. It stated that the officers, in spite of their determination to defend the legal status of the professional civil service, could not offer the requested assurance. They recognize that civil servants do not have the right to strike. The resolution, however, raises the question as to whether they should seek to change the law. This is a matter of basic policy, which cannot be decided by the officers alone without determining the wishes of the member organizations. The officers cannot guess the present views of the member organizations on this question. A few months ago there was certainly no interest in strike legalization, but there has been a vast change of opinion on this point as a result of the unfortunate pay policy of the federal government and the recent bitter disillusionment of the civil servants in seeing that the government will grant justified demands only in the face of a strike threat. This was the substance of the DBB reply. The minister had unwittingly "asked for it."

In later years the government has not repeated the mistake of treating its civil servants less well than its other employees. For example, in the autumn of 1969, when the Interior Minister was negotiating with the ÖTV and DAG on a lump-sum bonus after wildcat strikes, assurances were given from the outset that the civil servants, judges, and soldiers would receive any benefits that might be granted to the other employees. The DBB has therefore returned to its original strike policy. It not only opposes use of the strike by civil servants, but would also oppose any attempt to legalize the strike for them.

The DAG, whose membership consists overwhelmingly of salaried employees, is legally free to call a strike in case of a deadlock in negotiations. It has not felt it necessary to take this step. The question arose most recently in January 1970, when the ÖTV set a date for a strike vote. On that occasion DAG officials decided not to take similar action. It may be noted that the principal demand raised by the ÖTV at that time was the setting of a 100 DM minimum for the impending pay increase. The DAG had little interest in this demand since the overwhelming majority of its salaried employees were already scheduled to receive more than that amount.

As will be seen later, there have been a few instances of slowdowns that included certain groups of salaried employees and occasionally civil servants. So far as can be determined, most of these involved persons belonging to independent unions that have a working relationship with the DAG but are not actually a part of it. It appears that the DAG did not sanction or support these actions. It did sanction a slowdown in a single instance—a 1968 case involving air traffic control, where it claims to represent two thirds of the salaried employees.

The ÖTV has not officially sanctioned any public sector strike since a one-day stoppage by municipal workers in March 1958 and a two-day shutdown of the air traffic control service in June 1962, but it has occasionally made effective use of a strike threat. It took a strike vote during the 1967 negotiations, resulting in an affirmative majority of over 90 percent; and in 1966 and 1970 it set dates for strike votes that were subsequently canceled. It should be noted that, whereas some unions in other countries think they strengthen their bargaining power by taking a strike vote early in the negotiations or even prior to them, the ÖTV has, by use of clever timing, been able to make an effective weapon out of the mere setting of a vote date.

The other DGB unions that have many public employees— the DPG, the GdED, and the GEW—have also recently become involved in strikelike activities during the life of an agreement. The same is true of a few independent unions. These actions have in some cases involved civil servants, as well as wage-earners and salaried employees. They will be discussed in the following section.

There has been almost no instance of any attempt to discipline employees involved in any of these illegal actions. The growing tendency of unions to sanction or condone work interruption by public employees probably results in large part from the reluctance of government officials at all levels—federal, state, and local—to take any action against strike leaders or participants.

History of Public Employee Strikes

Strike action by German government employees has been

so rare that it is possible here to sketch almost all such instances that have occurred.

The first civil servant strike of significance took place in the spring of 1920. This was purely a political strike for counterrevolutionary purposes. A group of army officers on March 13 attempted a coup—the Kapp-Putsch—to overthrow the constitutional government. The DBB of that period, which had been first established on December 4, 1918, called a strike of all members. Other unions took similar action, resulting in a general strike, which was largely responsible for the failure of the coup within four days. The general strike continued for an additional three days pending agreement between the previous government and the unions concerning eight demands. The agreement resulted in the replacement of the Ministers of Defense and of the Interior. It also involved commitments to the democratic process and the enactment of social legislation. The unions were accused of putting undue pressure on the government by the prolonging of the general strike, but they contended that they were only counteracting the influence of the coup in order to assure the return to full democratic rule. The general judgment was that the civil servants had not breached their obligation by their work stoppage, but rather had fulfilled their duty to defend constitutional government.[10]

The first significant economic strike of civil servants came in February 1922. All civil servants had received a pay increase on January 12. It was generally regarded as inadequate, but the best that could be expected under the existing national budgetary situation. Only the National Union of German Railway Civil Servants (an affiliate of the DBB) refused to acquiesce. On January 27 it issued a five-day ultimatum demanding automatic adjustment of pay to cost of living and withdrawal of an hours-of-work bill, which provided certain exceptions regarding railway employees.

The government responded on January 29 by issuing an official statement setting forth the details of the dispute, indicat-

10. DBB, *DBB: Ursprung, Weg, Ziel,* pp. II/34–35; DBB, *Die Beamten und das Streikrecht,* p. 11.

ing the current state of deliberations in the Reichstag, and asserting its determination to take "the sharpest measures" against any striking employee and to protect those who remained true to their obligations. It followed this with an ordinance of February 1 asserting the illegality of any civil servant strike, providing fine and imprisonment for participation in a railway strike, and authorizing the Minister of Transport to take all necessary measures to assure continued operation in case of strike.

In disregard of these warnings the railway employees union called a strike for February 2. This union, having taken this step alone, waited in vain for support from the other DBB unions and its parent federation. The rest of the labor movement, through the other three labor federations, publicly denounced the strike on its third day. All other workers except Berlin municipal wage-earners, remained on the job. In the absence of further support, the strike collapsed after one week.

Two months later the convention of the DBB reelected its national chairman (Wilhelm Flügel) after he had reiterated his opposition to any civil servant strike. "A civil servant who strikes ceases to be a civil servant. Whether he will become one again, and whether under retention of his well-earned rights or under loss of them, depends on the outcome of the strike. . . . Every civil servant strike contains the danger of the loss of the basic civil servant rights." Thereafter, the leaders of the railway employees union found themselves largely excluded from effective participation in the activities of the DBB. In June they withdrew and attempted unsuccessfully to establish a new, competitive civil servant federation.

The government did not seek to discipline those who were guilty only of participation in the strike, but it proceeded energetically to penalize those who had engaged in any sabotage or had urged others to strike. Its action against a civil servant who had persuaded another to cease work was upheld on appeal by the National Court on October 30, 1922.[11] The court based its approval of the disciplinary action not only on the special ordinance of February 1 but on the

11. Ibid., pp. 19, 21.

173

general illegality of any civil servant strike as inconsistent with the special obligations of the civil servant to the public, with the special nature of his lifetime career, and with the need for uninterrupted performance of the functions of the state.

This ruling still continues to the present time as the controlling decision on this question. It is because of the decisive disciplinary action taken by the government and the supporting opinion of the high court that work stoppages by civil servants have been almost unknown since that time.

During the remaining years of the Weimar Republic there were no serious public employee strikes.[12] Those that did occur from time to time generally involved municipal wage-earners and were mostly the result of Communist agitation or of resistance to wage reductions during the desperate economic depression in the tumultuous political period immediately preceding the Nazi takeover.

For thirteen years following the end of World War II there was no significant work stoppage of public employees. The first crack in this record came on March 19, 1958, with a one-day strike of municipal wage-earners in connection with the negotiation of their revised pay agreement.

Another challenge came in connection with the reluctance of the federal government to grant any increase during 1962. As has been mentioned, the municipal employees on May 11 received an increase effective as of April 1. The state and federal governments announced on May 30 their willingness to resume negotiations, and an agreement was reached on June 7. In the meantime the air traffic control personnel, then organized chiefly in the ÖTV, became impatient. They were largely salaried employees of the Federal Institute for Flight Safety. This Institute is under the control of the Transport Ministry, which replaces the Interior Ministry as government representative in negotiations. Most of these employees now

12. The refusal of work by railway employees in the Ruhr during 1923 was in accord with instructions from the government under its policy of passive resistance to the French occupation of that area, and was not an economic strike.

belong to the DAG, but many are members of the Association of German Air Traffic Controllers (Verband Deutscher Flugleiter or VDF). This association is not authorized to negotiate directly with the Transport Ministry. Its salaried employees are represented in collective bargaining instead by the ÖTV and DAG.

The ÖTV and VDF called a thirty-six hour strike for reclassification and higher pay on June 4-5, bringing a temporary halt to German air traffic except on the Berlin flights. It appears unlikely that the strike had any effect on the outcome of the general negotiations that had been already planned and were completed two days later. The terms of settlement were not very favorable to the employees, leading to the assumption that they were about what the government already had in mind when it offered to resume negotiations. This strike, however, led the government to invite these employees to accept civil servant status, so that they could no longer legally strike. It could not require such transfer, because entry into the civil service is always voluntary. About two thirds of the 1,400 employees accepted the transfer, and all subsequent appointments have been as civil servants. The continuation of many as salaried employees has been one cause of subsequent problems.

With the settlement of the 1962 pay increase for wage-earners and salaried employees, the unions directed their efforts toward winning an increase for the civil servants, and the DBB resorted to the unusual tactic of holding a series of protest meetings during June. When these meetings failed to win the desired result, the DPG and the GdED decided on further efforts. They called a three-day slowdown for mid-August. In an effort to circumvent the illegality of a civil servant strike they called this procedure "work by regulation." Because of the illegality, the railway and postal unions affiliated with the DBB refused to participate in these actions.

The GdED named its railroad tactic "Action Eagle," though one newspaper[13] commented that it should have been called "Action Vulture." Some irregularity of train schedules resulted

13. *Sonntagsblatt,* Aug. 28, 1962.

from widespread observance of all speed and other safety regulations. The DPG called its postal tactic "Action Hedgehog." Selection of this name will be understandable only to those who know that hedgehog dolls have a popularity in Germany that corresponds roughly to an imaginary American combination of Teddy Bear, Mickey Mouse, and Donald Duck. The slowdown resulted when some employees weighed all letters to assure correct postage, opened all "printed matter" mail to make certain that it contained no first-class material, and measured all parcels even when it was obvious that they were within the acceptable limits. Such finesse has apparently not occurred to American postal workers as a means of bringing their discontent to public attention without complete suspension of service.

It is highly probable that work by regulation does not successfully circumvent strike illegality. There is little reason to doubt that the courts would hold it unlawful as a labor conflict weapon or a modified strike. Nevertheless, the government decided not to invoke disciplinary measures, as might have been the case if the actions had lasted longer. The result of the government's forebearance was the encouragement of similar action by civil servants in the future. It was the first instance of the governmental "permissiveness" that has recently been weakening the no-strike tradition of the German civil service.

Yet it was six years before the tactic of work-by-regulation was tried again. Although its use had been encouraged by the failure of government officials to invoke disciplinary action, it had been discouraged by the lack of any demonstrable gains. Another major factor contributing to peaceful settlement of public employee relations problems was the economic environment. The period from 1962 until late 1966 was one of marked increase in productivity and employment, accompanied by substantial pay increases and only moderate advance in the cost of living. The unions were winning satisfactory gains for their members in private industry without strike. The average annual number of days lost by strike per thousand employees from 1964 through 1967 was only 5 for Germany, as compared with 30 for Sweden, 109 for England, 147 for France, and 447 for the United States. This period of phenomenal industrial peace found its natural counterpart in the public sector. It carried through the recession of 1967 and continued until the sharp revival of 1968.

The change that began to take place in late 1968 was apparently caused more by psychological than by economic developments. Many countries on all continents were beginning to witness an upsurge of public protest that frequently took the form of violence or other illegal action. In Germany there was widespread student revolt against the antiquated form of state university administration. In some instances, particularly at the Free University of Berlin, small groups of radical students became so extreme in their demands and so disruptive in their actions that they sought in vain for support from the labor movement. But some of the youngest union members began to feel that they were perhaps missing a piece of the action.

While student protest in its more violent forms had largely a negative effect on public opinion and union attitudes, protests in another area won wider acceptance. These were the protests against the increase of fares in local transport. The municipal bus and streetcar services were running at a deficit with the aid of public subsidy. They felt it proper and necessary to increase the pay of transit employees in line with other public employees, but sought to avoid increased deficits by fare increases. In Hannover, Cologne, and several other large cities protests begun apparently by students and resulting in the disruption of transit service won widespread support and participation from the local citizens and were successful in winning a rescinding of the fare hikes. This tendency toward public protest found increasing expression among German government employees toward the end of the 1960s, though to a much lesser extent than in most other industrialized nations.

The first evidence appeared among the air traffic controllers— a group that has evinced considerable discontent in several countries. Since most of them were now civil servants, they adopted the tactic of work-by-regulation. On October 28, 1968, they began a slowdown that continued until December 12. The background situation in this case was unusually complex. As previously mentioned, although many of the controllers belong to the independent VDF, the ÖTV and DAG have insisted on representing in negotiations those who are salaried employees, as they do in the case of all other public salaried employees except those in the postal and railway services. One problem has been that the negotiating unions have felt that some of the demands were unjustified and have been unwilling to press for them because the achievement of them would result in serious inconsistency with the conditions of all other public salaried employees.

Another complicating factor has been the difference in terms of employment between the salaried employees and civil servants doing the same types of work. As indicated earlier, after the brief strike in 1962 the government invited the staff to change from salaried employee to civil servant status. It also decided to make transfer more attractive by discontinuing advancement training for salaried employees—a decision that has increased dissatisfaction.

Nevertheless, there remain some 600 original employees who have declined the transfer. As salaried employees they receive appreciably higher current pay than the corresponding civil servants, though their pension plan is contributory. This situation is very disturbing to the civil servants. Though they may realize that their long-run prospects are relatively attractive, they cannot help but resent their lower current pay. In addition, there is a discrepancy between the old and new civil servants. In order to reduce the contrast between the current pay of those who accepted transfer and those who declined, the former were given a type of red circle rate that is not applicable to those newly hired.

In addition to the demands for salary adjustment and promotional opportunities are the requests for an increase in the size of the work force, a reduction of the retirement age to fifty, a readjustment of work schedules, and special annual recuperation leave.

Ten days after the start of the slowdown, negotiations were resumed. They were discontinued without result on November 9, at which time the ÖTV and DAG approved continuation of the slowdown. On November 12 the president of the Federal Institute for Flight Safety (the employing agency) announced that disciplinary measures would be taken. The following day the Transport Minister—a former union president—made a very strange statement in the Bundestag: "I cannot find . . . a single point in the conduct of the civil servant air traffic controllers, concerning which I can point out to them that they are violating valid law, and thus make possible an intervention by the federal government."

Thus the slowdown continued without penalty, but also without appreciable impact on negotiations. On November 21 the cabinet issued a statement disavowing its Transport Minister: "Work regulations are to be followed not literally but in accord with their meaning and purpose. 'Work-by-regulation' is therefore nothing other than an intentional improper and absurd application of work regulations. It cannot be reconciled with the obligations of civil servant law, and thus fulfills the conditions of conduct subject to discipline." However, there were still no signs of disciplinary action.

During early December there were indications that the Transport Ministry was inclined to advance the civil servant air traffic controllers to a higher career level, but this was opposed by the Interior Ministry. As the Christmas season approached, public resentment toward the slowdown increased. The VDF announced on December 10 that it was discontinuing the slowdown for one month. At the end of that time it seemed likely that the government would soon make some concessions. The slowdown was not resumed. In view of the unrealistic character of some of the VDF demands, the eventual settlement left widespread employee discontent.

Another slowdown in late 1968 illustrates how strong emotions may be generated regarding a relatively minor matter when a feeling of injustice exists. It represents also the first instance in which a slowdown in public service apparently achieved its purpose.

The issue concerned the amount of the Christmas bonus for civil servants. Such a bonus had long existed for wage-earners and salaried employees, but had been extended to civil servants only on July 15, 1965. The amount had been set at one third of a month's earnings through 1968, one half in 1969 and 1970, and two thirds thereafter. On October 17, 1968, the TdL and VKA agreed with the unions to increase the bonus for that year to 40 percent in the case of wage-earners and salaried employees. The federal government followed suit on October 23. It was widely assumed that this increase would be granted also to civil servants. On November 13 the federal government announced that its finances would not permit the application of this increase to all civil servants, so that it would be granted only to those whose basic salary was less than a stated amount. This cabinet decision came especially as a surprise because it apparently had not been discussed either with the unions or the state governments. It was widely regarded as a strange and unfair decision.

The DPG called immediately for a slowdown in the postal service. The DBB's postal union did not participate, because of the DBB position on the illegality of such action. On November 21 the cabinet instructed the Finance Minister to make another thorough check on the availability of funds. About four days later he reported the discovery that sufficient monies existed in the unexpended budgets of various ministries. The extension of the increase to all civil servants then seemed assured, and the slowdown ceased after a two-week duration.

It appeared that a slowdown had at last been effective. Many government officials regretted this. For example, a speaker in the Bundesrat stated: "I shall not discuss whether this slowdown was appropriate with respect to a mere 6⅔ percent addition to the Christmas bonus. But what is disturbing especially for us who are striving to find an understanding for the interests of the public services is that a literal following of work regulations in the final analysis perverts the meaning of the public services. As romantic as it may sound, 'service' still in the twentieth century has something to do with 'serving.' "[14]

It soon became clear, however, that the federal government had perhaps yielded as much to parliamentary as to union pressure. The likelihood of parliamentary approval of its original bill had been diminishing. This loss of support may have been due in part, but not entirely, to the slowdown. It was surely the result also of dissatisfaction on the part of the state governments and of the lobbying activities by the DBB. When the revised bill came up for discussion in the Bundesrat on December 6, it was reported that the Committee on the Interior had earlier decided to propose the adoption of the following resolution with reference to the original.bill: "It is the opinion of the Bundesrat that, in the interest of equal treatment for all members of the public services, the special bonus foreseen for 1968 under the law of July 15, 1965, should be fixed for all active and retired civil servants at 40 percent of their monthly payments."[15]

The spring of 1969 witnessed the first strikelike activity involving school teachers. Many teachers felt that the federal civil servant pay bill then under consideration in the Bundestag did not provide appropriate special provisions for the members of their profession. The leaders of the Hesse state branch of the GEW—the teachers union—called a protest meeting in Frankfort for the late morning of a school day, February 13. Similar meetings were subsequently held in several other of the larger cities in that state, in spite of strong warnings of disciplinary action from the state Ministry of Education. The union claims that some 6,000 of its 17,000 members in that state—about a sixth of the total teaching staff—participated in one or another of these meetings, which involved a refusal to work for about a half day.

On April 11 it was announced that the Education Ministry was planning disciplinary action. The main issue of conflict then shifted from the legislative proposal to the question of discipline, which had not seriously arisen in any of the previous

14. DBB, *Die Beamten und das Streikrecht*, p. 47
15. Ibid., p. 48, or DGB, *Geschäftsbericht 1965–68*, p. 676.

postwar strikes or slowdowns. On April 28 the union issued a call to its members to display their solidarity with their colleagues who were threatened with discipline, promised the latter legal representation in the courts, and asserted that new protest actions would soon be set. On May 13 it was announced that no general disciplinary measures would be taken and that the union had discontinued plans for further protest. The participating teachers would be sent a letter of disapproval, which would not be entered in their personnel files. It appears that nearly all of them had made up their lost work time and that the remainder were docked for their absence.

This case was the closest that any government agency has come in the postwar period to obtaining a court ruling concerning the strike rights of civil servants. This opportunity was lost when the government authorities, in spite of their strong legal position, finally capitulated. The union won its point on discipline, but not on its original legislative issue.

The next significant instance of public service strikes was a flurry of brief wildcat stoppages by municipal wage-earners in September 1969, already mentioned. In this instance the interruptions in local public services were the outcome of a unique outburst of wildcat strikes in private industry. The municipal strikes were widely considered in Germany to be a spontaneous outburst of the employees beyond the control of their union. It is clear, however, that they were not directed against the union or the local employee representatives, as had been the case two weeks earlier in the Ruhr. In fact, President Kluncker of the ÖTV has since admitted privately that the public service strikes were at all times under complete union control. He claims that employee unrest was so serious that there would have been an explosion if this safety valve had not been used to permit the controlled blow-off of the steam. This claim is of course a matter of judgment. Granted that I have had no contact with his rank-and-file, I still find it difficult to accept his claim. It seems to me incredible that this union, whose members had never previously challenged union discipline or shown any tendency to strike, could not have held them on the job for three months until the expiration of their current agreement and the introduction of new rates.

These demonstration strikes, involving transit employees, trash collectors, and dock workers and lasting from an hour to a day, took place in at least a dozen cities within the course of a week. Noteworthy is the fact that they did not represent an antiunion revolt, but were instead unofficially planned or sanctioned by the ÖTV. They met with equal but less immediate success. They have probably lent encouragement toward future interruptions in public service. Several such instances took place during the next six months.

In September 1969, four days after the municipal wildcat in Berlin, the kindergarten teachers in the Kruezberg district of that city went out for a day. These salaried employees publicized demands for higher classification, better working conditions, and smaller classes. Here we see perhaps the first instance of protest on behalf of demands regarding issues that would not be covered by a labor agreement. Since some of the demands did relate to issues regulated by agreement, the stoppage was illegal, and the local GEW found itself obliged to disassociate itself from their action and publicly denounce it. There was a similar one-day strike of kindergarten teachers and municipal welfare workers in the city of Kassel on November 27.

A new protest technique was introduced by doctors in the Bonn University hospitals in November 1969. Involved were the "medical assistants" or doctors engaged chiefly in hospital duties and medical research, in contrast to the "head doctors" engaged also in administration or teaching. The former took a free day (except for emergency duty) on November 21 and again a week later, declaring it to be compensatory time off for overtime performed in that week. They devoted these days to a general assembly for discussion of their problems.

The most basic of their complaints centered on this matter of overtime. The assistants are civil servants on revocable appointment. (The hospital director states that the appointments must be terminable because most of these doctors are narrowly specialized and it is necessary to make occasional changes as the research emphasis in the hospital changes.) As civil servants they are expected to work whatever overtime is necessary to the performance of their duties. If the overtime is considerable and regular, they should receive compensatory time off within six months. If they were salaried employees—as are many doctors in public service—they would get compensatory time off or overtime pay.

The regular workweek in public service is 43 hours—42 hours after January 1, 1971. The assistants claim that they are on duty an average of about 70 hours a week. The protest placed as much emphasis on the need for a larger staff as on overtime pay. It was directed at the state government rather than the hospital administration, because the latter had requested 130 additional positions in the last budget and received only 36. As civil servants some of these medical assistants belong to the DBB. Many of them choose instead to affiliate with the "Marburger Bund." This latter is an association of salaried-employee and civil servant doctors, which is attractive to many of the latter because of its complete focus on their profession. The association is not authorized to negotiate for its salaried members, so it had formed a working relationship with the DAG, which serves as its bargaining representative. In such sessions an official of the association is always present as an expert, but not as negotiator. It is this association that was active in the winter of 1969-70 in pressing demands and promoting protests on behalf of the medical assistants.

The Minister of Education in North Rhine-Westphalia proposed that the doctors regularly take their compensatory time off, but they said this was impossible without neglect of their duties. Then on November 23 he ordered extra pay of 350 DM a month. They considered this inadequate for so much overtime. The state government finally decided to pay a lump sum of 2,000 DM to each doctor for overtime performed during 1969 and to make certain other adjustments in the future.

The state of Baden-Württemberg had earlier met the same problem by agreeing to pay the doctors at the universities of Heidelberg, Tübingen, and Freiburg hourly overtime, as though they were salaried employees. It issued this order on a temporary basis until such time as the several states could agree on a uniform method of handling the situation. This overtime payment to university doctors in these two states is of particular interest because it may represent the beginning of a gradual crumbling of the special status of the civil servant. There had been earlier changes in the terms of the civil servants that had made these more similar to those of the salaried employees, such as the granting of a year-end bonus in 1965; but the payment of overtime strikes at the heart of the special status of the civil servant and moves it in the direction of an employer-employee relationship.

The days off at Bonn were followed on December 9 by a brief strike of the medical assistants in the clinics of the universities of Marburg and Giessen in the state of Hesse, where the demands were much the same.

A week later there was a one-day "warning strike" at Marburg. This differed in two respects from the earlier protests. Its participants were not only doctors, but most of the 900 scientific assistants in all of the various laboratories. Its demands were not economic but political. The Hesse state legislature was considering a revision of the law on university governance, and the assistants—under the leadership of an organization called the Hesse State Assistants Conference, whose parent national organization (the BAK) was formed only in 1968— were advocating changes that would give them much more authority at the expense of the professors. The state Minister of Education and the legislature were not inclined to yield to their demands. The strike was resumed on February 21 and continued for nine days.

While the Marburg interruptions were, in effect, a strike of assistants against professors, the Free University of Berlin experienced what might be called a strike of some professors against assistants and students. The city-state of Berlin revised its law on university governance in the summer of 1969. The new statute provided, among other things, that the universities would no longer be headed by a professor-elected rector with little authority, but by a president named for a seven-year term, whose powers would be more comparable to those of his American counterparts. He is designated by a selection committee of 114 members, composed of an equal number of representatives of professors, assistants, and students, plus a few delegates of the nonacademic employees. The selection of the first president at the Free University took place in November 1969. The professors and the Berlin government were unable to persuade anyone of high repute to seek the appointment. The nonprofessorial delegates caucused for several days and finally agreed on a candidate—a thirty-year-old graduate assistant—who was duly elected. The Berlin cabinet ("senate") has the legal authority to veto the selection, but it concluded that it would be impractical to exercise this power.

Disruption of some lectures by small groups of Marxist students, which had been taking place from time to time during the previous two years, continued. They focused now on a member of the economics department, who was accused of being a propagandist for capitalism. A major demand was the appointment of a Marxist assistant to provide a balance for students in that area. The new president sought to mediate the conflict, but was immediately denounced as a traitor by radical students. In January, nearly all of some thirty professors in that department went on strike for a week in protest to the continuing disruption of their colleague's classes. The disruptions ceased, at least for the time being, when a new assistant was appointed.

Another dispute involving civil servants started in February 1970. It was a recurrence of the continuing dissatisfaction of the air traffic control staff. Negotiations of the ÖTV and DAG with the Transport, Finance, and Interior ministries broke down on February 24, and the earlier tactic of work-by-regulation was promptly reinstituted. Operations returned to normal on March 11, when the government agreed to retirement at age 55 for control-tower personnel, and the unions dropped their insistence that the change apply also to other branches of the air safety staff.

Finally, in early 1970 even the police began to show signs

of unrest, especially toward a Bundesrat proposal to introduce maximum limitations in the police personnel budgets. In recent years the police in most of the states had been raised two or three steps to higher pay groups, which has led to some lack of uniformity of police pay in the various states. The proposal to set uniform maxima was viewed by the police as a threat to the prospects of future pay gains, although such uniformity applies to most state civil servants.

The Police Union (GdP), an unaffiliated organization whose mid-1970 membership of some 120,000 includes about 90,000 officers or two thirds of the total, decided to seek to exert pressure by conducting a membership referendum on various possible tactics during the week of February 16. It asked how many would be willing to refuse voluntary overtime work, to refuse training, to refuse use of firearms, to reject responsibility for record keeping, to participate in a sit-in, or to give only oral warnings instead of collecting fines from traffic violators. There was the further rhetorical question as to how many would follow a union strike call, provided such action were legal and were necessary to achieve major union demands. It was subsequently announced that, of the 83 percent who voted, from 69 to 93 percent expressed willingness to adopt one or another of these various measures. In mid-March the union was threatening only demonstrations in case of rejection of its demands for a national or interstate structuring of the police, the creation of a research institute, modernization of equipment, and extension of training. It will be noted that these demands go beyond the terms of employment, but there is no request that they be covered by collective agreement.

The refusal of many teachers in North Rhine-Westphalia to perform overtime work for three weeks in May 1970 has been mentioned earlier.

Analysis of Strikes

This review of most of the postwar strikes and quasi-strikes in the public service shows a trend toward increasing resort to use of this weapon, even though the level of work interruption remains much lower than in most other western nations. This trend is not the result of growing organization of public employees or of efforts to win union recognition, as in some other countries. Government employees have long been highly organized, and union recognition has been no problem. The causes may lie rather in the widespread malaise of recent years, the increasing practice of public protest on nonindustrial issues, and the German awareness of the rising incidence of strikes in the public service of many other nations. And surely the trend has become inevitable in light of the almost complete absence of any effort to take disciplinary action against either the participants or their unions.

Although there is a wide area of strike legality in the public service, there has been scarcely any use of the legal strike. Only the one-day strike in March 1958 and the first strike of the air traffic controllers in 1962 were permissible. All work interruptions since that time were probably illegal, although no attempt was made to test them in the courts. Either they involved civil servants, who have no strike right, or other employees during the terms of their collective agreements. At times when the strike would be legal—during a negotiation deadlock on a new agreement—the mere threat to take a strike vote has provided adequate pressure.

The tendency toward an increasing number of work interruptions in the public service can scarcely be attributed to their success. In general we must conclude that government negotiators and legislators have not been overly influenced by union efforts to apply special pressure, except in the municipal strikes of September 1969. The one instance where capitulation clearly led to a rash of strikes—in August 1969—occurred in the private sector.

Up to the time this is written, only three actions by public employees appear to have won clear-cut concessions. The first was the postal slow-down in late November 1968 to win for some civil servants a small Christmas bonus increase that had already been granted to all other public employees. This extension, however, would probably have been granted without the slow-down, because of the logically untenable position of the federal government, the relatively minor cost involved, and the insistence of the state governments. The second instance was the municipal wildcats of September 1969 to win a lump-sum pay increase for the last quarter of their contract year. In this case an objective was won that surely would not have been achieved without the strikes and particularly the threat of further strikes. The imminence of the national election was undoubtedly one reason for the panicky response of many municipal officials. Whether the 300 DM per employee was worth the breach of the peace obligation and all the commotion may well be questioned. It seems more likely that the main objective of the ÖTV was to strengthen its prestige with its members.

The third instance was the compensatory time-off holiday by the doctors at the University of Bonn and elsewhere. Here the success resulted primarily from the clear indication of a serious, justifiable grievance in the tremendous amount of regular overtime work that was required by the circumstances.

By and large the municipalities and their bargaining agent, the VKA, appear to have been more influenced by work-interruption threats than the state and federal governments. The possibility of a temporary stoppage in government administrative operations does not seem to cause great public concern, although in principle it is the most serious threat to state sovereignty. A complete interruption of the federal postal or railway services or the state police services would doubtless cause much more concern. It is the possible cessation of municipal services, such as local transit, trash collection, and utilities, that causes the most immediate concern. Both union and government officials believe that the cities, especially the large ones, are more vulnerable to union pressure tactics than either the state or federal governments.

It is hard to understand why municipal officers are so fearful of strike action. They seem to think that public resentment would be directed toward them rather than toward the union. In the light of experience in other countries, one may doubt whether brief interruption to municipal services is as much of a catastrophe as most German city officials believe. Perhaps it is the slight extent of such experience that leads them to be so susceptible to strike threats.

The thought is bound to occur that their relative readiness to yield may have a political explanation, since the large cities tend to have a Social Democratic administration. There may be some validity to this hypothesis, but it seems impossible to make a conclusive case in support of it.

ARBITRATION

There is no arbitration of public-sector interest disputes in Germany. Accommodation in negotiating the terms of employment for government wage-earners and salaried employees has always been achieved by the parties themselves without resort even to mediation, let alone arbitration. No provision has been made by legislation or agreement for the use of third parties in the settlement of disputes of interest in the public area—and there appears to be no need for it.

For some years there has been occasional suggestion in the literature that there should be some form of third-party determination available to civil servants, in view of their lack of a right to strike. A strong, and probably a convincing, case can be made for such a procedure in most countries that prohibit public employee strikes. In Germany the need for such an arrangement is less obvious.

One reason why German civil servants have little need for arbitration or fact-finding is that their terms of employment are customarily adjusted in line with the terms applicable to public wage-earners and salaried employees, which latter terms are set by negotiation where the right to strike does exist. The result is that civil servants tend to get the benefits of the strike right of the other public employees without incurring the losses suffered by strikers. It is chiefly with regard to special problems of one or another particular group of civil servants that a pattern may be unavailable.

The other main reason why they have little need for the strike right or a strike substitute is the assurance of fair treatment that results from the phenomenally high proportion of sympathetic union members in the Bundestag and the state legislatures. The situation in the Bundestag is especially important since federal legislation can set the framework for state legislation on this subject. When 163 of the 518 Bundestag members are civil servants, when a clear majority of all the legislators are union members, and when many of them are prominent union officials, it is difficult to believe that civil servants in general will not get a fair deal without a strike substitute, even though some union officials complain that union members in parliament often do not follow the union line.

The meagerness of support for arbitration of interest disputes may be due not only to the absence of any demonstrable need but also to the unfortunate experience with this procedure during the period of the Weimar Republic. Under the tumultuous economic and political conditions of the middle 1920s, the use of poorly conceived arbitration procedures became the general rule, with unfortunate consequences for collective bargaining and mediation.[16] Although this unhappy experience resulted in large part from very special circumstances, memories of it may perhaps dampen any enthusiasm for a return to arbitration.

16. Frieda Wunderlich, *Labor under German Democracy: Arbitration 1918–1933*. New York: New School for Social Research, 1940.

·VI·

Prospective Changes in Public Employee Relations

THE period of 1969-70 has witnessed considerable change in public labor relations in the United States and several other countries. It might be expected that this would be less true of Germany, where a very high proportion of government employees has long been organized, where the status of civil servants has for decades been firmly established along traditional lines, and where the pattern of collective bargaining for public wage-earners and salaried employees has been fully developed for at least fifteen years. Such an expectation, however, would be erroneous, for the German system at this time is highly dynamic and is rapidly undergoing significant change in almost every aspect.

There is much discussion of the possible revision of almost all of the legislation in this area. Revision of the Federal Staff Representation Act and the corresponding laws in several of the states appears imminent. The Federal Civil Servant Pay Act may well be next in line for some basic changes, not counting the periodic modifications in its rates. Even the fundamental Federal Civil Servants Act seems likely to undergo significant revision within the next few years.

In the area of collective bargaining, all of the basic agreements governing public wage-earners or salaried employees have been opened for renegotiation, which takes place only infrequently. Such negotiations are quite separate from the annual renegotiation of pay rates and certain bonuses. Bargaining on the basic agreements is a slow process. It will probably be several years before the task is completed this time, but some of the resulting modifications may prove to be quite significant.

STAFF REPRESENTATION LAWS

Mention has been made in Chapter IV of some of the recent changes in the staff representation laws of several states, and of current efforts toward revision of the federal act. Each union of public employees has long had its list of desired changes, which is revised from time to time. The Social Democratic Party (SPD) drafted its own proposal for a revised law in 1968 and introduced it in the Bundestag in December of that year, too late in the session for serious consideration. It was assumed that the bill would be reintroduced the following autumn, but meanwhile the party's status shifted from that of minor to major coalition partner. The party, therefore, decided to await the introduction of a bill drafted by the Interior Ministry and supported by the cabinet. The timing of this action is not yet clear. Perhaps action on this measure will await revision of the Works Councils Act relating to private industry.

An analysis of the SPD bill gives some clues as to the possible directions of future change. Only the revisions that appear most significant can be mentioned here. Some of these involve the relationship of the unions to the staff representation system. The bill would permit submission of nominee lists by unions having members on the council. Such unions could send a representative to act in an advisory capacity at council meetings upon request by one fourth (rather than a majority) of the council members and at staff assemblies without invitation. Council members would be allowed to carry out union duties in the workplace.

Several major revisions concern council operations. Separate election of council members by the three groups of employees would in general be retained, but council decisions regarding members of only one group would be by the full council rather than the representatives of that group. A local council could invite a delegate of a district or central council to attend its meetings. Relief of council members from their regular occupational duties would be extended. The present general provision that they will be relieved to the extent necessary for the performance of their duties would be replaced by a requirement that one be entirely free if there are 300 employees in the unit, two if there are 500, three if there are 1,000, four if there are 2,000, etc. The council's right to information would also be increased. It would have the right to see not only documents necessary to the performance of its duties, but all those that were available to the administration in reaching a decision on its proposal. The present limitations on access to individual personnel files—available only to one member of the council's executive committee and only on approval of the employee—would be continued. Council members would receive compensatory time off with pay for all time spent outside of working hours on staff representation activities or on training for such activities.

The discussions in staff assemblies would no longer be limited to matters within the competence of the council, but might include any union, economic, or social policy matters related to the agency or its employees.

The participation rights of the councils would, of course, be considerably expanded. Final decision on matters subject to cooperation, on which agreement is not reached, would be made not by the district administrator but by the head of the agency, thus permitting one additional appeal. Nearly all matters now subject to cooperation would become subject to codetermination. Subject to cooperation would be all other—unspecified—social matters. The basis for objection to proposed staff actions would be unlimited, instead of narrowly limited. Protection against discharge would be strengthened. Dismissal without notice (i.e. for serious cause) would be allowed only after prior consultation with the council and, in the case of council members, only with approval of the council.

The DGB proposals for revision, as of August 1968, were very similar to those of the SPD. They differ chiefly in ways designed to strengthen the role of the unions or to give some special advantage to the larger unions. A few instances will serve to illustrate the general nature of the variations.

There is no provision for direct nomination by unions, since the DGB affiliates have no problem in obtaining as nominators for their lists the necessary 10 percent of the electorate. A council could invite the representative of one union to attend its meetings without including the other unions that have members on the council. If a fourth of the council members belonged to the same union, that union could send a representative to any meeting of that council without invitation. Instead of council members being elected normally in separate elections by the three employee groups, there would be a single election by the merged groups unless a majority of the eligible voters in one group voted to hold separate elections. A council's executive committee would no longer consist of a representative from each of the three groups, but only of the council's chairman and vice-chairman, so that usually one of the three groups would not be represented. Release of council members from occupational duties would be even more liberal than under the SPD bill. The number to be free of duty would not be specified according to the number of employees. Instead, the council would have the right of final decision as to the number to be released. The rights of the councils to participation in internal administration are very similar in the two bills.

The DBB revision proposals of 1968 and 1969, like those of the DGB, would extend the right of codetermination to nearly all social and staff actions and remove the limitations on the grounds for objection to proposed appointments, promotions, transfers, etc. Agency organizational matters would also become subject to codetermination. On the other hand, the DBB would strongly oppose any reduction of the minority-protection provisions, such as the termination of separate group elections and group voting within the councils or the allowing of attendance of one union at council meetings without similar permission to the other concerned unions.

UNION PARTICIPATION IN THE ENACTMENT PROCESS

Since the conditions of the civil servants are determined entirely by legislation, the right of the federations to participate in the drafting process is of great importance. The statement of this right in Section 94 of the Federal Civil Servants Act (p. 101) is general and imprecise. The elaboration by the Interior Minister on July 20, 1963, gave the legal provision much more specific meaning, but the federations seek some revisions. On this point the DGB and the DBB find themselves largely in accord. They emphasize that true participation requires an involvement from the very outset, even before a first draft has been achieved. They seek to extend and clarify the subject matter, in order to make sure that their participation shall apply not only to new legislation but also to new administrative regulations or ordinances that affect the social, economic, or professional status of the civil servants. When they spell out their position on a proposal that is nearing its final form, they want assurance that their views will not remain within the Interior Ministry but will be conveyed to the cabinet (if it has occasion to discuss the measure) and to the parliament (as an attachment to the government's bill). And finally, they would like to see it clearly enunciated that the parliament, as well as a ministry, has an obligation to consult them. They are reasonably well satisfied with the present practice of parliamentary committees in giving them a hearing on matters of interest, but would like assurance of participation in the formative stages on proposals that may originate in parliament rather than in the ministries.[1]

When it comes to long-range planning on revision of union participation in the enactment process, the two federations part company to some extent. The DGB advances a far-reaching proposal, which is adopted only in more general terms by the DBB. The DGB suggests[2] that civil service legislation should be divided into two categories of *Statusrecht* (basic provisions) and *Folgerecht* (derivative provisions). The former would include, for example, the nature of the basic pay claims of the civil servants, while the latter would cover the actual amount and forms of their pay. The former would be drafted and enacted substantially in the manner now used, with the minor revisions stated in the preceding paragraph. The latter, however, would be developed jointly by the Interior Ministry (with cabinet approval) and the federations, so that the bills

1. DGB, *Geschäftsbericht 1965–68*, pp. 616, 633–37; DBB, *Geschäftsbericht 1969*, pp. 24–25.
2. *Geschäftsbericht 1965–68*, p. 635.

presented to the parliament for its consideration would be in the form of agreements that had been reached between the government and the major unions.

This concept is a very interesting proposal of a compromise between collective bargaining and legislative enactment. If it were adopted, the procedure for determining the details of the periodic pay revisions of the civil servants would be very similar to the negotiation method now applicable to the pay changes for public wage-earners and salaried employees, except that the former would be subject to approval or revision by the Bundesrat and Bundestag. Under these circumstances revision of the agreed bill during enactment would be most unlikely. It may be assumed that agreement between the government and the two federations would normally be achieved, as is the case in negotiations concerning the other two employee groups. What might happen in case of a conceivable deadlock is not so clear, since the civil servants do not have the right to strike. It seems doubtful that the proposal would really benefit the unions and their civil servant members. To be sure, the bills submitted to the parliament might be somewhat more favorable, but the unions, by advance agreement, would in effect have surrendered their present important right to seek revisions during the enactment process. Under an alternative union proposal the agreements would not need parliamentary approval.

The **DBB** is somewhat more cautious and less specific in its voicing of a similar demand. It suggests that, in the absence of the right to strike, there is a need for a continuous negotiation structure that will enable the civil servant federations to deal on equal terms with the government and parliament. It urges that parliament should limit itself to setting the basic principles governing the allocation by the government of the financial resources it approves and should give the government greater negotiating leeway, especially in matters of pay and pensions.[3] With the **DBB** and **DGB** both working in somewhat the same direction, the next few years

3. Resolution, DBB Triennial Congress, Nov. 1969.

may witness some interesting experimentation in the procedures used for adjusting civil servant pay.

CIVIL SERVANT STATUS

As previously indicated, the status of the civil servant has been appreciably modified during the last two decades. It will probably be changed much more significantly within the next decade, if not much sooner. The development will first affect various details of the civil servant's position, but the end result may well be a fairly complete restructuring of the present three groups of government employees.

There is already considerable sentiment in both union and government circles for modification of the present career-level structure of the civil service to facilitate advancement to higher levels on the basis of experience and ability without the necessity of taking time off for formal education toward an advanced degree. This could be achieved by relaxing the present rigid educational, age, and length-of-service requirements for advancement and providing additional facilities for in-service training or training specifically for public service other than the present law curriculum. An alternative proposal favors the abolition of the separate career levels while retaining the several entrance points. After initial entrance, less emphasis would be placed on formal education and more on individual ability and achievement. The result might make little difference to the great majority of civil servants, but it would permit the more rapid advancement of those who demonstrate exceptional ability, without the need for granting a special exception in each case.

The granting of more civil service credit for nongovernment employment is frequently advocated on the grounds that it would encourage more frequent interchange between public and private employment.[4] It is true that government recruitment of mature individuals with valuable experience and special skills might be facilitated in this way. Some of those who advance

4. It appears that this may be done in 1971 by means of replacing the length-of-service increases in each pay group with an age supplement.

this proposal, however, emphasize that civil servants would be less reluctant to transfer temporarily to industrial employment. It is not at all obvious that this result would be beneficial to the government in many instances. Some who transferred might not return, and in any case industrial experience might prove to be of no more value than continuing governmental experience. There is probably a stronger case for granting credit to those entering the civil service than to those temporarily leaving it. At least that would be much more in line with American thinking, where the emphasis is placed on attracting persons in private employment for periods of government service rather than on encouraging civil servants to seek a period of employment elsewhere.

Any far-reaching changes in the career structure must probably await further development of the changes now taking place in the educational and administrative systems. Significant experiments are already under way with reference to reorganization of secondary education and the development of new specialized institutions of higher education, which will eventually require adjustment of career regulations. In the meantime there is the possibility of making many changes of the types just mentioned. Some have already been embodied in a Federal Career Ordinance of April 1970.

These changes in the operation of the civil service system should increase the attractiveness of the service to its more competent members. They should also somewhat reduce the degree of difference between civil servants and the other two types of government employees by basing rank and salary less on educational achievement and more on task and performance. Further reduction of the contrast in other ways is imminent. Current renegotiation of the basic master agreements governing public wage-earners and salaried employees will surely bring to these groups some new terms of employment that have heretofore been applicable only to civil servants. This will be merely a continuation of a trend that has been in process throughout the 1960s. It is the major aim of the negotiating unions, and they will surely be at least partially successful.

At the same time civil servants may be gaining some advantages that have as yet been applicable only to the other groups. The best illustration of this is the previously mentioned recent move toward payment of overtime to some civil servants who habitually work long hours. This leaves the denial of the strike right as a major distinction that the DGB, but not the DBB, is eager to eliminate. There is no present indication that the civil servant strike ban will be lifted in the foreseeable future. More likely is the gain of some compensatory advantage. This could conceivably take the form of the introduction of advisory arbitration. There has as yet been very little mention of this possibility, but the increasing use of arbitration for other purposes, such as in connection with the codetermination right of staff councils, may lead to greater interest in its applicability to this problem.

As the contrasts in the terms of employment of the three groups of government employees gradually diminish, the probability of an eventual restructuring of government employment increases. There is widespread agreement that the traditional view of the civil servant as a servant of the state rather than an employee is largely obsolete. It is also recognized that the sharp distinction between employees who are and who are not civil servants is often illogical and that the frequent use of both types on the same tasks creates difficult personnel problems. There is as yet, however, no crystallization of views as to the best method of obtaining a more rational structure. There is already some talk of the possible discontinuance of the civil servant status at some time in the distant future. At the close of World War II the American Occupation Forces sought to discourage the reestablishment of the civil service in its traditional form. The framers of the new constitution finally decided otherwise, but there are reports of some subsequent change of opinion. Any partial or complete termination of the civil servant category might conceivably take the form of integrating that group into the other two. An alternative less objectionable to the civil servants might be the merger of the three groups of public employees into a single new group. In August 1970 the Minister ("senator") of the Interior for West Berlin advocated such a merger into a new group to be known as *öffentliche Bedienstete*. Either of these steps would require, of course, a basic alteration of German labor law and public law concepts, which would not come easily and would surely face bitter opposition from the DBB.

A more generally acceptable development, in the opinion of this author, would be the gradual elimination of the lower career levels and pay groups of the civil service. These are the groups where the assignments have the least identity with the exercise of the state's sovereignty and the greatest incidence of duplication of tasks delegated to wage-earners and salaried employees. Assuming that it would be difficult, if not impossible, to withdraw civil service status from anyone already holding it, the lower grades could nevertheless gradually be phased out by ceasing to accept new entrants and using only wage-earners and salaried employees to fill future vacancies at those levels. Then with the passage of time the number of civil servants in the lower pay groups would gradually decline as a result of retirement, promotion to higher levels, and the voluntary acceptance of transfer to the status of wage-earner or salaried employee. Such voluntary transfer would be encouraged by the gradual improvement of pensions and other fringe benefits for the members of these two categories. It might also be motivated by a desire to escape the civil servant strike ban and the liability to discipline for off-the-job conduct.

An indication of the growing attention to this problem was the establishment in May 1969 of the Association for Administrative Reform as a research organization to study the possibilities of revising the structure of government employment to eliminate ultimately the distinctions between the three groups of employees. Most of its initial financial support came from some of the DGB unions. The extent of its future activities will depend upon the attraction of further resources.

A final indication of the increasing concern for revision of the status of the civil servant was the decision of the Bar Association to place the subject on the agenda for its congress (*Juristentag*) in September 1970. For this purpose it invited a presentation by Professor Werner Thieme on the subject of the desirability of reorganizing civil servant law in view of the changes in state and society.[5] Since Professor Thieme's treatise is the most comprehensive discussion that has appeared in this field and since it was presented under such prestigious sponsorship, it will presumably have a strong impact in accelerating and guiding the change that has thus far been only gradual. It is therefore appropriate to conclude this chapter with a brief summary of some of Thieme's principal conclusions.

He believes that there is a need for revision not only of civil servant legislation but also of Article 33, Sections 4 and 5, of the Constitution (see p. 95). The exercise of sovereign authority cannot be clearly distinguished from other functions of public employees; the concept of a public-law service relationship is cloudy; the obligations of a relationship of loyalty are not defined and in practice rest only on the civil servant and not equally on the public employer; and finally, the traditional principles of the professional civil service cannot forever be an adequate guide for up-to-date civil servant legislation.

After removal of these barriers to basic statutory revision, extensive changes in civil servant legislation would be possible. He proposes the merger of the four career levels, with entrance at any point appropriate to a person's education and training. He suggests relaxation of promotional limitations to reward performance and acquired abilities. For the higher ranks the present requirement of legal training might better be replaced by one of administrative training that is not now available in German universities. More credit might be given for relevant experience gained in the private sector. The present meaningless position titles should be replaced by function titles. Pay should be based on systematic job evaluation. Payment for overtime should be sanctioned. The location bonus should be discontinued, with corresponding increases in base pay and the children's bonus. The extent of the pay differentials in any

5. *Empfiehlt es sich, das Beamtenrecht unter Berücksichtigung der Wandlungen von Staat und Gesellschaft neu zu ordnen?* (Gutachten D zum 48. Deutschen Juristentag). Munich: Verlag C. H. Beck, 1970.

one pay group based on length of service should be reduced. Present limitations on political activity and moonlighting might well be relaxed. The eventual merging of the three types of public employees, or at least of the civil servants and the salaried employees, should be a long-range goal. Progress in this direction might best take the form of gradually achieving uniformity in the terms of employment for these two groups. With regard to the extent of the codetermination rights of staff councils, these might well be broadened for civil servants to match those now granted for salaried employees and wage-earners, with the major exception that it should not apply to appointments, promotions, or transfers to top positions. Union demands that codetermination rights be extended from social and personnel matters to economic matters, as in private industry, should be rejected because of the basic differences between the employer-employee relationship in the private and public sectors.

It will be noted that the recommendations thus far listed are not inconsistent with the views expressed in this present study. When it comes to the method of setting civil servant terms of employment, however, Thieme's views are in sharp contrast to those of the present author. Thieme accepts the DGB proposal to introduce a distinction between *Statusrecht* and *Folgerecht*, with the former to be determined by legislation and the latter, including pay rates and other economic matters, by negotiation (see above, pp. 196-97). He admits that there is no clear basis for a distinction between the proposed categories, but suggests that a few items be shifted to negotiation to begin with and that others be added from time to time as experience may indicate. He claims that pay in the public sector has been consistently less than in the private sector, but offers no supporting evidence. He states that parliament is obviously not in a position to raise civil servant remuneration to industrial levels against the pressure of numerous interests, that civil servants as representatives of the state are unpopular, and that they are always the first to suffer from budgetary stringency. All of these statements are highly questionable. The enacted pay raises of civil servants have apparently been commensurate with the negotiated raises of other public employees. Equally conclusive is the fact that the tendency of parliament is to raise rather than reduce the amount of pay increases recommended by the administration. No instance of a cut in the recommendation is known to this author, while there have been many instances of an upward revision. Thieme further expresses perhaps a naive faith that the pressure of public opinion would make it impossible for the unions ever to obtain unreasonable demands for the civil servants, even by resort to strikes. To be sure, the increases accepted by the unions for other public employees have not been unreasonable, but this in no way proves that unreasonable demands could not be achieved in the future. Thieme correctly states that the unions have a real impact on the drafting of civil servant legislation and that the government makes a genuine effort to satisfy union demands in such drafting, but he fails to draw the appropriate conclusion from these facts.

Thieme surprisingly makes no clear recommendation concerning the legalization of civil servant strikes. He shares the general view that they are now illegal and apparently favors continuation of the ban, since he says that civil servants through the use of work-by-regulation and other forms of slowdown have had as much success as other public employees who have the right to strike:

It will be interesting to watch the reaction to Professor Thieme's analysis and proposals, which will surely attract widespread attention. It seems probable that many of his recommendations will be adopted in whole or in part, but at this point in time we can be sure only that the German civil servant system is in the midst of a very dynamic period and that, in addition to the many recent changes that have been noted in this study, others of an even more basic character may be anticipated in the near future.

·VII·

Impact of
Public Employee Unionization

THE effects and consequences of unionization are at best difficult to judge, and they are doubly so where, as in Germany, unionism is a long-established and universal institution. Any attempt to contrast postunion and preunion conditions would carry us back to incomparable times, and a look at the nonunion interlude during the Nazi regime would scarcely be meaningful. Nor is it possible, as in some countries, to contrast union and nonunion sectors of public employment, since all government wage-earners and salaried employees (except those in a few small villages) are covered by collective agreement. Nevertheless, it is possible to make some tentative judgments regarding certain respects in which the unions appear to have had, or not to have had, a significant influence.

IMPACT ON SUPERVISORY ATTITUDES

An appraisal of supervisory attitudes was undertaken in connection with the earlier analysis of the actual operation of the staff representation system. It was found that supervisors in general did not object to the role of the staff councils in decisions on social and personnel matters, even though there are few, if any, other countries that grant such a far-reaching role to public employee representatives. It is safe to assume that their attitude toward the role of the unions in negotiating collective agreements on behalf of the wage-earners and salaried employees and in participating in the drafting of legislation on behalf of the civil servants is still more favorable. As a result of experience with public employee unionization during the Weimar Republic and even earlier, there was no reluctance to recognize public employee unions and deal with them when the Nazi regime came to an end in 1945. Such a development was taken as a matter of course, in sharp contrast to the strong opposition of many state and local agencies to union recognition even today in the United States. The fact that such unions in the past had demonstrated a fairly high degree of responsible behavior was doubtless a factor in the government's ready reacceptance of them.

The impact of unionization on supervisory attitudes is undoubtedly strengthened by the high degree of support that the public employees at all levels have given to' their unions. They too have accepted unionization as a matter of course, as shown by the high rate of union membership in the public service. Surprisingly, membership support is just as great or greater in the higher ranks of the service than in the lower ranks.

Unionization and its accompanying staff council system have caused all agency supervisors to give serious attention to the interests of the employees in reaching all decisions that affect them. As has been noted, an earnest effort is almost always made to reach an agreement with the unions and with the staff councils. The staff council must by law be accepted as a partner in the making of many types of administrative decisions, but we have noted that it is generally granted a role of somewhat greater influence than the law requires. It is commonly consulted before a decision is reached on both major and minor matters affecting the employees. And the unions are consulted in the drafting not only of legislation but also of ordinances and administrative regulations.

A brief comparison with earlier times will not help to prove causation, but will serve to underline the extent of the change in managerial attitudes. Unfortunately, the contrast can be based on little more than the author's general impressions. Prior to World War I the Germans were widely regarded as a highly disciplined people. The parade goose step of the German soldiers was thought to be symbolic of general regimentation. It can probably be said that there was an industrial as well as a military goose step. There had been a significant degree of unionization but very little union recognition and very few collective agreements. At the time of the author's first German research in 1928 and 1931, union membership was widespread, collective bargaining was the rule, and the Works Councils Act of 1920 had brought substantial rights to the employees in private industry. But Germany's experience with political and industrial democracy had been too brief to effect any great change in management attitudes toward the employee. Many supervisors were still inclined to be domineering, and subservience was generally expected from the employees. The Germans had a phrase for the traditional attitude that was dying so slowly—they called it the *Herr-im-Hause* (master-in-his-own-house) attitude. Most firms had extensive employee welfare programs, but the typical attitude was highly paternalistic.

Soon after World War II a decided change was evident. Employees and supervisors in the steel industry interviewed in 1952-53 testified to the transition. One worker stated: "What codetermination means to me is that now workers are regarded as men." And another said: "The greatest improvement over the earlier days is the disappearance of class deference. . . . In the old days I always had to stand and bow with my cap in hand. Nowadays there is more friendliness, regardless of differences in schooling and position. Supervisors talk things over more with their subordinates in the plant." This change of attitudes was perhaps brought about in part by union development and legislation regarding works councils and codetermination. It may have been partly a reaction to the industrial as well as political subjugation of the Nazi era. It seems probable, however, that this replacement of the traditional master-servant relationship by more cooperative attitudes was primarily the result of the recent common disaster, the urgent need to rebuild a prostrate industrial system, and management desire for union support in dealings with the occupation forces.

Whatever the causes of the change, there is no reason to believe that it was confined to private industry. It is probable that the old master-servant attitudes were as characteristic of public service as of the steel mills, but few traces of them can be found today. In fact, the change of attitude is not limited to the employment relationship, but has permeated the entire citizenry. Regimentation and discipline are no longer widely regarded as ends in themselves. The formerly ubiquitous *"ver-*

boten" signs are now nearly extinct. Walking on the grass in the parkways is seldom considered treason. And most citizens do not hesitate to disregard pedestrian traffic lights in the absence of traffic. In fact, Germany, like many other countries, seems recently to have moved far away from a disciplined society in its reluctance to prosecute violent protest demonstrators, its failure to protect academic freedom at some universities, and its inability to guarantee freedom of speech to unpopular campaigners.

IMPACT ON CIVIL SERVICE LEGISLATION

From what has been said it should be clear that the German public employee unions have a considerable influence on the drafting, enactment, and application of civil service legislation. On major bills they normally formulate their chief proposals, publicize them, and discuss them with high staff members in the Interior Ministry long before any drafting begins. When a tentative draft has been completed, or soon thereafter, copies are handed to them and they have the opportunity to comment on them orally and in writing in whatever detail they wish. Any subsequent major revisions during the preparation of the government's final draft bring a new chance to comment. While any threat of the use of force would be illegal, there is full opportunity for suasion and rational argument. It has also been noted that union influence is considerable during the enactment process in the parliament. After enactment, the administrative participation rights of the staff councils give the local employee representatives, and to some extent the unions, a strong role in checking on the administration and application of the laws.

While it is easy to see that the unions have a variety of opportunities to exert their influence, it is impossible to measure in any precise way the extent of their impact. For example, their efforts to influence the drafting of a bill in the Interior Ministry could conceivably fall on deaf ears. Though the degree of impact at this stage of the prelegislative process cannot be measured, it is obviously considerable. It is clear that the staff members of the ministry do seek to satisfy the unions to the extent that they feel able to do so consistently with the principles of sound administration. In fact they must make every reasonable effort toward agreement, because to do otherwise would increase the likelihood of revisions by the parliament. Similarly, the results of union lobbying activities directed toward the Bundesrat and the Bundestag, their committees, and their party caucuses cannot be actually measured, but again it is obvious that the impact is considerable in view of the close working relationships of the unions to one or another of the parties and the number of active union officials among the Bundestag members.

The extent of union influence will clearly vary from case to case depending on several factors. One determinant is the relative strength of the various political parties. The DBB has had for years a fairly close relationship with the FDP and the majority wing of the CDU/CSU and has been able to lobby very effectively when those parties were in power. There is a widespread belief that the DGB and DAG unions have gained in political effectiveness since the Social Democrats became the senior coalition party in the fall of 1969. Another determinant is the degree of uniformity in the objectives of the unions. The unions of Germany, like those of other democratic countries, have a greater legislative impact when they are in a position to present a united front. This tends to be the case with reference to the periodic pay-increase legislation for civil servants. Agreement on union objectives is less customary, however, in the public service than in private industry. The frequent disagreements result from the fact that in the public service unionization extends to higher administrative levels than in industry. The DBB, as the chief representative of the civil servants in the higher, if not the highest, ranks, necessarily takes a different stand than the DGB and DAG on some issues.

A brief survey of union activity in the enactment of a bill whose provisions were the subject of sharp union disagreements will show the complexity of the tactics used in such a case. The civil service measure that caused the greatest controversy was the Staff Representation Act, which created the staff council system.[1] Work on this bill covered a five-year period from 1950 to 1955. It will be recalled that the Codetermination Act, affecting the steel and mining industries, was adopted in May 1951, and the Works Councils Act, applying a modified form of codetermination to the rest of industry, was enacted in October 1952. The drafting of a companion bill covering public employment was begun in the Interior Ministry in late 1950, before either of the other measures had been enacted.

A first draft, somewhat revised after consultation with the state governments and with national associations of county and municipal governments, was submitted to the unions for comment and discussion in April 1951. The DGB and DAG at first refused to participate in conferences on the measure. They were still devoting their efforts to an unsuccessful attempt to extend coverage of the Works Councils Act to public employment and were therefore opposed to any separate bill. The DBB was at first also opposed to the coverage of the bill for a different reason. It preferred a measure that would apply only to civil servants rather than to all three groups of government employees. However, it soon recognized the futility of this objective and directed its best efforts toward obtaining an otherwise favorable bill, at a time when the DGB and DAG were still devoting all of their political efforts to the other two codetermination measures. The bill presented by the government to parliament in March 1952 was acceptable to the DBB in most respects. In reviewing the actions in the prelegislative stage, it may be noted that the total union impact at that point was less than is usually the case and that some of it came later in the stage than is customary. Another unusual feature is that there was no union initiative. The government began its drafting before the unions

1. An excellent study of the efforts of the various unions to influence the measure, illustrating the legislative impact of German interest groups, is to be found in Otto Stammer et al., Verbände und Gesetzgebung, Cologne: Westdeutscher Verlag, 1965 (Schriften des Instituts für Politische Wissenschaft, Vol. 18). An analysis of the impact of the DBB on this measure and on the salary demands of 1962 is contained in Schoonmaker, The Politics of the Deutscher Beamtenbund, chs. VI and VII.

were ready to consider the measure and without the normal union prodding.

The bill was considered first by the Bundesrat, which recommended several changes. Some of these were in line with the wishes of the DGB in that they would treat the staff council more as a single entity with less differentiation between the three groups of public employees. The bill then received its first reading in the Bundestag in September 1952, a month prior to the enactment of the Works Councils Act. Bundestag leaders decided that the press of other legislation already under consideration would make it impossible to complete action upon so controversial a measure prior to adjournment for the national elections in the following year. Consequently the bill received no serious committee consideration at that time.

It might have been expected that this bill, considering which there was such sharp disagreement between the political parties, would be a major issue in the 1953 election. It appears, however, that no particular attention was paid to it by the campaigners.[2] Nevertheless, the outcome of the election undoubtedly had an effect on the final form of the act. In the first election in 1949 the SPD had received about 29 percent of the votes, the CDU/CSU 31 percent, and the Bundestag had elected Adenauer as Chancellor by a one-vote margin; but this time (1953), with the SPD percentage virtually unchanged, the CDU/CSU percentage rose to 45 and Adenauer was reelected by a substantial majority. The government was therefore in a position to press strongly for the ultimate adoption of its draft, even though it encountered an early setback.

The bill was resubmitted to the new parliament and reconsidered by the Bundesrat. It had its first reading in the Bundestag in March 1954, and was referred to the Labor and Civil Service committees, which established a special joint subcommittee. A majority of the subcommittee members were receptive to the views of the DGB unions. These unions and the DAG focused their lobbying efforts on the subcommittee, where they met with very considerable success. The DBB, soon realizing that its views would not prevail at

2. Stammer, *Verbände und Gesetzgebung*, p. 216.

the committee level, directed its activities chiefly toward the leaders of the parliamentary party caucuses and the appropriate caucus committees ("work groups"). The government even went so far as to announce that the committee's revision of the bill was unacceptable. At the second reading of the bill in the Bundestag in March 1955 the debate was prolonged and bitter. Most of the major changes that had been recommended by the committee were overruled by margins of about fifty votes. Elements of compromise began to appear at this stage as all of the unions realized that they could not achieve their full goals and that they could continue to be influential only if they were flexible enough to adjust their aims. The many and varied tactics of the unions set forth in the Stammer and Schoonmaker books are not listed here, since they are necessarily similar to those used in matters of great concern by interest groups in other democratic countries.

The action during the third reading in June showed the results of extensive discussion in the party caucuses, in which the unions had played a considerable role. Since some who had voted for revisions during the second reading would now be voting against adoption of the total bill, support from nearly all members of the CDU/CSU would be needed for passage. The majority right wing of these parties made several concessions in order to obtain the support of its left wing, and the measure passed by a majority of 26 votes, which closely followed party lines. One of the most important of the final changes concerned the last step for resolving disagreement on issues subject to codetermination. The government bill had proposed a final decision by the appropriate minister. The committee had favored establishment of a permanent Federal Personnel Committee under the chairmanship of the president of the Federal Accounting Office as a permanent board of arbitration. The final decision adopted the CDU caucus proposal for *ad hoc* arbitration boards.

The conflict did not end at this point. The bill had to be sent back to the Bundesrat for concurrence. That house refused approval and referred the measure to conference committee with request for modification of sixteen sections. Union activity continued even at this stage, with the DAG making an especially vigorous effort to influence the committee in favor of the Bundestag version. Fifteen changes were made in this final stage, but they did not seriously modify the provisions that were of most concern to the unions.

This summary of the legislative action on the staff representation bill shows the variety of steps that may be involved in the enactment of a measure in the German parliament and the many stages at which the unions may seek to exert their influence. Since the Bundesrat consists of representatives of the state governments, the lobbying on a crucial matter such as this one takes place not only in Bonn but in all the state capitals. The state branches of the unions are therefore called upon to play a significant role. It will also be noted that the highly organized and well-staffed party caucuses play an important part in the legislative system and are therefore a major target of union tactics. Union access to the caucuses and committees is facilitated by the presence of a considerable number of union officials among the members of the Bundestag. As with lobbying everywhere, personal contacts may have a greater effect on legislation than the flood of press releases and official written communications.

Relations between the unions are also an important part of the total process. The DGB had the task of coordinating the action of its several unions in the public service area. This is usually accomplished on an informal basis, but in this case it established a "Small Commission" to assure unity of objectives, to plan strategy, and to develop arguments and supporting materials. The DGB and DAG were also able to form and maintain a united front on nearly all provisions of the bill except those dealing with minority protection, which were favored by the DAG and DBB. The DBB, on the other hand, found itself in disagreement with the DGB and DAG on a number of major provisions, which consequently became the most controversial items in the measure. Here there was little opportunity for interunion cooperation until it came to the final stage of desperate compromise. On the contrary, there was continual friction. At one early stage an effort to influence public opinion took the form of an open letter from the executive committee of the DGB to the chairman of the DBB, claiming that the latter was "attempting to downgrade the civil servants to second-class citizens."[3]

The importance of constant government contact and the lobbying function has led most of the unions whose national headquarters are elsewhere to establish branch offices in Bonn. The DGB, with headquarters in Düsseldorf, the ÖTV in Stuttgart, and the DAG in Hamburg all maintain a small staff in the capital city. The DBB, on the other hand, is the only major union that has the good fortune to have located its national offices in the recently merged cities of Bonn-Bad Godesberg.

IMPACT ON WAGE AND FRINGE BENEFIT LEVELS

The extent of union impact on the wage and salary levels of government employees cannot be determined or even estimated on the basis of the available data. An analysis of the overall situation tends to suggest that the impact has been minimal or at least has been less than the union impact in private industry. For example, the DBB has estimated that it would have required a 12 percent increase in the average pay of civil servants in 1963 and 19 percent in 1969 to bring them up to the increase in national income per economically active person since 1957. The existence of some lag is generally accepted, though there is disagreement as to its extent. There is no clear indication that public wage-earners and salaried employees have fared better than the civil servants.

An analysis of individual instances of public employee pay increases, on the other hand, suggests that there may have been a union influence. Union rejection of increase proposals has on some occasions led reluctant governments at the federal or state levels to raise their offers. There is, for example, no obvious reason to believe that the actual increase in 1970 would have been any higher than the original proposal in

3. Ibid., p. 71.

the absence of union pressure, even though it is conceivable that the government could have been holding something back for bargaining. It seems probable that there has been a union impact, but that it has been less than in the private sector. It is unlikely that the influence has been great enough to have caused any change in the allocation of the nation's resources or to have raised pay to the extent of reducing the volume of public employment.

IMPACT ON THE ELECTORAL AND POLITICAL PROCESS

While the unions in the public sector, as previously noted, have had a considerable influence on the legislative process and on the policies of political parties, they have not had a significant impact on the political or electoral process. As organizations, they have remained fairly true to their professed political neutrality. So far as is known, union funds are not contributed to political campaigns. The federal government apportions federal campaign funds among the parties in proportion to the number of votes they receive. There is no official endorsement of a particular party or particular candidate. With balloting on the basis of proportional representation, there is not very much possibility of favoring individual candidates or "splitting the ticket."

On the other hand, individual union members and officers have played prominent political roles to a much greater extent than in most other countries. Ten of the fifteen present federal ministers carry a union card and two of them are past presidents of DGB national unions. It has also been noted that a majority of the Bundestag members belong to a union and that quite a few of them are or have been union officials. It is believed that the picture is generally similar at the state and local levels, with the exception of the more rural areas.

No evidence has been found of any instance in which a matter of public labor relations was treated by the parties as a major campaign issue. Some of the parties have issued statements on public employment or civil service as a part of their platform, but these have been phrased in general terms without reference to specific issues and appear to have received little attention. There are, however, a few instances in which government action at the state or local level appears to have been influenced by the imminence of an election. The state of North Rhine-Westphalia in 1962 and again in 1970 enacted pay increases for civil servants in a spirit of urgency only a few days before statewide elections. The 1970 action appears to be illegal following a constitutional revision and the passage of federal restrictions in May 1969. It will not be surprising if the federal government challenges this state action in court, as it has already done in the case of an act of early 1970 by the state of Hesse to increase judicial salaries. The fact that North Rhine-Westphalia acted in apparent defiance of federal legislation is additional indication that the election may have been one of the motivating factors. Perhaps original sponsorship of the measure by the SPD was in the hope of gaining some credit even if the measure was defeated, and last-minute support from the CDU may have been due to a desire to offset such a result. On the other hand, strike action by some civil servants in the educational system was undoubtedly another motivating factor.

One other probable instance of government action being influenced by an impending election involved the municipal wildcats of September 1969. The eagerness of many cities to capitulate quickly to union demands for a 300 DM lump-sum payment across the board was due in part to their abhorrence of interruption of public services, but the immediacy of the federal election may have been a contributing factor.

Public labor relations matters are less likely to become a campaign issue in Germany than in some other countries. At the federal level such matters are sure to be outweighed in importance by other issues. It is only at the local level and occasionally at the state level that they may be of major concern to the voters. In Germany the municipalities and counties have very little "say" in labor relations, and decision-making at the state level is much controlled by the federal government.

These considerations lead to the general conclusion that the public sector unions have had little or no direct impact on the electoral or political process, though government action in a few instances may have been influenced by expectations that the action would influence the voting of some civil servants.

·VIII·

Conclusions

HAVING described both the structural organization and the actual operation of the German public employee relations system as thoroughly as possible within the time limits set for this study, it remains to draw such conclusions as may be of particular interest to the German or American reader. The German reader may seek an evaluation of his system, if he will pardon the temerity of a foreign appraiser. Since the material that would permit a comparison of the German system to those of other countries has not been presented here, it will be necessary to evaluate that system in and of itself. The American reader will perhaps be more interested in suggestions as to those aspects of the system that might well be kept in mind as the corresponding system in his own country develops through its present transitional stage.

EVALUATION OF THE GERMAN SYSTEM

In order to appraise the German system in and of itself as it functions in actual practice it is necessary to decide on the criteria to be used as a basis for judgment. We must ask, "What are the characteristics of an ideal system?" so that we can see in what ways the German system does or does not approach that ideal. Any attempt to construct a perfect model must necessarily involve a large measure of value judgment and a considerable element of incompleteness. Many readers may well dispute the appropriateness of some of our criteria. Those who approach the analysis with different values can readily make the necessary adjustments to reach their own conclusions. Agreement on the relative importance of the various criteria is inconceivable, but fortunately such agreement is quite unnecessary as long as we have no interest in trying to derive a numerical score for the system. Our criteria, while doubtless incomplete, are surely numerous enough to permit a comprehensive appraisal.

Our model is built around the framework of three very general characteristics of a public employee relations system, namely its equity or fairness to the employees, its efficiency, and its balance. Two miscellaneous considerations are added. As subheadings under these characteristics we list the sixteen criteria that are proposed as the basis for appraising the quality of the system. They are presented as questions so phrased that a highly affirmative answer will, in the author's opinion, indicate one aspect of the system that is very desirable or successful. While this model is designed in part to emphasize certain aspects of the German system, it should with slight modification be equally applicable to the appraisal of the public employee relations system of any country with a democratic form of government. Most of the criteria would be equally appropriate for evaluating an employee relations system in the private sector, while others are applicable only to the public sector. Questions in the first group involve matters of particular concern to the employees. Those in the second group are of special interest to the administrators and the employing public. But of course the whole evaluation can be approached only from the point of view of sound public policy and the public interest, recognizing that this interest includes a fair deal for the employees as well as efficient operation and a well-balanced system that infringes in no way on the concern of the total citizenry for the integrity and sovereignty of its government.

The complete list of the criteria that comprise our model is as follows:

Equity

Do the employees have a voice in their terms of employment?
Are pay levels reasonable as compared to the private sector?
Is the impact of tight budgets on pay levels held to a minimum?
Are the terms of employment uniform?
Are grievances settled fairly, promptly, cheaply?
Is there adequate job security?

Efficiency

Is there adequate incentive for high performance?

Is there adequate leeway for adjustment at the lower levels of government?

Is the time spent on negotiations held to a reasonable level?

Is the time devoted to employee relations within the agencies reasonable?

Are work stoppages and slowdowns held to a minimum?

Is the scope of negotiations confined to employee relations?

Balance

Is the bargaining power of the parties well balanced?

Are government and union negotiators equally sophisticated?

Other Considerations

Are the attitudes of the parties cooperative?

Is the system well adapted to the peculiarities of the public sector?

The nature of the German system with respect to each of these criteria will now be briefly reviewed in order to differentiate between its stronger and weaker aspects, as viewed from the perspective of the author's value judgments.

Do the employees have a voice in their terms of employment? It is suggested that in an ideal employee relations system the employees would have a significant voice in rule setting and rule enforcement if they so desire and that such a voice is obtainable only collectively through employee organization. Freedom of association is thus a first requisite. That is granted in the German constitution. A second requisite is the ready granting of union recognition and acceptance of the unions' role as a participant in negotiations or in legislative enactment. This is also universal in Germany in the sense that no government agency at any level anywhere in that country refuses to recognize a union. Almost every one of the more than 1,700,000 public wage-earners and salaried employees is covered by the terms of collective agreements. It has been noted, however, that negotiation is largely in the hands of the major affiliated unions, so that some of the independent unions are forced to have their bargaining conducted through officials of some major federated group. The German system thus tends to discourage the formation of independent unions.

The civil servants also have the right of union membership. Since their terms of employment are set by law rather than by agreement, they are the beneficiaries of an unusual legislative right to be fully consulted in the drafting of such laws and regulations. And we have seen that they also have a considerable influence in the legislative process.

Our estimate that roughly 75 percent of all public employees are union members indicates that these employees believe that they have a real voice through their unions. The high membership serves to strengthen the effectiveness of that voice. Clearly the German system closely approaches the ideal with respect to our first criterion.

Are pay levels reasonable as compared to the private sector? Opinions differ as to the appropriate relationship between earnings in the public and private sectors. There are those who believe that they should be higher in the public sector, with the government leading the way toward better remuneration and setting an example for private industry. There was perhaps more justification for that view a few decades ago than there is today. When unions were weak and their bargaining power was no match for that of the industrial employers, there was good reason for government to lead the way as a model employer. Today in most industrialized countries government can be a good employer without necessarily heading the procession. Some think that in a prolonged period of labor shortage and inflationary pressure, such as Germany has experienced during most of the past decade, the government should hold back on wage increases and hope that its example will lead private employers to do likewise. It seems unreasonable, however, to ask public employees to bear the main brunt of antiinflation policy in this way. Our criterion therefore implies the judgment that in a "good" public employee relations system in an industrialized nation the levels of pay and benefits would approximate those in private employment, both for the whole and for comparable groups.

Unfortunately, no data have been found that provide a definite answer to our question. We know the DBB claim that civil servants in late 1969 would have needed a 19 percent increase to give them an increase over 1957 equal to the rise in national income per economically active person during that period, but even if the claim is valid it relates only to relative gain rather than relative level. The government, however, has not argued that 1957 is not an appropriate base period. In fact, the Interior Ministry contracted in April 1970 with a private research firm for a study of the increase since 1957 in earnings of civil servants as compared with other occupational groups. Analysis is complicated by the difficulty of comparing total remuneration of civil servants with that of wage-earners and salaried employees. The DGB and DAG do not claim that their public wage-earners and salaried employees are less well paid than those in the private sector. In the annual negotiations they always try to insist that the public employees receive an increase equal to the typical increase for private employees in the past year, but there has been no talk of a lag or any need for a catch-up. A sound judgment with regard to the criterion of comparability to private sector pay must be deferred pending the results of the current contracted study mentioned above.

Is the impact of tight budgets on pay levels held to a minimum? In an ideal system, public employees would not be denied increases that were otherwise justified, just on the grounds of financial stringency. Denial on this basis is often unavoidable in the private sector, because some firms have only a limited control over their receipts, even though others may be in a position to raise prices when wages are increased. Governments also cannot hope to achieve the ideal implied in our criterion, but their taxing power does give them some flexibility in this regard. We have noted that German public negotiations are well timed with respect to budget formulation, that the federal and state governments are unusually flexible in adjusting the distribution of tax receipts, and that governments at the various levels aid each other financially in time of need to a remarkable extent. The conclusion is therefore warranted that in respect to this criterion the German system comes just about as close to the ideal as is humanly possible.

Are the terms of employment uniform? Another measure of the quality of a system is the extent to which comparable employees within the system receive similar remuneration. The concept of uniformity does not preclude the payment of certain supplements, such as geographical differentials. Nor does it preclude a desirable flexibility in relative pay levels of various groups to adjust to changes in the supply or demand. The uniformity in Germany is exceptionally high. Take, for instance, the single pay agreement for all county and municipal wage-earners and another similar one for the wage-earners of all the states and three nearly identical ones for the wage-earners of the federal railways, the postal service, and all other federal agencies. For the salaried employees the agreement structure is even more centralized, with the federal agencies and the states combined in one agreement. For the civil servants the state laws cover also the county and municipal employees, and the federal legislation largely controls the state laws (assuming that the federal government will be able to enforce its guide lines in spite of the recent challenges from Hesse and North Rhine-Westphalia). It has been noted, however, that the federal government believes there is growing diversity in civil servant remuneration and has proposed a constitutional revision to increase its control. Uniformity is greater in the public than the private sector for at least three reasons. In the latter there are different negotiating parties and separate agreements in each major industry. Second, most agreements are regional rather than national. And third, the pay scales constitute minima, which are supplemented to varying degrees by most employers, whereas in the public sector they are the rates actually paid. Lack of uniformity exists chiefly in the differences of terms of employment between the public wage-earners, salaried employees, and civil servants. These differences have been diminishing and further reduction appears imminent. Such differences may well be desirable in the case of the higher levels of the civil servants, but are particularly objectionable at the lower levels where similar work is often performed by more than one type of employee. These latter differences could be gradually eliminated by ceasing to appoint civil servants to positions that can be performed by wage-earners or salaried employees. The July 1970 agreement on a monthly wage for public wage-earners has practically eliminated the remaining differences in the pay of such employees at the federal, state, and local levels and has largely equalized their pay with that of comparable salaried employees. Uniformity in the terms of employment of comparable employees in the government area is not complete, but it approximates the ideal.

Are grievances settled fairly, promptly, cheaply? Grievance settlement within an agency is a function of the staff council. It has been noted that the councils have not only the right to challenge staff actions as being in violation of law or agreement, but they have the much greater rights to prior consultation on all but the most routine actions, to one-step appeal in case of disapproval of some types of actions, and to an equal voice in decision regarding certain others. Grievances that cannot be settled at any of the several administrative steps in the agency may be appealed to the disciplinary courts, the administrative courts, or the labor courts, depending on the nature of the claim and the type of employee involved. Although no data can be presented, it seems probable that settlement within the agency is usual and that appeal to the courts is far less frequent than in the private sector. Court settlement is reasonably rapid and inexpensive. The German public system clearly meets high standards as regards the criterion of grievance handling. Whether the additional rights of cooperation and codetermination make it a better system or not is a complex question, concerning which opinions will vary widely and sharply. This author's view is that these rights in their present federal form have worked very successfully in their German context, but that the desirability of their recent further extension in a few states is highly doubtful, except from the unions' point of view.

Is there adequate job security? Most civil servants have a high degree of job security. This is not true of the few who hold a revocable or a limited-time appointment, nor of the beginners who hold a probationary appointment. The vast majority of them, however, are on lifetime appointment which is normally attained at age 27. They will not be dismissed even for incompetence. On the other hand they, unlike other government employees, are subject to penalty for aggravated misconduct off the job, under regulations that many may well consider outmoded. Job security of public wage-earners and salaried employees is at least as great, and probably greater, than that of their counterparts in private employment. They appear to be entirely free from any threat of loss of job for political reasons. The patronage or spoils system is not practiced in Germany. Political considerations may have an influence on many appointments, and some reassignments, but apparently not on dismissals, except at the highest level. To assure that top officials are in accord with government policy, it is permissible that civil servants in the top pay groups B 9 to B 11 be placed in premature retirement subject to recall. Very little use is made of this possibility except in the case of the "state secretaries" or deputy ministers. Judging from newspaper accounts, it appears that the total number of employees so retired as a result of the change in the federal government in the autumn of 1969 was much less than fifty; and even this amount gave rise to considerable protest. All in all, the German system scores quite high on job security.

Is there adequate incentive for high performance? Turning now to criteria related to the efficiency of the system, the first one concerns the general level of staff performance. Here the question of incentive is of major significance. Incentive is related not so much to the operational aspects of the system—the rule-making process of negotiation and legislative enactment—as to its structure. Under conditions of high job security, regulations regarding promotion are a major determinant of incentive. In the case of wage-earners and salaried employees there seems to be adequate opportunity for promotion in recognition of experience, training, and good performance. There have been frequent complaints that the same is not true for civil servants. Some steps to remedy this situation were taken with the issuance of the Federal Career Ordinance of April 27, 1970.

It has been noted, however, that the amount of earnings depends not only on occupation and merit but also on other factors such as length of service, location, size of family, and, in the case of civil servants, especially on the amount of formal education. All public employees receive a length-of-service increase every two years until they reach the top of their group. Prior to October 1970 the maximum for wage-earners was five raises, so there was little overlap between the base pay of a long-service worker and a younger one in a higher pay group.[1] Salaried employees, however, receive in some cases as many as ten raises and civil servants as many as fourteen, so that the old-timers may well receive more than an employee who is as much as four grades higher. Financial recognition for length of service is certainly desirable within limits and contributes to the morale of those who do not warrant promotion, but there is some question as to whether it has been carried to the extent of reducing the motivation for high performance. There may also be some question about the children's bonus in this regard. In addition to this monthly bonus of 50 DM or 60 DM per child there is a similar supplement incorporated into the location bonus and a further incentive for large families in the provisions for employee capital savings. These bonuses continue to be increased from time to time, leading to the conclusion that the Germans have not yet become as concerned as Americans about the dangers of overpopulation, even though their density of population is tenfold higher.

The question of motivation is particularly serious in the case of the civil servants, since formal education is such a major factor in their salary determination and performance until now has been only a minor factor. The very high degree of job security must also have a negative influence. It would seem that performance must suffer to some extent

1. Under an agreement of July 10, 1970, the top of the range for each pay group will be raised each October 1, until in 1972 it will equal the top for comparable salaried employees. This will result in a substantial overlap between pay groups.

when reassignment and refusal to promote are the only penalties that can be invoked for unsatisfactory service. On the other hand, job security may improve the quality of the service by protection against improper influence. The German civil service has long been considered in other countries as a model of efficiency, but this efficiency appears to result more from the character of its personnel than from the incentives built into its structure.

Is there adequate leeway for adjustment at the lower levels of government? This criterion needs examination only in systems characterized by a high degree of centralization and uniformity. There is not much opportunity for a German municipality to raise its rates to draw employees from neighboring communities in a tight labor market or to reduce its rates to ease a tight budgetary situation, but that is all to the good. Some flexibility is desirable to assure equity in special situations and to maintain employee morale. That is obtained mostly by the process of slotting the actual jobs into the various pay groups. Special position bonuses are also permissible to a limited extent. So much has been said in this study regarding the uniformity of the German system that it is essential to emphasize at this point that a considerable and apparently adequate degree of flexibility remains.

Is the time spent on negotiations held to a reasonable level? This criterion and the next two concern the extent to which performance of the basic mission of government agencies is interrupted by the operation of the system. The first is perhaps less important than many of the others, but it deserves consideration because the German system is so outstanding in this respect. The centralization of bargaining and the considerable uniformity of terms of employment make possible a substantial saving in total negotiating time. We have seen that at the time of a major negotiation concerning the pay of nearly all public wage-earners and salaried employees, except those in the railway and postal services, as many as 300 persons may be present in the vicinity waiting to be consulted when the spokesmen recess for instructions, but this is clearly very much less of an involvement than would be necessary if each state, county, and municipality conducted its own bargaining. The participation of only four unions also contributes to simplification. The tendency to keep all occupations at the same relative position on the pay scale rather than competing against each other annually is another factor that makes for efficient negotiation. And finally, it normally takes only a very few days of meetings to achieve consensus on the pay agreements, even though the occasional renegotiation of the basic agreements may be spread out over a period of months.

Is the time devoted to employee relations within the agencies reasonable? Here we must consider the time spent by both agency and employee representatives in the operation of the staff council system. We know that the local councils normally meet weekly for a few hours, while the district and central councils tend toward monthly meetings. The council chairmen must devote considerable additional time to their function. In some cases they are relieved of all professional duty. Since the councils have the unusual right of prior consultation on a wide range of personnel actions, it must be assumed that a great deal of time is used for this purpose by government and employee representatives. It may well increase still further as legislative revisions expand the number of actions subject to cooperation and codetermination and as unions seek to extend the number of representatives excused from all other duties. Thus the amount of time devoted to employee relations within the agencies is relatively large and growing larger. No evidence was found that any Germans consider the present amount unreasonable.

Are work stoppages and slowdowns held to a minimum? This criterion probably involves more of a value judgment than any other, for views differ widely as to the appropriateness of strike action in the public sector. This author believes that a total prohibition is desirable provided some substitute procedure such as advisory arbitration is made available. He is not impressed by the argument that the prohibition would sometimes be violated. If we enacted only laws that could be completely enforced, our statute books would be bare. It may also be noted that some countries, like Germany, have made little recent effort to enforce their strike bans and that such efforts as have been made in other countries often involve the penalty of brief imprisonment rather than the probably more effective one of a fine on the individual or the organization. Nor is he impressed by the argument that some public positions are not essential, at least for a limited period of time. The fact remains that many are essential at all times and many others cannot long be dispensed with. Yet any attempt at legislative demarcation can scarcely be successful, and the alternative of asking the courts to judge in each case the essentiality of the function or how long it may cease before it becomes essential is to place on the courts a tremendous and unreasonable burden to be performed by judges whose views on the problem may differ as widely as those of other citizens and who cannot be given an adequate set of guidelines. Since it is generally agreed that many governmental functions are essential, it seems better to apply the strike ban to all public employees rather than to attempt to make in each case a distinction which, though perhaps valid in principle, is indeterminable in practice. Coverage of the less essential functions is not unreasonable so long as an alternative procedure is made available. The basic justification for a general prohibition of strikes and related actions in the public service rests not on the essentiality of many of the services but on the fundamental need to safeguard the orderly process of democratic government. Attempts to coerce rather than persuade government officials or legislative bodies is incompatible with our concept of democracy.

What is important here is not the author's views, but a summary of the German experience. After the railway strike of 1922, the instigators, but not the mere participants, were penalized effectively. The various courts involved in those cases all agreed that the traditional concept of the civil servant precluded the right to strike, even in the absence of specific legislative provision. Except for slowdowns by air traffic controllers and some postal and railway employees, there was no significant work interruption by civil servants from that time until a few instances in early 1970. On the other hand, public wage-earners and salaried employees do have the right to strike in case of deadlocked negotiations. This right has seldom been exercised, but there appears to be a recent trend toward more frequent interruptions. Those at the municipal level in September 1969 and some others at the state level in 1970 occurred even during the life of the agreement. German experience does not indicate that a strike ban is unenforceable, since no attempt at enforcement has recently been made. However, many of the strikes, including partial interruptions, have thus far been unsuccessful. The prohibition concerning civil servants tends to assure continuity of governmental administration, but it is the threat of strike by wage-earners in the municipal services that is most feared by government officials. In summary, the German system as it operated up to 1969 stood exceptionally high on the criterion of continuity of operation. Since then the record is weaker as a result of illegal strike actions and the failure of government to penalize them. The system itself falls short of our model in permitting strikes of public wage-earners and salaried employees.

Is the scope of negotiations confined to employee relations? The chief issue here is whether the interest of the public in maintaining control over decision-making in matters of governmental policy is threatened in the actual operation of the system. For government agencies decisions on policy regarding the mission of the agency (but not its personnel policies) belong in the same category as matters that are considered as management prerogatives in private industry. As yet there are no signs of any attempt to subject to union negotiation questions of agency policy outside the personnel and employee relations areas. Collective agreements deal only with matters that are clearly related to the terms of employment, and there has been no obvious attempt to extend them beyond this limit. Some unions, especially in the educational field and more recently in the public safety field, have presented demands involving governmental policy concerning the operation of the agency, but there has been no suggestion that such issues be incorporated in collective agreements. There would seem to be no logical basis for objecting to unions presenting such demands just as might be done by any other citizens or interest groups. In fact, agency employees and their organizations may well be better qualified than most others to make sound policy suggestions. It is only when public employees attempt to dictate public policy by resort to force, such as the strike or any of its lesser variations, that the public interest is endangered. Unfortunately, there have been a few instances of this in the last two years. Such cases may be regarded and condemned as political strikes, though the borderline between that and misuse of bargaining power is hard to draw. Where there is a resort to force, it would be a mistake to condone it on the grounds that it takes place outside the negotiating procedure, for it makes little difference whether the forced change of policy is incorporated in an agreement or a unilateral agency announcement. We conclude that the public interest has until recently been well protected with reference to the scope of bargaining, but that it is now subject to serious threat in this respect.

Is the bargaining power of the parties well balanced? It is difficult to justify the use of collective bargaining as a means of determining equitable and economically desirable terms of employment unless there is approximate equality in the bargaining power of the parties over a period of time. If either side is able consistantly to dictate the terms of the settlement, the results cannot be justified. There is no method for precise measurement of relative bargaining power. One can look only to the negotiation process and to the results of that process over a period of time. From our study of the conduct of bargaining, it is evident that the unions are in a reasonably strong position, but are not able to dictate the outcome. Also our analysis of the equity of the system tends to indicate approximate equality of bargaining power. Perhaps the most that can be said in this imprecise area is that there is no sign as yet of any serious imbalance.

In countries where negotiations are less centralized it would be impossible to give just a single answer to our question. There might be imbalance in either direction in some situations and not in others. In Germany a single answer is appropriate. To be sure, the employees appear to have somewhat more bargaining power at the local than at the state and federal levels, but with a uniformity of outcome the influence of any one group of public employees tends to redound to the benefit of all—or perhaps it would be more accurate to suggest that there is in practice a sort of averaging of the influence of the various groups.

With reference to the civil servants also there appears to be a good balance of influences. The union influence is not exactly one of bargaining power, but we have seen that it is considerably more than just lobbying power.

Are government and union negotiators equally sophisticated? With most of the negotiating centered in the hands of relatively few persons on both sides and with those few engaged in fairly continuous bargaining on one agreement or another, it is clear that the parties have a wide choice in selecting their spokesman and that those selected get lots of experience. It may also be observed that there tends to be a high degree of continuity rather than frequent change in the identity of the persons selected. Under these conditions, bargaining is inevitably in the hands of old pros. The situation that can arise in countries with highly fragmented negotiations where bargaining may be an almost constant experience for the union spokesman but just a once-a-year experience for the representative of the government agency cannot occur in Germany. Some readers may think this criterion to be of very minor significance, but consideration of possible widespread ramifications of mistakes that may be made by the amateur or novice, especially in an immature system, shows that it should not be undervalued.

Are the attitudes of the parties cooperative? The attitude of government administrators was discussed in Chapter VII. Less has been said about the attitudes of union officials. In reviewing the decade of the 1960s with regard to union demands and tactics, it appears that union leaders in the public sector have generally been aggressive but not hostile. Like their counterparts on the government side they have usually adopted a problem-solving approach and appear to have been motivated by a desire for accommodation. As a result of the tendency toward the attitudes of each party tending to pull those of the other party in their direction, the fact that the typical attitudes of both parties lie at about the same point on the hostility-collusion continuum tends to make the attitudinal relationship a stable one in this case.

We conclude that the dominant attitudes of both parties may best be described as cooperative. Some observers believe that German negotiations often contain even an element of collusion. This study could not probe deeply enough to permit evaluation of this view. The author did not detect any indication of collusion, except in one instance. This involved the all-night negotiations with the VKA on September 24-25, 1969, on the union demand for a flat monthly bonus of 100 DM at the time of the brief wave of municipal strikes. The number of telegrams received by VKA officers from municipal officials urging that union demands be granted in full, if necessary, to obtain an immediate settlement certainly justifies a suspicion that many mayors or city councils were not taking an appropriate adversary position. With regard to the regular negotiations, any appearance of collusion may belie the reality. It is true that much conferring between the parties takes place outside the formal bargaining sessions and that each party when it enters a formal session has a good idea of the position that will initially be taken by the other party. But this does not indicate collusion. Real negotiation can take place in the informal as well as the formal meetings. The amount of consultation that takes place within the government and within the unions between sessions and the duration of many of those sessions tends to indicate an absence of collusion. For example, during the pay negotiations of January 1970 the Interior Minister gave the ÖTV President enough indication of the government's coming offer to induce the latter to cancel announced plans for a strike vote, so both parties knew the approximate terms on which agreement would surely be reached at the next session. Yet it still took the parties thirteen hours of negotiation in the formal meeting to work out the details to their mutual satisfaction.

There are some recent signs of increasing hostility on the labor side. This refers not just to some rise in militancy but to the occasional refusal of some union leaders to abide by the rules of the game. It seems strange that most of these signs should have appeared during the first year of the dominance of the SPD in the federal government and particularly in those states where that same party is in control. An increasingly cordial union-government relationship might well have been anticipated, at least in the short run. An explanation of this anomaly must await further perspective.

Is the system well adapted to the peculiarities of the public sector? The purpose of this final criterion is to call attention to the fact that, as pointed out by John Dunlop,[2] an employee relations system that works well in a country's private sector is not necessarily appropriate for its public sector. As distinctions between the two sectors that are significant for employee relations, Dunlop mentions that the government agency confronts not a market but a budget authorized by elected representatives, that many of the terms of employment are mandated or prescribed by authorities outside the agency, and that strike action may be prohibited. (The last of these considerations appears to be a difference not so much in the characteristics of the sectors as in the systems themselves, resulting from more basic public sector characteristics, such as the essentiality of much of the work, the necessity of assuring the continuity and integrity of democratic government, and the consideration that action hostile to a democratically controlled agency is action against the democratic form of government and the expressed will of the people.) Another environmental difference (i.e. difference in the relevant social institutions that form the environment in which the system operates) is that the agencies are operating for public service rather than for private profit.

Some of the relevant differences between the two sectors are brought out by Professor Thieme in explaining why the

2. In Gerald Somers (ed.), *Essays in Industrial Relations Theory.* Ames: Iowa State University Press, 1969, pp. 28–32.

scope of codetermination should not be the same in both areas:[3]

In private industry the two factors of production, labor and capital, work together to create the product of the enterprise. This fact justifies granting to both factors an influence on the regulations of the enterprise. This raises the questions of democratization and the limitation of power. In the case of the state the questions are basically different. Here labor faces not private capital but governmental authority that is democratically legitimized and constitutionally limited in its powers. The products produced by the administration serve to obtain benefits not for capitalists but for the general public. . . . It is appropriate to give the employee in a private plant an influence on the decisions of the enterprise, since he shares the many risks of economic decisions. His fate is linked with that of the plant and is largely dependent on its prosperity.

In contrast, the influence of civil servant representatives on basic decisions means an influence on democratic administration, i.e. a curtailment of the influence of the parliament and of the government that is responsible to the parliament. . . . Thus codetermination in the public service can never be characterized as "administrative democracy" in the same sense that many like to characterize codetermination in industry as "industrial democracy."

One aspect of the adaptation of the German system to the environmental peculiarities of the public system is its provision for a special type of employee under public law. Though the German concept of the civil servant seems outmoded in some respects and is of doubtful appropriateness for the lower levels of employment, the system is sound in its provisions for a special type of employment at the higher levels, with a strike prohibition, with terms of employment set by legislation rather than negotiation, and with additional job security. The German system also shows adaptation in that its staff council

3. *Empfiehlt es sich, das Beamtenrecht unter Berücksichtigung der Wandlungen von Staat und Gesellschaft neu zu ordnen?* Munich: Verlag C. H. Beck, 1970, p. D57.

system is different from the works council system. Some variation is well justified because of the complete difference in the motivation of and control over the administrators in the two sectors. Some unions argue for certain changes in the staff council system partly on the grounds that these would make it more similar to the works council system. Some revisions may be desirable, but the argument that this would be desirable just because it would increase the similarity of the public to the private system is untenable. In general, the German system shows that the persons responsible for its structuring were well aware of the special environment of the public sector.

The foregoing evaluation of the German public employee relations system indicates that it merits its high international reputation. To be sure, it is still capable of improvement in some respects. Some revision in both the nature and the scope of civil service status appears desirable and is presently under consideration. Also, it seems impossible at present to prove that pay plus benefits in the public sector are equal to those for similar work in the private area. The aspects of the system that relate to incentive and motivation toward high performance can be and are being improved. With respect to most of the other criteria, the German system must be rated very high. Indeed, on some aspects, such as minimizing the impact of budgetary limitations, the efficiency of the negotiation system, the balance of bargaining power, the attitudes of the principal parties, and adaptation to the peculiarities of the public sector, the German system approximates the standards of our ideal model. A review of probable revisions of the system in the near future shows some that will surely bring further improvement and others that may result in injury. But even with some injury, the system should remain for the foreseeable future strong and viable and should continue to operate very successfully within the total German context.

SIGNIFICANCE FOR THE UNITED STATES

Every discussion of the applicability of the experience of one country to another begins with the caveat that the organization and procedures developed in one nation for social problem-solving cannot appropriately be transferred to a different institutional environment. This time-honored tradition will not be violated here. It is hoped that enough has been said about the history of German public employee relations and the special characteristics of their political and economic background to make clear that these differ in many respects from conditions in the United States, and that therefore some aspects of the German system that operate very successfully in their own context might not be appropriate or desirable in our setting.

This caveat, however, is often overemphasized. The people of any nation tend to be so absorbed in their own institutional development that they fail to take maximum advantage of the experience of others. The possibility of such benefit is especially great in the case of immature social systems. We expect countries with less developed economies to look to us and other countries for pointers. In the area of public employee relations, however, we are one of the relatively under-developed countries. Our system is in a stage of rapid transition, and we cannot afford the luxury of ignoring the experience of other countries, especially one like Germany, which is in many respects somewhat similar to our own. We can reasonably expect to get some good pointers from them, even though we must check carefully on the applicability of their methods to our problems.

For example, one aspect of the German system of public employee relations that has little significance for us is their staff council structure and its rights of cooperation and codetermination. That subsystem is the logical extension of a half-century experience in development of a works council structure, which results in part from their frequent lack of a separate union entity at the plant level and is thus something of a substitute for our union locals. In addition, their rights of cooperation and codetermination are quite out of line with our conception of the role and function of local employee representation. From our point of view their procedures result in some inefficiency and the waste of considerable time of administrators and employees in discussion of routine individual personnel actions. What we do gain from this aspect of the German system is a verification of the long-established maxim of personnel administration that much misunderstanding and dissatisfaction can be avoided by advance consultation.

On the other hand, there is much to be learned from other aspects of the German system. The extent of the possible usefulness of their experience cannot be fully probed without a detailed exposition of our own system and its setting, which is not practicable in this study. Instead, we shall mention some of our problem areas that are currently the subject of extensive debate and suggest certain respects in which German experience may provide guidance. It must be emphasized that benefit may be gained by considering some aspect of a system without necessarily adopting in whole that particular aspect. In many cases it may be preferable to take first a few steps in a particular direction than to go the whole way.

Union Recognition. Many students of the American system are saying that it is no longer a question of whether public employee unions shall or shall not be recognized, because it is clear that unionization has now at last come to the public sector as it did to the mass production industries in the 1930s. Yet at this writing there are still many agencies at the local and even state levels that deny union recognition regardless of the wishes of the employees. German experience shows how much more simple it is, how many disputes are avoided, and how much employee dissatisfaction is reduced when union recognition is universal or at least is readily granted upon majority request.

Union membership for supervisors. There is much discussion as to where the line should be drawn in various agencies between positions whose incumbents are or are not eligible for union membership. The question of possible conflict of interest is of major concern. German experience indicates that this whole question is perhaps somewhat less important than we think. The German unions draw a rather tight line in the private sector, much as we do, but no line is drawn in the public sector. It may be assumed that nearly all employees with supervisory functions have civil servant status. Some of the unions appeal particularly to one or another of the three types of public employees, but there is no clear-cut demarcation. The DBB membership consists of about 90 percent civil servants and 10 percent salaried employees. For the DAG public employees, the percentages are reversed. Over half of the ÖTV members in government employment are wage-earners, but more than 10 percent are civil servants. In the railway and postal services there is even less union focus on any one type. A high proportion of all three types of the employees within their respective jurisdictions are enrolled in the GdED and the DPG.

When these last two unions and the ÖTV and DAG negotiate on behalf of the federal salaried employees, for example, they are presumably not unmindful of the fact that their membership also includes civil servants and, usually, wage-earners. Some of the government negotiators may be union members, but not those who bear responsibility for the final decisions. When it comes to drafting civil servant legislation, the staff members performing this function are themselves civil servants and perhaps members of the DBB, which has a consultative role in the drafting. There is no indication that supervisors' union membership has affected the integrity of negotiations or that either the government or the unions object to this situation. Nor has any indication been found in the German experience that this condition prejudices day-to-day employee relations at the local level. It appears that supervisors normally consider that they have a responsible job to do and that they perform it conscientiously regardless of union membership and without any evidence of a conflict of interest. The only exception to this generalization arises perhaps in the special situation where the head of an agency has been a prominent union official. The German practice largely resolves the perplexing question of how to provide for representation of the interests of supervisory personnel when they are excluded from union membership.

On the other hand, German experience concerning the organization of supervisors is not completely applicable to the American setting, because of other differences in the two systems. Where negotiations are so centralized, the government is represented at the bargaining table by officials at the highest levels, so that it is highly improbable that any who are responsible for final decisions are union members. Another difference is the absence of union membership meetings. Thus there is no danger that membership in the same union might result in undue influence being exerted by supervisors on the rank and file or vice versa, as could occur at local union meetings in the United States.

In view of these differences, German experience probably provides little guidance on this American problem beyond an indication that at least lower supervisory ranks may safely be allowed membership in the same union.

Size and scope of the bargaining unit. The area of the bargaining unit is one of the most important aspects of a country's public employee relations system. In this respect Germany and the United States are at opposite poles. Germany's units are about as large as could be envisioned, whereas it is almost impossible to conceive of a system where the units would be more fragmented than in ours. The high degree of centralization of bargaining in Germany clearly has some major advantages. It is highly efficient with respect to the time involved, whereas ours, in a nation that prides itself on efficiency, is the extreme of inefficiency. It provides highly sophisticated negotiators, whereas our local school board members are not chosen for their bargaining expertise, and the vast army of union negotiators required by our system must necessarily include many who are less qualified than the best. It results in a high degree of uniformity in the terms of employment of comparable employees and a fairly stable relationship between different groups, with the consequent gain of greater equity to all public workers. The German system does not indicate that we should go to its extent in expansion of the bargaining unit and centralization of negotiations, but it very strongly suggests that we would have much to gain by moving a considerable distance in that direction.

Arvid Anderson, speaking to the U. S. Conference of Mayors in Denver on June 14, 1970, said: "One effect [of collective bargaining in the public service] could be to speed the consolidation of local government units." That is undoubtedly correct, but the German system proves that it is not necessary to merge government units in order to obtain centralized bargaining. What is to prevent, for example, joint negotiations on behalf of teachers and the local school boards of one county or even one state, if the parties recognize the advantages to be gained from such a change? Or to prevent a city from negotiating jointly for most or all of its employees rather than separately for each of several groups? What does prevent this at present is chiefly the habits of thought of government administrators and union leaders plus the practice of regulatory agencies of establishing mini-units and designating only a single local union as the bargaining agent. The single-union designation is not too serious an obstacle, since we are fortunate in having in the public sector at least two major unions whose membership includes a wide variety of employees at the federal or lower levels. The German experience shows that, even when two different unions are involved, it is entirely feasible to conduct joint negotiations. The designation of an exclusive bargaining agent is a firmly established part of the American system, but it need not prevent the parties from subsequently broadening the number of participants and the size of the unit. Indeed, some unions in our private sector have already begun moving in this direction, most notably in the electrical appliance industry. We already have a considerable tradition in our private area of negotiation with industrial unions, and we have some industrial unions in our public sector. Why then do we persist in establishing public bargaining units on a craft basis? What is needed as a first step is an extensive merging of the bargaining units under any one employing agency. The original designation of small units is probably unavoidable at our youthful stage of growing unionization, but it need not preclude the parties from a consolidation of units as union recognition spreads. A second step toward a more rational structure would be a move toward multiagency negotiation by administrators and union officials who are willing to use some imagination and inventiveness. Negotiation on such a broadened base need not cover all the issues. German experience indicates the possibility that centralized negotiation may leave some matters for local determination just as our company-wide bargaining normally leaves some issues for settlement at the plant level.

The obligation to meet and confer. We see and hear much discussion of the proposal for legislative requirement that public administrators meet and confer with unions as an alternative to negotiation. Our analysis of the German system suggests that, whether or not such a requirement is applied to the bargaining relationship, it might well be adopted with reference to the drafting of all civil service legislation at the federal and state levels. A great deal of such consultation takes place at present. Perhaps it would be well to make it mandatory. The meet-and-confer procedure might also be applied to policy matters concerning the agency's mission, which are not considered appropriate subjects for collective bargaining.

Differentiation of the right to strike. As has been mentioned, this author believes that total or partial work interruption should be prohibited throughout the public sector. Those who advocate only a partial ban usually suggest differentiation on the basis of essentiality. Examination of the German system suggests that, if strikes are to be permitted in some cases and not in others, it might be more practicable to distinguish the two areas on the clear and precise basis of level of employment rather than the difficult and vague basis of essentiality. If we must experiment with distinction based on essentiality, at least that should be supplemented by a ban applicable to the higher levels throughout the public service in order to give better assurance of the continuity of governmental administration.

Mandating. There is currently much debate on the extent to which the higher levels of government should mandate the terms of employment and other aspects of employee relations for agencies at the lower levels. It has been shown that in Germany mandating is practiced very extensively in the area of civil service legislation. State legislation invariably sets all of the terms of employment of civil servants at the county and municipal levels. And since the constitutional change of 1969 the federal parliament has extensive control over the pay levels as well as the other terms enacted by the states. At this point one question of institutional environment must be considered. The relationship between the state and local governments is somewhat different in the two countries, and this is even more the case in the federal-state relationship, but the differences do not appear to make the German experience with mandating inapplicable to the American scene. We already follow this practice at both the federal-state and state-local levels to a very limited degree, and there appears to be no constitutional barrier to extending the degree if we so desire. The German experience with mandating suggests that we might wisely move much further in this direction to obtain a higher degree of uniformity and equity. This is not to suggest that matters that might be determined by negotiation at the lower level be settled instead by legislation at a higher level. Rather it proposes that terms of employment, whether appropriately determined locally by legislation or by negotiation, might preferably be determined by the same process at a higher and broader level.

Revenue sharing. If we do extend our practice of mandating, it may become increasingly necessary to give careful consideration to the German method of flexibility in revenue sharing among the various levels of government. It has been noted that the German fiscal system is characterized by a remarkable degree of such flexibility. Perhaps we should consider adopting some of their practices for aiding hard-pressed governmental units, quite aside from any question of mandating, but we will leave that question to the political scientists. It seems clear, however, that a desirable extension of mandating would necessitate some adaptation of our fiscal practices. German methodology reveals many such possibilities.

Patronage. The practice of the spoils system is a uniquely prominent aspect of the American public employee relations system that seriously jeopardizes the job security of a large portion of our public employees. It was noted that this practice, as applied to dismissals, is unknown in Germany. It is ironic that, whereas American workers have much greater job security than their German counterparts in the private sector, the opposite should be true for many in the public area. Americans can scarcely dispute the German view that our patronage system is a barbaric remnant from frontier days.

Arbitration. Fortunately we are beginning to have considerable experience of our own to shed some realistic light on our long-debated question as to whether arbitration of disputes of interest may undermine the will of the parties to reach agreement through negotiation. As stated, the German system has no arbitration of this type. It does, however, include provision at the federal level and in some states for arbitration as the final step in their codetermination system. We have noted with considerable surprise that almost no use is made of this final step in their procedure because of the strong preference of both parties for working out their own settlements. It may be that their reluctance to arbitrate is due in part to their unfamiliarity with this method in contrast to its widespread use here. If this difference in institutional environment does not entirely invalidate the applicability of German experience, we could conclude that, at least in the case of grievances, providing for the use of arbitration need not necessarily lead to its abuse.

In view of the fact that we have so many serious problems during this dynamic and transitional period in the development of our public employee relations system, it is fortunate that we can obtain many helpful insights on possible solutions from the experience of Germany and other countries if we will but put aside a natural tendency to rely on introspective analysis, broaden our horizons, and escape from the rut of traditional views, including the view that the employee relations system in a nation's private sector is necessarily appropriate for its public sector.

Bibliography

BOOKS AND PAMPHLETS

Blum, Albert A. *Teacher Unions and Associations: A Comparative Study.* Urbana: University of Illinois Press, 1969. (Chapter 4 on "West Germany" by Wolf D. Fuhrig.)

Blumenthal, W. Michael. *Codetermination in the German Steel Industry.* Princeton: Industrial Relations Section, 1956.

Böttcher, Reinhard. *Die Politische Treupflicht der Beamten und Soldaten und die Grundrechte der Kommunikation.* Berlin: Duncker und Humbolt, 1967.

Bourier, Karl. *Disziplinarrecht.* Regensburg-Munich: Valhalle und Praetoria Verlag, 1964.

Däubler, Wolfgang. *Der Streik im öffentlichen Dienst.* Tübingen: J. C. B. Mohr, 1970.

Ellwein, Thomas *et al. Mitbestimmung im öffentlichen Dienst.* Bonn-Bad Godesberg: DBB, 1969.

Fitting, Karl, Hermann Heyer and Uwe Lorenzen. *Personalvertretungsgesetz: Kommentar.* (3rd ed.) Hamburg: R. v. Decker's Verlag, 1964.

Fürst, W. *Beamtenrecht.* (Division II, Vol. 30 in the series: Schaeffers Grundriss des Rechts und der Wirtschaft.) Stuttgart: W. Kohlhammer Verlag, 1968.

Furtwängler, Franz Josef. *ÖTV: Die Geschichte einer Gewerkschaft.* Stuttgart: Union Druckerei, 1955.

Galenson, Walter (ed.). *Comparative Labor Movements.* New York: Prentice-Hall, 1952. (Chapter 4 on "Germany" by Philip Taft.)

Guillebaud, C. W. *The Works Council.* Cambridge: Cambridge University Press, 1928.

Hofstätter, Peter R. and Werner H. Tack. *Das Bild des Beamten in der Öffentlichkeit.* Bonn-Bad Godesberg: DBB, 1963.

Hueck, Alfred, H. C. Nipperdey, and Eugen Stahlhacke. *Tarifvertragsgesetz.* (4th ed.) Munich: Verlag C. H. Beck, 1964.

Kley, Gisbert. *Codetermination in Coal and Steel: Replies to the DGB's Demands.* Cologne: BDA, undated.

Lauxmann, Frieder. *Öffentlich-rechtliches und Privatrechtliches Dienstverhältnis im Hinblick auf die Grundrechtliche Stellung der Angehörigen des Öffentlichen Dienstes.* Stuttgart: Ritter-Drucke, 1961.

Limmer, Hans. *Die deutsche Gewerkschaftsbewegung.* Munich: Günter Olzog Verlag (an ÖTV publication), 1966.

Potthoff, Werner. *Die Mitbestimmung der Beamten im öffentlichen Dienst.* Doctoral dissertation, University of Münster, 1965.

Ramm, Thilo. *Das Koalitions- und Streikrecht der Beamten.* Cologne: Bund-Verlag, 1970.

Schoonmaker, Donald O. *The Politics of the Deutscher Beamtenbund: A Case Study of a Pressure Group.* Ann Arbor: University Microfilms, 1966.

Schuster, Dieter. *Die Deutsche Gewerkschaftsbewegung.* Düsseldorf: DGB, 1969.

Shuchman, Abraham. *Codetermination.* Washington: Public Affairs Press, 1957.

Spiro, Herbert J. *The Politics of German Codetermination.* Cambridge: Harvard University Press, 1958.

Stammer, Otto *et al. Verbände und Gesetzgebung.* (Schriften des Instituts für Politische Wissenschaft, Vol. 18). Cologne: Westdeutscher Verlag, 1965.

Sturmthal, Adolf (ed.). *White Collar Trade Unions.* Urbana: University of Illinois Press, 1966. (Chapter 4 on "Germany" by Günter Hartfiel.)

Sturmthal, Adolf (ed.). *Contemporary Collective Bargaining in Seven Countries.* Ithaca: Institute of International Industrial and Labor Relations, 1957. (Chapter 5 on "Collective Bargaining in Postwar Germany" by Clark Kerr.)

Thieme, Werner. *Empfiehlt es sich, das Beamtenrecht unter Berücksichtigung der Wandlungen von Staat und Gesellschaft neu zu ordnen?* (Gutachten D zum 48. Deutschen Juristentag). Munich: Verlag C. H. Beck, 1970.

von Münch, Ingo. *Rechtsgutachten zur Frage des Streikrechts der Beamten.* To be published by the GdP in 1970.

ORGANIZATION REPORTS

Wunderlich, Frieda. *Labor under German Democracy: Arbitration 1918-1833*. New York: New School for Social Research, 1940.

DAG. *Tagungsbericht, 9th Bundes-Kongress*. Hamburg: DAG, 1967.

DAG. *Tätigkeitsbericht der Bundesberufsgruppe Öffentlicher Dienst, 1962-1966*. Hamburg: DAG, 1966.

DAG. *Zum Verhältnis DAG-DGB*. Hamburg: DAG, 1968.

DBB. *Deutscher Beamtenbund: Ursprung, Weg, Ziel*. Bonn-Bad Godesberg: Deutscher Beamten-Verlag, 1968.

DBB. *Die Beamten und das Streikrecht*. (DBB Dokumente No. 4). Bonn-Bad Godesberg: DBB, 1969.

DBB. *Die Besoldungs Tragödie 1962*. Bonn-Bad Godesberg: DBB, 1962.

DBB. *Geschäftsbericht der Bundesleitung, 1969*. Bonn-Bad Godesberg: DBB, 1969.

DBB. *Vorschläge zur Änderung des Personalvertretungsgesetzes*. Bonn-Bad Godesberg: DBB, 1970.

DGB. *Codetermination: A Contemporary Demand*. Düsseldorf: DGB, 1966.

DGB. *Codetermination Rights of the Workers in Germany*. Düsseldorf: DGB, 1967.

DGB. *Geschäftsbericht, 1965-1968*. Düsseldorf, DGB, 1968.

DGB. *Vorschläge zur Änderung des Personalvertretungsgesetzes*. Düsseldorf: DGB, 1970.

DPG. *Geschäftsbericht, 1965-1968* (also *1963-1965*). Frankfort: DPG, 1968 (and 1965).

GdED. *Geschäftsbericht, 1965-1968*. Frankfort: GdED, 1968.

KAV. *Geschäftsbericht 1968*. Stuttgart: KAV in Württemberg-Baden, 1969.

ÖTV. *Geschäftsbericht, 1964-1967* (also *1961-1963*). Stuttgart ÖTV, 168 (and 1964).

ÖTV. *Tagesprotokoll, 6th Ordentlicher Gewerkschaftstag*. Stuttgart: ÖTV, 1968.

ÖTV. *Tarifaktion '69 der ÖTV im Spiegel der Presse*. Stuttgart: ÖTV, 1969.

BIBLIOGRAPHY

ÖTV. *Tarifverträge, 1968.* Stuttgart: ÖTV, 1969.

ÖTV. *Zwanzig Jahre ötv.* Stuttgart: Verlagsanstalt Courier, 1966.

GOVERNMENT REPORTS

Mitbestimmung im Unternehmen (Bericht der "Mitbestimmungskommission"). Deutscher Bundestag, Drucksache VI/334.

Stable Money—Steady Growth. Report of the Council of Experts on Economic Development. Stuttgart: W. Kohlhammer, 1964.

Herbst, Fritz. *Notice of Dismissal and Protection Against Dismissal.* Bonn: Federal Ministry of Labor and the Social Structure (Social Policy Monograph No. 13), undated.

Klein, Alfons. *Codetermination and the Law Governing Works Councils and Staff Representation in the Public Services.* Bonn: Federal Ministry of Labor and the Social Structure (Social Policy Monograph No. 23), 1963.

Sahmer, Heinz. *The Labor Courts.* Bonn: Federal Ministry of Labor and the Social Structure (Social Policy Monograph No. 24), undated.

Schelp, Günther. *The Contract of Service.* Bonn: Federal Ministry of Labor and the Social Structure (Social Policy Monograph No. 12), 1965.

Reichel, Hans and Otfried Wlotzke. *Collective Bargaining and the Law Governing Collective Agreements.* Bonn: Federal Ministry of Labor and the Social Structure (Social Policy Monograph No. 19), 1963.

Reichel, Hans and Hanns Zschocher. *Conciliation and Arbitration and the Law as Applied to Labor Disputes.* Bonn: Federal Ministry of Labor and the Social Structure (Social Policy Monograph No. 20), 1963.

COLLECTIVE AGREEMENTS

Bundes Angestellten Tarifvertrag (BAT). Düsseldorf: Werner-Verlag, 1969.

Lohntarifverträge für die Arbeiter des Bundes, der Länder, der Gemeinden. Stuttgart: ÖTV, 1969.

Mantel-Tarifvertrag für Arbeiter des Bundes (MTB). Stuttgart: ÖTV, 1961.

Index